OF MERMAIDS AND ROCK SINGERS

CURRENT RESEARCH IN ETHNOMUSICOLOGY
VOLUME 2

CURRENT RESEARCH IN ETHNOMUSICOLOGY
OUTSTANDING DISSERTATIONS

Edited by
Jennifer C. Post
Middlebury College

A ROUTLEDGE SERIES

CURRENT RESEARCH IN ETHNOMUSICOLOGY
JENNIFER C. POST, *General Editor*

1. NEWLY COMPOSED FOLK MUSIC OF
YUGOSLAVIA
Ljerka V. Rasmussen

2. OF MERMAIDS AND ROCK SINGERS
*Placing the Self and Constructing
the Nation through Belarusan
Contemporary Music*
Maria Paula Survilla

OF MERMAIDS AND ROCK SINGERS

Placing the Self and Constructing the Nation through Belarusan Contemporary Music

Maria Paula Survilla

Routledge
New York & London

Published in 2002 by
Routledge
29 West 35th Street
New York, NY 10001
www.routledge-ny. com

Published in Great Britain by
Routledge
11 New Fetter Lane
London EC4P 4EE

Routledge is an imprint of the Taylor & Francis Group
Printed in the United States of America on acid-free paper.

Copyright © 2002 by Routledge

All rights reserved. No part of this book may be reprinted or reproduced or utilized in any
form or by any electronic, mechanical, or other means, now known or hereafter invented,
including photocopying and recording, or in any information storage or retrieval system,
without permission in writing from the publisher.

10 9 8 7 6 5 4 3 2 1

Library of Congress Cataloging-in-Publication Data
Survilla, Maria Paula.
  Of mermaids and rock singers : placing the self and constructing the nation through
Belarusan contemporary music / by Maria Paula Survilla.
    p. cm. — (Current research in ethnomusicology ; v. 2)
Discography: p.
Includes bibliographical references (p.) and index.
  ISBN 0-415-94014-1
    1. Popular music—Belarus—History and c riticism. 2. Nationalism—Belarus. I. Title.
II. Series.
  ML3499.B38 S87 2002
  306.4'84—dc21
2002002528

For ancestors past, present, and future
Janka, Ivonka, Anton, and Vaalik

&

For Eric

Contents

List Of Illustrations	xi
Notes to Accompanying CD	xiii
The Transliteration of the Belarusan Language	xvii
Acknowledgments	xix
Preface	xxi

1.
"Žyvie Bielaruś!": Nationalism, Critiques, and Cultural Responses — 3

Identity and Nation — 5
Explanations of Identity Construction: Eastern Europe in the
Western Press — 8

2.
Terminology, Controversy, and the Interpretation of History — 17

Steps Towards Independence — 18
Terminology — 21
National Origins and the "Golden Era" — 22
Aggressive Colonization — 27
Rebellion — 29
The Twentieth Century — 31

3.
"Stand in the doorway": Entrances and Exits in Urban Belarus — 41

Singular Visions and Multiple Directions in Urban Belarus — 42
The Public and the Private — 44
Expectations for Change in Belarus — 45

ix

x   *Contents*

"And what please, is a please . . . ?"	48
Popular Culture Without a Marketplace: Perfume, Lipstick, and the Soaps	51
Red Wine and Radiation: Chernobyl in Everyday Life	53
Conclusion	56

4.
From Legislation to the Renaissance: Belarusan Rock and Urban Folklore — 61

Generalities and Specifics of the Soviet Rock Scene — 65
The Pieśniary [Songsters]: From VIA to "Pieśniarok" — 68
Defining the Elements of "Good?" Belarusan Rock — 77

5.
Of Mermaids and Rock Singers: Ethnography and Shifting Authority in Pałac's "Rusałki" — 87

Culture Contact and the Expedition — 88
"Young girls, our sisters . . ." — 92

6.
Ulis: "America is Where I am" — 109

Group Dynamics and the Practice Space — 110
Defining Ulis and Belarusan Rock — 111

7.
From Bard to Rock Star: Kasia Kamockaja — 125

Gender and Belarusan Rock — 126
Novaje Nieba's Kasia Kamockaja: from Bard to Rock Star — 129
Image, Belonging, and Association — 132

8.
National Republic of Mroja [Dream]: Quotation and the Kangaroo — 141

9.
Rock and Revolution: Performance and the Mediation of Rock — 149

Rock and Revolution: Performance and the Mediation of Rock — 150

Bibliography	163
Discography	175
Index	177

List Of Illustrations

FIGURES

2.1 Map of Modern Belarus	18
2.2 The Belarusan Flag and the Belarusan Coat-of-Arms, Pahonia	20
2.3 Map: The Grand Duchy of Lithuania, Ruś, and Samogitia	23
2.4 Map: Vilnia (Vilnius) Region Given to Lithuania in 1939	27
2.5 Map: Annexation of Belarusan Territories in the Eighteenth Century	28
2.6 Radioactive Pastures	34
3.1 "The Face of Contemporary Democracy"	46
4.1 Pieśniary Album cover, front	70
4.2 Pieśniary Album cover, back	71
5.1 Waiting for the Local Experts	91
5.2 Pałac Cassette J-card	102
6.1 Ulis in concert, Miensk	118
7.1 Basovišča '93, logo	126
7.2 Kasia Kamockaja in concert, May 1993	133
7.3 Kasia Kamockaja in concert, September 1993	133
9.1 "Rockin' Lenin," concert logo for "Rock Against the Revolution"	155

MUSICAL EXAMPLES

4.1 Melodic basis for the Pieśniary's "Pierapiołačka"	73
4.2 Introductory segment for "Pierapiołačka"	73
4.3 First manifestation of layering in "Pierapiołačka"	75
4.4 Ostinato transformation in "Pierapiołačka"	75

xi

xii   *List of Illustrations*

5.1 Melody and text distribution for the traditional version of
       "Na Hrannoj Niadzieli"   97
5.2 Melody and text distribution for Pałac's "Rusałki"   97
5.3 Rhythmic underpinning for Pałac's "Rusałki"   99
5.4 Guitar response pattern as established in the introduction
       of Pałac's "Rusałki"   99
5.5 Recurring keyboard pattern in Pałac's "Rusałki"   99
6.1 Melody for Ulis' "America is Where I Am," Verse One   120
7.1 Refrain excerpt from Novaje Nieba's "Żachlivaja Pryhažość" 135
8.1 Introduction and Interlude for NRM's "Aŭstralijskaja Polka" 143
8.2 Melody and guitar counterpoint for NRM's "Aŭstralijskaja
       Polka," Verse 1   144
8.3 Chorus for NRM's "Aŭstralijskaja Polka"   145
8.4 "Lavonicha" excerpt as heard in NRM's "Aŭstralijskaja Polka" 145
8.5 "Hey Jude" quotation in NRM's "Aŭstralijskaja Polka"   146

SCHEMAS

4.1 Melody / Chorus and Drone elaborations in "Pierapiołačka"   75
5.1 Mapping of the Pałac version of "Rusałki"   96
5.2 Live and Electronically-generated elements in a Pałac
       performance   100
8.1 Mapping of Mroja's "Aŭstralijskaja Polka"   146

TABLES

9.1 A Summary of Rock Concert Activity in Belarus (1993)   152

Notes to Accompanying CD

1. "Pierapiołaćka." *Piesniary: Byelorussian Traditional Songs Arranged by V. Muljavin*, Pieśniary (1988). Melodija 33 C 60—11287-88. Used by permission.

This setting of a traditional Belarusan folk song offers an eclectic mixture of styles, timbres, and instrumentation that define this performance as Belarusan art rock. Traditional flute, hurdy-gurdy, and a classical violin cadenza initiate the listener to a theme and variations treatment of the folk melody that is further explored through richly voiced vocals, electric bass, guitar, and keyboard improvisation. With each verse the group increases the texture and the complexity of the polyphony driving the music to a dramatic climax before returning to the style heard at the beginning of the selection. (For transcription and further analysis see Chapter Four)

2. "Na Hrannoj Niadzieli." Field recording by Maria Paula Survilla. Janava, Vietkoŭskaja Region, Belarus, 1993.

The excerpt included here serves to underscore differences in structure, phrasing, and performance between a rural version of the ritual mermaid folk song "Na Hrannoj Niadzieli" and Example 3 that follows. This recording is not the one used by Pałac for their subsequent popular hit. However, the asymmetrical phrasing, staggered entrances, uninterrupted flow within the verses, and vocal polyphonies are shared amongst regional variants. (For further discussion see Chapter Five)

xiii

xiv   *Notes to Acompanying CD*

3. "Rusałka." *Palace Folk-Modern Palac*, Pałac (1996). Vigma 0360. © Juraś Vydronak, Used by permission.

This first hit for the rock group Pałac illustrates well the synthesis between traditional and contemporary resources that defines their music. The fusion of acoustic, electric, and digitally-managed sounds supports a male vocal performance that mimics the techniques heard amongst women singers in Belarusan Paleśsie (South-western Belarus). The changes to verse structure and to flow are evident in this rendition, as is the level of appropriation including Jazz-influenced brass interludes (punches) and English-language rap. (See Chapter Five)

4. "Ameryka." *Dances on the Roof '93*, Ulis (1993). Dainova n.n. Used by permission.

In 1993 Ulis' style combined the energy of driving guitar and drums, an active bass line, throaty aggressive vocals, and lyrical introspective texts. The initial moments establish a sense of urgency especially through the pitched drum ostinato and the anticipation created by the electric guitar. The melodic line offers a sharp contrast with the instrumentals through short lyrical phrases that stretch borrowed triple divisions over quadruple time. The melodic line and instruments are unified by a bass line that alternates between driving the rhythm and lyrical lines, particularly at the end of a phrase. (For further discussion see Chapter 6)

5. "Żachlivaja pryhazość." *Son i tramvaj*. Novaje Nieba (1993) Kovcheg. n.n. Used by permission.

This early example by Novaje Nieba illustrates the avant-garde element in Belarusan rock. The angular melody of the refrain, the driving mechanistic character of the verses, and the use of traditional and synthesized elements are further punctuated by Kasia Kamockaja's full alto. The band's interest in production techniques in this cassette album, such as the incorporation of rural or urban soundscapes, is also evident in this selection. (For further discussion see Chapter 7)

6. "Prezydent idzi damoŭ." *Go Home*. Novaje Nieba (1995) Novaje Nieba. n.n. Used by permission.

Novaje Nieba's 1995 critique of president Lukaśenka is evidenced in this aggressive call for the politician to "go home." The song is also a commentary on the inaction of Belarusans to determine a political and cultural future. (For musical and text analysis see Chapter 7)

Notes to Acompanying CD xv

7. "Aŭstralijskaja Polka." *28th Star*. Mroja (NRM) (1990) Melodija, C60 30401 001.

This early example from Mroja's repertoire illustrates the hard edge of their rock style as well as the social commentary embedded in their music. The hard rock polka tells of a young man who must choose to emigrate to Australia or stay in post-Chernobyl Belarus. The use of stylistic and melodic quotations from traditional folk and Western popular music signals the band's black humor as well as their facility with a variety of genres and idioms.

The Transliteration of the Belarusan Language

THE BELARUSAN LANGUAGE CAN BE WRITTEN IN CYRILLIC AND IN THE LATIN alphabet. In this document the spelling of terms, cities, and persons is based on the Belarusan variant of terms and proper names as written in the Latin alphabet. Note that each term may have several spellings as a result of the different languages used in the Belarusan territory, as well as any mandated changes due to government policies. Zaprudnik (1993, xvii) offers the following examples:

Skaryna	Skoryna	Skorina
Kalinoŭski	Kalinowski	Kalinovsky

The Latin version of the Belarusan alphabet is given below with approximate pronounciations (xviii):

LETTER	PRONOUNCIATION
a	(ah)
b	b
c	ts
ć	ts (palatized)
č	ch
d	d
e	e (glen)
f	f
g	g (glad)
h	h (hope)
i	i (machine)

xvii

j	y (boy)
k	k
l	l (million)
ł	l (table)
m	m
n	n
ń	n (onion)
o	o
p	p
r	r
s	s
ś	s (palatized)
š	sh
t	t
u	u (rule)
ŭ	w (how)
v	v
y	y (mary)
z	z (zero)
ź	z (palatized)
ž	s (pleasure)
ch	ch (chutzpah)
dz	(adze)
dž	j (jet)

Acknowledgments

FIELD WORK CAN BE A TRANSFORMING EXPERIENCE FOR THOSE WHO HAVE faced the adaptations, joys, and frustrations of research in another environment. The relationships that develop from this kind of endeavor are numerous and varied. Throughout my field work in Biełastoćcyna, Poland and in Belarus I had the privilege of working with many individuals who contributed to my understanding of their local knowledge and of their musical lives. There were also many individuals who provided moral support through their friendship and involvement in my day-to day life in the field. I am grateful to the musicians who offered me access to their rehearsal spaces and who included me in their backstage camaraderie, their social lives, and their family celebrations. The members of Pałac, Mroja (NRM), Novaje Nieba, Ulis, and Krama were generous with their time, their resources, and their friendship, especially Kasia Kamockaja, Lavon Volski, Juraś Vydronak, Veronika Kruhłova, and Dzima Vajciuškievič. I also thank Kasia for asking me to join the band and experience rock from the other side.

I am deeply thankful for having developed some deep friendships throughout my field work. In Poland Mirasłava Panfiluk, Yolanta Panfiluk and Valenty Sielviasiuk were a constant source of support. Their generosity, concern, and friendship softened my initiation to field work. I thank Sakrat Janovič and his wife for their time, their insight and for my visit to Krynka. In Miensk Alena and Vacłaŭ Bahdanovič offered me their hospitality and their friendship. I am grateful for Alena's enthusiasm for my project and her efforts in helping me connect with Miensk musicians. Valancina Tryhubovič was a quiet presence who made sure I was managing and who was poised to help. Nadzia Kudrejka and Villi Simaška shared their views on the rock scene and gave their time and resources. I also wish to thank Aleś Lozka. For includ-

xix

xx   *Acknowledgments*

ing me in their research trips and cultural events I thank Vasil Lićvinka and Rehina Hamzovič. I very much enjoyed the long conversations, the eggs, and the brandy I shared with Zinajda Mažejka. I also wish to thank Leanid Šymaniec. I am especially indebted to Tania Markaviec whose generosity, ingenuity, and resourcefulness led to many wonderful and rewarding experiences.

I owe my intellectual debts to four people. Jocelyne Guilbault who introduced me to the field of ethnomusicology in the first place and whose continual support, enthusiasm, and friendship have been invaluable. Judith Becker whose direction and patience defined my graduate school experience and who has remained a source of inspiration and insight throughout the completion of my dissertation. My parents Janka and Ivonka Survilla inspired me through their example. They have always provided their emotional, their intellectual, and their practical support. Although I was grappling with deconstructing an aspect of their cultural identities they refrained from directing my work and consistently supported my choices. I will always be grateful.

I would also like to thank the members of my doctoral committee, Judith Becker, Michael Kennedy, Travis Jackson, and Joseph Lam, for their suggestions and critiques, and for their contribution to my understanding of this research.

I am very fortunate to have a partner who shared my frustrations and accomplishments throughout graduate school and my field research. He experienced my field work at a distance and faced his own transformations. He continues to be a source of support, encouragement, and love.

Throughout the preparation of this book I was once again reminded of the generosity of the musicians who have provided their recordings for inclusion in this volume and who facilitated my access to music and musicians. I especially thank Kasia Kamockaja and Juraś Vydronak for their logistical and moral support and Valancina Tryhubovič for her invaluable help.

Finally I would like to acknowledge the Fulbright–Hays Doctoral Research Abroad program which generously supported my research in 1992–1993.

Preface: Insider/Outsider: "But you don't understand, I'm supposed to ask the questions."

I ARRIVED IN MIENSK[1] IN EARLY MAY OF 1993 AND STAYED UNTIL LATE November. During these first few weeks I would begin to interpret this city as a complex layering of opposing ideas, of contrasted lifestyles, and unequal opportunities. The city's urban energy, an accurate reflection of the blinding rate of social change, was in sharp contrast to another impending yet predictable process, the steady arrival of Spring.

I watched these energies at work from my apartment window as I listened to the broadcasts on Belarus Radio. I took notes on producers, on the music, and on the style of the programs. As I began to record some of the programs, I recall being annoyed that the radio seemed permanently attached to the wall above the kitchen table. I asked Rita, my roommate, about the impractical placement of the device and smiling she unplugged it to show me a strange dedicated plug: "Every apartment has one," she said, "it guaranteed that the voice of the State was always heard."[2] Clearly, the radio now provided a voice of exploration. The national media was involved in an advertising campaign, broadcasting in the Belarusan language, producing ethnographic programming, and highlighting traditional and contemporary musical culture. My interest in radio programming led me to contact a reporter who made arrangements for my first interview with one of the producers of Belarusan Youth Radio programming [Biełaruskaje Maładziožnaje Radyjo].

One trolley ride to the Metro and another quick ride to the center of Miensk placed me along the newly-named Skaryna[3] Boulevard (formerly Lenin Boulevard).[4] I walked up the hill from Victory Square and arrived at Belarus Radio Studios with notes and recorder in hand. In the dark marble foyer of the imposing building a uniformed militia officer asked for my pass-

xxi

xxii   *Preface*

port. I produced it gingerly from its permanent hiding place underneath my blouse. He made a phone call, pointed to the red vinyl seats, and told me to wait.

Eventually I was led to a small studio where I took out my notes and proceeded to re-check my recorder and microphone. I smiled at the technician in the neighboring sound booth. He looked at me with keen interest and no doubt was wondering what I thought I was doing. In little time I was introduced to a staff reporter. I nervously began to strike up a conversation (in Belarusan) explaining the kind of information I was interested in. I hardly got one sentence out. Instead, she briskly thanked me for coming in, said we were going live across the nation in about 5 minutes, and proceeded to elaborate on the types of questions she was going to ask me. My mouth went dry.

* * *

The reversal of roles, from researcher to subject, became a typical part of my field work experience. As often as I sat down to interview my new contacts, I would find myself exposed on the public airwaves. Questions about the new Belarus were always interspersed with questions that established my cultural identity, and suggested my authority to the public: "Why is it that you speak the Belarusan language although you were not born here?" or "Tell our listeners how your upbringing reflected your Belarusan background?"

I had become the *immigrant daughter come home* and newspapers, television, and radio became involved in a media blitz of this constructed me. The public me interfered with my work, and placed a level of responsibility on me that I did not want and could not avoid. As much as I was studying and getting to know this Belarus, these Belarusans were studying and defining me within a cultural and national context.[5] While this afforded me access to many people, musicians, artists, journalists, and scholars, I was increasingly feeling a crisis of intent. How would my own cultural identity, my definition of Belarusan affect my role as an observer, chronicler, and interpreter of Belarusan culture?

My immediate absorption into the public sphere was the first indication that my field work expectations would be contradicted by my field work experience. Prior to my arrival in Belarus, I had anticipated that my field work would be a coming home of sorts, a long-awaited arrival to a familiar cultural destination. My expectations were based on my familiarity with the Belarus I had known since childhood, the one celebrated and lived by my parents, and the one lamented and passionately remembered by the members of the Belarusan immigration in Toronto and in Ottawa, Canada.

In the Belarusan-Canadian immigrant community, the conscious expression of cultural heritage was central to community celebrations as well as part of private lifestyles. Community events included historically-relevant

Preface *xxiii*

ceremonies (Belarusan Independence Day, March 25 [1918]), traditional celebrations (*Kupalle*– Summer Solstice), as well as religious observances. In the home and during community events it was always clear that the most important element in cultural education was language. I had grown up in a household where the Belarusan language was always heard. I responded to its rhythms and inflections as I listened to discussions, laughed at the humor, wondered at the ever-present metaphors, and sang songs central to the immigrant repertoire. All of these expressions were presented within a lifestyle package that consistently illustrated the value of Belarusan cultural identity for our parents and for the Belarusan community.

Despite my familiarity with Belarusan expression, logic and education told me that I would experience culture shock going out into the field. What I did not expect was that most of my field work adaptation would center on understanding a very differently-defined Belarus. While cultural contrasts can generate compelling questions for any researcher, I was left with a mixture of emotions. My own cultural history became a source of cultural discomfort and confusion. I was compelled to reach beyond the literary romanticism of the Belarus I had come to understand, and to accept attitudes and choices about being Belarusan that were as much recognizable as they were unfamiliar. The intent of this Preface is to explain the source of my voice as a researcher, to explain the definitions of self and nation that determined my research choices, and to explain how I came to understand this new, unexpected Belarus through the lens of my own cultural identity.

* * *

Belarusaness refers to an awareness of being Belarusan. In the immigrant environment, this awareness has developed through a conscious process that articulated what being Belarusan actually **means**. Attitudes towards language, history, ritual, music, religion and politics have been openly displayed, prescribed, and explored through consistent community activity. These activities have also been documented and legitimized through publication and through the establishment of academic circles.[6]

How this Belarusan culture is articulated is related to a connection with both pre- and post-sovereignty Belarus (1991), and is guided by a philosophy of separation and the longing to return to the homeland. The immigrant definition of Belarusan that I have come to know is constructed and maintained through: (1) the valuation of cultural memory including the acknowledgment of shared historical conflict and (2) the assertion of cultural differentiation through conscious, public acts of self-definition.

In the immigrant community cultural memory and group cohesiveness was strengthened by the acknowledgment and remembrance of shared cultural conflict. Sources of that conflict include knowledge of the colonization of Belarus throughout its history, the subjugation of the Belarusan language and culture before emigration, the shared trauma of migration, and the loss *xxiv*   *Preface*

of cultural distinction imposed upon the immigrant community by those outside Belarusan group boundaries.

For many immigrants in the Belarusan Diaspora, cultural conflict[7] had defined their experiences in the homeland and was the reason why many had been forced to emigrate. Conflict was also defined by the knowledge that Soviet-era Belarus was facing increased political, linguistic, and cultural assimilation. The emotional significance of this knowledge most affected those members of the community that fled Belarus in their youth. Although early migrations were motivated by economic factors, most of the emigration during and after World War II was due to cultural and political persecution. These cultural and political refugees represented many facets of rural and urban life. Many were young intellectuals who were to become the historians, chroniclers, activists, writers, and artists of their immigrant communities. The conflict that defined their early cultural experiences helped to determine their sense of cultural identity and commitment in their adopted environments.[8] For some, the emotional ties with the homeland were so strong that they refused to pursue new citizenship. They hoped to someday return to Belarus.

In their adopted countries Belarusans congregated in mutual support. They shared cultural practices, celebrated rights of passage, and organized political and academic organizations to address issues of cultural, linguistic, and political survival. Their community centers, often doubling as church spaces,[9] were remarkable rooms. The sacred space could be transformed into a political space, a forum for academic debate, an art gallery, a restaurant, or a performance hall. Within such mutable spaces, Diaspora Belarusans[10] who retained a Belarusan-specific linguistic and cultural identity concentrated their energies on (1) perpetuating and expressing their imported cultural knowledge and (2) informing those outside their communities about Belarusan history and contemporary issues.[11]

Belarusans who had fled Belarus as a result of cultural persecution considered the immigrant community to be a repository for the cultural knowledge that had survived processes of Russification and Sovietization.[12] As a result, Belarusan cultural practices and repertoires were consciously protected through the regulation of culture change. Such regulation required the definition and preservation of *authentic*[13] expression. As a defining criteria for expression, authenticity underlined the importance of cultural uniqueness as a means to validate Belarusan culture. Authenticity was central to the immigrant concept of *Belarusaness* by stressing differentiation and the need for cultural survival. Through its application the community had a consistent reminder of shared cultural history and could contribute to a sense of cultural continuity. Authenticity includes,

Preface xxv

1. the use of the Belarusan language (pre-Stalin orthography and grammar, see Chapter 1),
2. the validation of what was considered traditional performance practice in vocal and dance performance (evaluated according to the experiences and memories of community members),
3. the validation of literary, musical, theatrical, and dance repertoires.

Language choice, traditional performance practice, and authentic repertoire became part of the community canon through application in community life. Most performance contexts, such as the celebration of Belarusan Independence in 1918, prescribed the function of much of the musical repertoire as overt, communal expressions of identity. The importance of such communal expressions is particularly evident in the emotional responses to musical and literary repertoire with the homeland as theme.[14] The thematic content of Belarusan literary and musical repertoires often echoes the longing for a nostalgic homeland. In such expression, the Belarusan language as well as references to "Belarus" as theme are consistent, if not necessary, components.[15]

One of my earliest memories in the Belarusan community places me at age seven on a small stage in the Belarusan Community Center in Toronto, Canada. Standing in traditional costume with my older sister Hanna, we sang to a crowd that was moved to tears. They weren't moved by the performance, but rather by the song we were singing. The melody by Viačaslaŭ Kačanski with words from a poem by Kanstancyja Bujło (1898-1986) remains a classic anthem in the Belarusan Diaspora:[16]

Lublu naš kraj, staronku hetu	I love our country
Dzie ja radziłasia, rasła,	Where I was born, where I did grow
Dzie pieršy raz spatkała ščaście	Where for the first time I felt good-fortune
Ślazu niadoli praliła.	Where first I shed a tear of misery.
Lublu narod naš biełaruski	I love our Belarusan people
Chaciny ŭ zieleni sadoŭ	Cottages nestled in blooming orchards
Załočanyja zbožžam nivy	Shining, golden fields
Šum našych hajaŭ i lasoŭ	The murmur of our groves and woods.

This song is representative of the tone of literary and musical expression embraced by the immigrant community. Much of the repertoire is taken from turn-of-the-century Belarusan poetic literature that romantically speaks of longing, suffering, and traditional life, eloquently maintaining a cultural memory for the community. The emotional relevance of this repertoire is *xxvi*   *Preface*

deeply connected to the articulation of shared identity. As Simon Frith writes: "only music seems capable of spontaneous collective identity [. . .] a personally felt patriotism."[17] Raised to anthem levels, such songs represent the participatory repertoire for the Belarusan community and are usually performed before and after official community events. As a member of the community that had been born abroad, such songs could not echo my own cultural memories. Sung in the first person, almost like a sacred credo, the words reflected the passions and memories of my parents' and grandparents' generations. Nevertheless, the emotional responses of the adults around me validated not only being Belarusan, but a very specific definition of what being Belarusan meant. The focus on survival, differentiation, identity, language, and authenticity remain central to this immigrant definition.

My family was also actively involved in political and cultural aspects of community affairs.[18] We were always aware of symbols and events that were relevant to Belarusan identity. When the Belarusan hockey team first used the traditional Belarusan flag over the Soviet version, the phone lines buzzed in celebration. Other symbols, a stand of birch trees, traditional weaving patterns, the corn flower were all part of a repertoire of powerful cultural icons. My father, usually stoic and controlled, could reveal deep emotions when responding to such symbols. Equally respected were icons from Belarusan history such as the outlawed coat-of-arms Pahonia (see Chapter Two). Such images and representations found continued relevance in my grandfather's and in my mother's paintings. For me, a consistently-articulated definition of Belarusaness resulted in a strong cultural confidence and a deep emotional commitment to this identity.

Beyond family and community experience, being Belarusan also meant asserting a Belarusan identity in the public sphere. In this public context Belarusan immigrant communities continue to respond to what is considered a marginalization of their culture in the West. Before the early 1990s when the fall of the Soviet Union and new media attention began a process of clarifying the previously enigmatic Eastern Europe, members of these cultures living in the West were faced with explaining their cultural identities. In the Belarusan case this had much to do with asserting what Belarus was **not**— that is, that it was **not** Russia. Such assertions were directed to the lay-man and the academician alike, dispelling views of a culturally and politically homogenous Soviet Union.

Much time and activity was spent teaching our own Canadian and American administrations[19] and public that Belarusan culture actually existed. As a result, Belarusan youth not only danced Belarusan dances but learned what lobbying meant. For many Belarusans in Canada and in the United States, the act of self-definition was based as much on cultural preservation as on political action.[20] For the Belarusan immigrant community such campaigns resulted in the conscious assertion of cultural differences, of the

Preface   *xxvii*

existence of Belarusan culture, and of the right to be recognized as such.[21] The need for differentiation was central to the Belarusan immigrant experience.[22]

The members of the Diaspora were focused not only on the survival and practice of cultural expressions, but on the abstract hope that the homeland would some day define its own "Belarusan" future. This future included the expectation that Belarusans in Belarus would define their identities in the same ways: a focus on cultural awareness, on Belarusan language education, and on a knowledge and an appreciation of cultural sources and histories. These aspects defined the cultural confidence that had been sheltered and maintained in the immigrant environment. This confidence, the basis of community continuity in the immigration, had been deeply eroded in Belarus through the Soviet experience (Chapter Three). The resulting contrasts between immigrant expectation and cultural exploration in Belarus were often stark and sobering. For example, when I heard that Belarus had declared its sovereignty in 1991, I remember thinking that now everyone would be able to freely speak Belarusan. I did not think of asking if they would want to.

My first cultural orientation in Miensk served to underline how my cultural positioning would contrast with many attitudes in Belarus. On my second day in the city I had to ask for information about bus routes. I chose the friendliest face I could find at the bus stop and asked the woman in my most respectful Belarusan which bus I needed to take to the metro. I had to repeat my question a few times. The woman only spoke Russian. Eventually she understood that I needed directions. I was left furious and confused. I had come to Belarus, and it seemed as though no one spoke the language. To add insult to injury, I couldn't understand which bus she had told me to take.

The increased flow of information between Belarus and the Diaspora also shapes what it means to identify with being Belarusan in the immigrant community.[23] Such information is significant because it allows for the formulation of contemporary opinion as well as the evaluation of past attitudes. In those communities where the homeland has been a focal part of identity as well as a catalyst for community activity, such first-hand information has a formidable impact. The immigrant intelligentsia began to travel to Belarus when sovereignty opened the lines of communication between the Diaspora and the homeland. They publicly supported identity-aware politicians, and offered commentaries on contemporary issues through participation in academic publications and conferences, culminating in the World Convention of Belarusans held in Miensk in July 1993. Underlying this activity was both a financial and emotional investment in the future of Belarus. The investment is enormous. Many members of the emigré intelligentsia have devoted their lives to the support, survival, and study of Belarus. The emotional impact of such new interactions has served to underline the contrast between cultural *xxviii*   *Preface*

assertion in immigrant circles and what must have seemed like cultural passivity amongst Belarusans in Belarus.[24]

The Diaspora Belarusans who traveled to Miensk for the 1993 World Convention seemed to share in one general experience: the truism that what they associated with their *Belarusaness* was not obvious to many Belarusans in Belarus. Their reactions were often anger and disappointment. Those who had returned to Belarus for the first time since they emigrated (my father returned after a fifty-year absence) were overwhelmed by the discrepancies between their memories and what they were seeing and experiencing in their homeland. Salman Rushdie describes the dilemma: ". . . exiles, or emigrants, or expatriates, are haunted by some sense of loss, some urge to reclaim, to look back even at the risk of being mutated into pillars of salt. But if we do look back, we must also do so in the knowledge—which gives rise to profound uncertainties—that our physical alienation [. . .] almost inevitably means that we will not be capable of reclaiming precisely the thing that was lost; that we will in short create [. . .] imaginary homelands."[25] Rendered imaginary by time and change, the homeland as a cultural and emotional destination remains at the core of an immigrant reality. Such reality is not only based on the recreation of a physical landscape. It is also about maintaining and encouraging a *Belarusaness*, supporting those movements in Belarus that work towards political and cultural self-determination, and reminding Belarusans about what "has been forgotten."

As a child of the immigration, the cultural curriculum that I carried with me to my field work was well-defined and well-learned. I had a passion for Belarus, but that passion was not merely appropriated nostalgia. That passion was based upon practical experience through language, music, lifestyle, education, and political action. Once in Belarus I was forced to assess this identity in isolation, without benefiting from my own community, nor my parents, nor from the Belarusans I had met in Belarus. By the end of my stay I managed to explain and to reconcile many of the same discrepancies that I had seen angering and devastating the older members of my community. My own sense of identity, my *Belarusaness*, had not really changed. I was still protective of the Belarusan language and I still directed my attention to the conscious movement towards cultural definition. But I was aware that my sense of belonging was in constant flux. I could no longer depend on the notion of being an insider in the immigrant community because my enthusiasm for Belarus was in direct contrast to the criticisms articulated by that same community. In Belarus, although I was sincerely embraced by many as a partial insider, I would never truly belong. My sense of place, my definition of the other, my notion of positive representation, and my own cultural memory could not guarantee a comfortable cultural position.

I entered ethnomusicology when issues of studying 'the other' were high on the list of theoretical concerns. The search for theoretical frameworks,

Preface   *xxix*

for representative abstractions, the need for political correctness and ethical decisions, and the struggle to balance the dreaded voice of authority were and continue to be important in our understanding of the study of culture. We have become conscious that we understand other cultures from the "outside" while we struggle to experience, theorize, and communicate about them. As a result, contemporary critiques of modern ethnography do not separate the responsibility of representation from the introspective analysis of the ethnographer himself. As a researcher that felt comfortable with what Belarus meant for the Diaspora, I have had many awakenings in the field. My own identity was shaped by this field work. I was constantly evaluating the lack of consistency between my cultural identity and the many attitudes and opinions I encountered in Belarus.

This inconsistency has come to represent a natural positioning—a positioning also felt by researchers and writers that have a place both within and outside their chosen field of study. The process has forced many issues, especially the awareness of the multitude of voices that speak and sing about *their* Belarus. I am conscious of alternative tellings and of the challenging of attitudes, as I attempt to understand the effects of, and the reactions to, hegemonic politics and the emerging authority of a variety of cultural voices. In the lonely and transforming business of field work I found myself being challenged to understand a homeland that did not reflect the cultural passion I had grown up with. In the end, I have come to see my own transformation and my field work frustrations as definitive contributions to that culture change. I have had to ask what my authority means as a cultural researcher who is privileged from a specific inside.

In "Outside In and Inside Out" Trih T. Minh-ha (1991) explores the mobility of difference in identity and in discourse about identity. It is for her a matter of location of self—a process that is always comparative, always selective, and must always strive to recognize the place of the other, whenever or why-ever that other might be identified as different. As a result, the concept of otherness is perpetual and in constant transformation according to the placement of the seer. I have become, as Minh-ha describes "both a deceptive insider and a deceptive outsider."[26]

I believe the strength of the following chapters lies in how my cultural frustration became comfortable in its persistence, and how I struggled to understand that the questions my own background prepared me to ask were often not the questions that were relevant to my field work environment.[27] As I became a fixture in the media, the sense of confidence in my own cultural identity became a reminder that I was deeply challenged in understanding this homeland. Moreover, I was not given the luxury of any methodical, patient contemplation on these contrasts. Instead, my interviewer asked, "Spadarynia [Miss] Paulinka [diminutive, affectionate form of Paula], tell the Belarusan public why you are here. How do you analyze the state of *xxx*   *Preface*

Belarusan culture? Is it what you expected? What do you see as the next step for this nation?" [28]

Such questions, including the expectation for a national diagnosis had to be addressed with solemn and earnest responses. I was really being asked to encourage and to validate current cultural explorations in Belarus, and I remember drawing my answers from my own immigrant-defined cultural experience. Through such public questioning, and through the often confusing and angering experiences I encountered, I realized that the Belarusan identities I was struggling to reconcile would once again be revealed, be solicited, and no-doubt criticized as a written document. The critical audience would include the immigrant community. The basis of their criticism would lie in the realization that my sense of homeland could no longer rely on what Salman Rushdie calls "a sense of loss, some urge to reclaim [. . .] imaginary homelands [. . .] of the mind" (10). While the core of my Belarusan self still responds to that learned cultural memory, I am as much a participant in the act of remembrance as I am a contributor to a new definition of *Belarusaness*.

NOTES

[1] The capital of Belarus.

[2] Margaret (Rita) Kumejša, conversations with author on May 15th, 1993, Miensk, Belarus; hereafter cited in text.

[3] Francišak Skaryna (ca. 1490–ca. 1552), the first Eastern European printer, remains a prominent and celebrated symbol of Belarusan history. The continued relevance of this Renaissance doctor of medicine, translator, and publisher is perhaps as much tied to his achievements as to his time. Skaryna is a reminder of what Belarusan historians consider as a Golden Era in Belarus' history, characterized by the development of vernacular publishing, the codification of an egalitarian legal system, and the flourishing of the education system.

[4] Changing Soviet place-names as well as street names to Belarusan-specific names was part of the process of redefining or reclaiming the city. At times, the juxtaposition of Soviet history and such redefinition was striking. For example, when arriving to the Metro station outside the Belarusan Parliament, newly named "Independence Square," one exited the train to see a huge bronze bust of Lenin. The station announcements were equally reflective of such physical transitions. Each station was announced using the old name in Russian, and then using the new name in Belarusan. By the end of my field work, most of these announcements had been converted to the Belarusan language and Belarusan station names.

[5] In many ways I became a "public ethnomusicologist" in that I was asked to mediate Belarusan culture. I engaged in "practical action in the world outside of archives and universities" as described by Jeff Todd Titon, "Music, the Public Interest, and the Practice of Ethnomusicology," *Ethnomusicology* 36 (Fall 1992): 315–321. Ironically, I was given this task in an unfamiliar environment where my

Preface

statements and my actions were always public and were used to affect policy and public sentiment. My activities often made the news in Belarus and, as a result, I had lost all anonymity even in the rural villages that I visited throughout my field work.

[6] For example, The Belarusan Institute of Arts and Sciences in New York.

[7] Discourse on the effect of conflict on group definition has been a popular issue in the social sciences. Long considered a negative social influence in the increasingly varied make up of modern societies, conflict is presently regarded as a productive aspect of group interaction: it is indeed a necessary ingredient in the process of the creation and maintenance of identity. See Anya Peterson Royce, *Ethnic Identity: Strategies of Diversity* (Bloomington: Indiana University Press, 1982), 45; hereafter cited in text; Donald L. Horowitz, *Ethnic Groups in Conflict*. (Berkeley: University of California Press, 1985), 70; hereafter cited in text.

[8] Belarusans who left Belarus during World War II were often forced to flee because they: (1) were actively participating in Belarusan-language education, (2) were members of organizations that supported and encouraged Belarusan-language publishing, (3) were members of municipal government, (4) were authors or artists. Members of Belarusan communities tell many stories of warnings and escape from execution. For example, in the 1940s, teachers who continued to teach in Belarusan were shot and municipal leaders were executed in order to debilitate regional infrastructures. Those that escaped saw their lives change as a result of their cultural, political, and artistic convictions and maintained the focus on their Belarusan identities once they had settled in another environment.

[9] The three principal denominations in the Belarusan community include the Autocephallic Orthodox Church (not based on Russian Orthodoxy), Uniatism (Catholicism with Eastern Rites), and Roman Catholicism.

[10] I use the term Diaspora to describe Belarusans living outside Belarus. The largest communities are found in the United States, Canada, Australia, Great Britain, France, and in Germany.

[11] In their activities to inform, many in the Diaspora saw their role as much more than a public affirmation of their historic experience. With Chernobyl in 1986, and Belarusan sovereignty in 1991, immigrants sought to affect Western policy for aid and for human rights monitoring in the homeland. As policy makers and lobbyists they fit the classical definition of an exiled intelligentsia. See Dick Flacks: "Making History and Making Theory: Notes on How Intellectuals Seek Relevance" in *Intellectuals and Politics,* vol. 5 of *Key Issues in Sociological Theory,* (London: Sage Publications, 1992), 3.

[12] Sovietization refers to the implementation of official nationalism, where populations were educated to accept a government-defined identity that obscured national and ethnic ties.

[13] The term "authentic" is problematic in the study of culture change because:

1. it implies the worth and genuine character of something while de-valuing any cross-cultural counterparts.

xxxii   *Preface*

2. it presupposes some sort of legitimization from an 'authoritative'
    source, be it historical, institutional, political, or economically-
    significant.

I choose to apply it here because supporters of a conscious *return* to Belarusan
expression use the term to differentiate what they see as genuine traditional
expression from what they consider as mediated expression. It is a basis for evaluating musical repertoire and musical performance. The search for the authentic,
particularly in rural practice, governs the way musical repertoire is preserved
and/or presented to urban audiences. Several scholars, for example Miensk ethnomusicologist Zinajda Mažejka, have produced ethnographic films as chronicles
of events with the conscious attempt to downplay the presence of the film-maker.
The evaluation and presentation of musical culture according to "authenticity"
varies amongst scholars, television producers, and popular musicians in Miensk.
However, the issues of culture change and of the search for the authentic reflect
the movement towards defining a distinct cultural identity, differentiated from
Russian practice and from Western influence.

[14] Maria Paula Survilla, *Music and Identity: Belarusans Making Music in North
America* (Masters Thesis, University of Michigan 1990); hereafter cited in text.

[15] Maria Paula Survilla "From Affirmation to Aesthetics: Belarus as Subject in
Poetic and Musical Texts" in *Zapisy 20* (New York: Belarusan Institute of Arts and
Sciences, 1992), 43–49. This paper was presented at the 1990 Learned Societies
Congress held at the University of Victoria, British Columbia, within the frame-
work of the Annual Conference of the Canadian Association of Slavists (May
30–June 1, 1990).

[16] For a full poetic translation in English, as well as poetic translations and bibli-
ographic information on Belarusan poetic literature see Vera Rich, *Like Water Like
Fire: An Anthology of Byelorussian Poetry from 1828 to the Present Day* (London:
George Allen and Unwin, 1977), 83; 94; 335; hereafter cited in text. Also see
Arnold B. McMillin, *Die Literatur der Weissrussen: A History of Byelorussian
Literature from its Origins to the Present Day* (Giessen: Wilhem Schmitz, 1977), 128;
hereafter cited in text.

[17] Simon Frith, "Towards an Aesthetic of Popular Music," in *Music and Society:
the politics of composition, performance, and reception,* ed. Richard Leppert and Susan
McClary (London: Cambridge University Press, 1987), 133–149.

[18] After Chernobyl in 1986 my parents founded the Canadian Relief Fund for
Chernobyl Victims in Belarus, of which my mother was President. She resigned
that position in 1997 to become the President in exile of the RADA (Council) of
the Belarusan Democratic Republic (Biełaruskaja Narodnaja Respublika [BNR]).

[19] Communities in France, Great Britain, and other Western countries are also
active in lobbying their government organizations. These communities are also
consistently involved in public education, through city and state folk festivals
such as *Caravan* (Toronto).

[20] The immigrant generation described here focuses upon those Belarusans that
emigrated during and after World War II.

Preface   xxxiii

[21] This became particularly important after the Chernobyl disaster, when international aid did not recognize the after effects of the explosion in Belarus, and those moneys that were offered by world bodies were channeled through Moscow politics without Belarusan representation. See for example *Canadian External Affairs Report on Aid to Developing Countries in Eastern Europe* (1996).

[22] Census and immigration statistics differ greatly in the number of Belarusan immigrants that entered Canada and the United States since the turn of the century. Most often these statistics are based on religious affiliation, that is, Catholics were labeled Polish and Orthodox (Greek or Russian) were labeled Russian. The impact of census categories on Belarusan community development in Canada are discussed in John Sadouski, *A History of Byelorussians in Canada* (Belleville, Ontario: Mika Publishing, 1981); hereafter cited in text; for the United States in Vitaut Kipel, "Byelorussians," in *The New Jersey Ethnic Experience,* ed. Barbara Cunningham (Union City, New Jersey: Wm.H. Wise and Co., 1977), 88–107; hereafter cited in text, and "The Early Byelorussian Presence in America," in *Zapisy 17: Proceedings of the Twenty-fifth Anniversary Symposium of the Byelorussian Institute of Arts and Sciences, February 1977,* (New York: St. Sophia Press), 113–131; hereafter cited in text.

[23] Anya Peterson Royce explains the importance of cross influence between the homeland and immigrant environments (1982). Royce writes that technology has shortened the distance between immigrant and homeland communities, placing recent information within the practical reach of most immigrant communities. This information expands the boundaries of events that stimulate identity assertion including the resources for cultural production.

[24] A knowledge of the immigrant passion for a Belarusan identity generated some interesting strategies amongst some Belarusans. Belarusan writer Sakrat Janovič spoke to me in Bielastok, Poland before my first trip to Miensk. He said: "Spadarynia [Miss] Paulina, take care of your Belarusan soul. In Miensk you will meet people who are as passionate about Belarus as can be, but they are not always sincere, don't get lost in their cultural schizophrenia," (conversations with author, March 1992). Although I did not fully understand his comment at the time, I quickly learned that Belarusan identity had many uses in Belarus. For some it was a commodity that could entice financial support from the immigrant community, while for others it was and remains a topic of exploration articulated through language choice, education policy, or more privately, as a conscious aspect of self-exploration.

[25] Salman Rushdie, *Imaginary Homelands: Essays and Criticism 1981–1991,* (Granta: Viking-Penguin, 1992), 10; hereafter cited in text.

[26] Trih T. Minh-ha, "Outside In and Inside Out" in *When the Moon Waxes Red: Representation, Gender and Cultural Politics* (New York and London: Routledge, 1991), 65–80.

[27] I take great comfort in the presentation given by Nazir Jairazbhoy where he generously offered a look at how his personal history shaped his ethnomusicology (SEM Conference; Charles Seeger Lecture: Saturday, October 21, 1995).

[28] From Radio Belarus interview of the author, Belarus Youth Radio, Miensk, April 28, 1993.

OF MERMAIDS AND ROCK SINGERS

1.
"Žyvie Bielaruś!": Nationalism, Critiques, and Cultural Responses

THE DINING TABLE IS THE RITUAL CENTER OF BELARUSAN HOME LIFE. THE preparation and sharing of food emphasizes family prosperity, however humble, while the ritualized behavior around the table reflects family hierarchy and order. As the focal center of the home, the table is also the stage around which guests are honored. The surface is covered with the best the family has to offer, displays of abundance consisting of food and drink that are methodically searched-for and saved for such occasions. While this important event often ends with unabashed celebration, the meal always begins solemnly with the liturgy of the toast: the vodka is poured, the shot glasses are distributed, and the host briefly expresses the hopes of those gathered together.

At one such meal, in an apartment in one of the outlying developments of Miensk, I sat at the table with a young couple and their son. Alena Bahdanovič was to become a great friend and was key in introducing me to many Miensk musicians. Her three-year old son Henik, normally full of agitated energy, sat quietly with us at the table. We were all poised to toast the beginning of the meal. I was expecting a traditional toast, a statement of thanks and of hope: "Daj Boža!" [may God provide]. Instead, Alena's husband Vacłaŭ turned to his young son and told him he could give the toast. Holding his juice in front of him with a grand gesture the boy loudly proclaimed, "Žyvie Bielaruś!" [Belarus lives!] and his parents answered, "Sapraŭdy žyvie!"[It truly lives!].

This affirmation of the nation resonated around many tables in 1993. The statement reflected sentiments of pride, commitment, and confidence that had grown during the two years following the declaration of independ-

4   *Of Mermaids and Rock Singers*

ence. This declaration could also be heard in the public sphere, during political rallies, rock concerts, and cultural performances.

As a kind of national antiphonal, "Žyvie Bielaruś!" signals the discrepancy between national sentiments and perceptions of Belarusan nationhood found in academic discourse and media sources. Such contrasts represent a central problematic in the study of contemporary Belarusan culture. Despite historical efforts towards national definition, Belarusan nationhood continues to generate controversy because of the complex historical relationships between countries in Eastern Europe. Some of the trends in such discourse reflect an indifference towards Belarusan efforts at national self-determination, an incredulity that asks rather than proclaims "Belarus lives?"

The construction of nation and the perception of nation are key issues in the study of Belarus. As cultural processes construction and perception are fraught with both contemporary and historical complexities. Steady efforts towards national definition seem to be the only constant in the varied analyses of successful national development. Franz Fanon writes: "a national culture is the whole body of efforts made by a people in the sphere of thought to describe, justify and praise the action through which that people has created itself and keeps itself in existence."[1] This definition of national culture underlines the importance of process as an accumulation of efforts (*the whole body*) that contribute to the definition and continued existence of a nation construct. It is this accumulation of efforts that best describes the process of nation definition in Belarusan history, where attempts at independence have often stalled, while the expressed desire for self-determination has persisted. This chapter addresses attitudes towards Belarusan nationhood. It serves to underline the perceptual legacy that affects world views of Belarus, the reasons for that legacy, as well as resulting responses in academic discourse.

While Eastern European nations have shared many parallel experiences since declaring independence, the path towards sovereignty has resulted in unique choices and situations for each country. Some of the choices made by these nations have perplexed Western scholars and political observers who had foreseen different models for change. If there is one constant in the literature produced about post-communist Eastern Europe, it is that political, cultural, and economic changes do not always reflect Western theoretical predictions.[2] The extraordinary and often frustrating historical moments experienced by these nations are defined by the sometimes shaky implementation of political choice, the uneven impact of a market economy, and the post-Soviet exploration of subjugated cultural identities.

Renewed access to Eastern Europe allows for a new understanding of these emerging nations. Past scholarship and media coverage of Eastern Europe continue to provide comparisons and points of contention against which to gauge new research. This is particularly true in the understanding of history, of cultural change, and in the articulation of national identity in each country.

The exploration of past and present politics and culture in Eastern Europe is often obscured by assumptions about the definition of nation and the process towards national identity. Writings on the Soviet Union rarely consider Belarus as a subject for cultural and political inquiry, depending instead upon a primarily russophile historiography of Belarusan history and culture. With its complex history (including that of its ethnographic territories Białastoččyna (Poland) and Vilnia (Lithuania) to the northwest), treatments of Belarus have produced a historiography of Eastern Europe underscored by a narrative that asks *who has the right to assert nationhood*.[3] Belarus' national identity is debated in several ways. Interpretations of history and nationhood reflected in Western, Polish, Russian, and Soviet scholarship often contrast with the internal exploration of what it means to be a modern nation as expressed by Belarusan scholars. Jan Zaprudnik maintains that part of outside perceptions of Belarusan nationhood have to do with a lack of informed critical scholarship about its history. He writes: "Traditionally, whenever Belarus was written about in Western source books it was treated as an "appendix" to a larger political unit [. . .] a description of a country as part of a larger whole [. . .] Such authors have failed to present the Belarusan nation from within, as it were, in the light of its own dynamics and aspirations" (1993, xiv–xv).

The most controversial and debated issues in the study of Belarus include a disregard of its distinct cultural and national identity, and are complicated by the fact that readings on the history of Belarus, as with any history, vary according to the placement of the historian. Developing histories are always mediated because the ownership or appropriation of any perceived historical moment necessarily redefines that moment in the history of another group. The politics of histories can be overt challenges to other histories or can be equally powerful through omission, conceptually eliminating the "other" by ignoring their significance. As James Clifford writes: "Every focus excludes, there is no politically innocent methodology for inter cultural interpretation."[4] Whatever the focus, it is clear that documenting histories is part of the process of justifying a national existence. Beyond adding to scholarly discourse, such documents also influence the character and articulation of cultural confidence and national identities.

IDENTITY AND NATION

Identity as a theoretical framework strives to answer the questions of *who am I?* or *who are we?* according to the many variables that the individual can choose to emphasize or to obscure.[5] These variables might include the importance given to heredity and/or to many other aspects of life choice and experience (social group; taste; sexual orientation; religious affiliation; etc.). While

6   *Of Mermaids and Rock Singers*

it exists as a highly individualistic concept, identity also includes the sense of connection to others.

For group definition, identity is the sense of similarity or of common origin that is fundamental to a sense of belonging. Group identity may be tied to the recognition of nation, in itself neither a simple nor a stable concept. Concepts of national origin and of nationality are understood according to the knowledge of common history, of shared conflicts, and of what are often perceived as collective achievements. This knowledge base can be maintained through language, historical narratives, cultural expression, and national symbols.[6]

When group stability is jeopardized due to internal conflict or external aggression, groups are compelled to define similarities, and behavioral norms as rules of conduct, traditions, and language become strategic tools for cultural defense (Royce 1982; Horowitz 1985). Such strategies for defense are often seen in countries that emerge from colonialism and begin to explore the impact of their pre- and post-colonial histories. One response to the stress of colonialism is the effort to establish distinction. Horowitz describes this reaction as a *movement of differentiation* recalling historic glories and "emphasizing cultural uniqueness" (115).[7] While identity can provide a fluid frame for cultural analysis, the concepts of nation and nationalism belong to a varied repertoire of scholarly discourse that attempts to understand this globally-manifested aspect of group definition.

Michael Ignatieff defines nationalism as a combination of political, moral, and cultural ideals that ultimately provide groups with identity boundaries leading to the historic and contemporary justification of assertion, including violent action.[8]

Despite the examples of violent nationalism in past and present world conflict (Chechnya and the former Yugoslavia), national identity and nationalist exclusivity are not parallel concepts. The ideal and practical construction of territorial boundaries based on ethnic ties can be an internal, conscious, historically-based process that groups rely on as a physical metaphor for identity. However, even without territory, or ethnicity, nationalism really struggles to answer questions of differentiation and to provide legitimacy according to cultural difference, according to "what we are not."

Benedict Anderson (1983) offers an analysis of nationalism from a developmental perspective. He theorizes that the nation is an "imagined political community" shaped in modern times through print technology and communication and perceived as a natural evolution, a historically-based, universally-accepted concept. While Anderson strives to understand the conceptual development of nationalism as a process, he stresses that negating the process as a "falsity or fabrication" obscures the overriding acceptance of the concept as a defining element of diversity and distinction in our global communities. He stresses the imagined state of communities bound by elastic

"Žyvie Bielaruś!": Nationalism, Critiques, and Cultural Responses   7

borders that exist partly on the basis of accepting the existence of a neighboring nation. Therefore the ideological hold of the *nation* exists because the root of the concept lies in the perceived connectedness between cultural practice and political differentiation, not in politics alone (14–40).

The reciprocal relationship between self-definition and outside acceptance is part of Belarus' national experience. Its history, tied to the national development of Samogitia (modern-day Lithuania), to the Polish Commonwealth (1569–1795), and to that of the Russian Empire, places Belarus in a tug-of-war for the ownership of history, for cultural distinction, and for the right to assert national identity.[9] Part of the outside perception is complicated by the perceived success of what Partha Chatterjee labels *official nationalism*.[10] In countries that have experienced colonization, for example pre-sovereignty Belarus, the notion of nation was being constructed by a political ideology that equally manipulated cultural choices. Chatterjee describes 'Russification' as a model of official nationalism which "involved the imposition of cultural homogeneity from the top, through state action" (165).

The manipulation of culture through state action was aggressively implemented throughout Belarus' history. One key example is connected to Joseph Stalin's definition of the nation and his subsequent manipulation of the Belarusan language. Stalin's nation doctrine had to justify the varied make-up of the Soviet construct. His definition stressed a historically constituted conglomerate of people who had lengthy and systematic connections, common territory, economic interdependence, and a definable spiritual complexion or national character.[11] These criteria were underlined by the perception of a national community based on language (Russian). Stalin's *official nationalism* altered the Belarusan language in a very specific way. In 1933, Soviet policy eliminated certain written elements in Belarusan orthography and grammar. Central to these changes was the outlawing of one letter, the "ь" [miakki znak]. The purpose was to bring the sonic characteristics of the Belarusan language closer to that of Russian, thus facilitating linguistic assimilation.[12] In addition to the manipulation of language, Belarusan demographics were also manipulated in the Soviet attempt to homogenize populations.

The Soviet mandate for the internationalization of populations in the Soviet Union led to many other colonial strategies including the displacement and conscious seeding of many groups into "other" geographic environments. In the case of Belarus this process was particularly aggressive because the system sought to "provide an ethnic Russian presence in an important Russian border region" (Clem 1990, 113). In addition to providing a military presence along the iron curtain this process was seen as a way to replace national and regional identities by the forceful adoption of a one-option Soviet nationalism based on Russian culture, language, and a centralized single-party rule. The psychological and practical effects of these experiences are seen and heard in contemporary Belarus. The freedom to react, to explore and assert a Belarusan national identity has also been defined by a knowledge of and reaction to the Soviet experience, and somewhat by the realization that world communities accept the definition of Belarus as outlined by Soviet scholars and politicians.

The contrast between national sentiment and historiography suggests key questions in the understanding of national identity in contemporary Belarus:

1. who controls the *current* definition(s) of national identity according to what agenda?
2. how are territorial boundaries, and conceptual boundaries for national identity accepted by neighboring nations (and the world community)?
3. how does a group define and articulate who they are and who they are not?
4. how does the loss of an ideology affect a population's sense of security and the search for and construction of a new belief system?

EXPLANATIONS OF IDENTITY CONSTRUCTION: EASTERN EUROPE IN THE WESTERN PRESS

European and American print media sources provide some of the most telling examples of the diverse interpretations of Belarusan identity and the post-Soviet process. This media represents one of the few resources that inform Western audiences about other cultural and political contexts. For Belarusans in the West, print media has the potential to educate the public about Belarus and emphasize the need for diplomatic and economic support. Conversely, the media can also dismiss Belarusan events and issues through the tone of representation, or by ignoring Belarus altogether. The representation of Belarus in media sources is influenced in three ways: (1) the level of attention given to current events in Belarus, (2) the analysis of these current events, and (3) the continuing trend of presenting Belarus in relation to Russia.

In comparison to central Europe and Chechnya, Belarus is rarely considered in American media sources. Despite the rising level of civil unrest and the increased political instability since Alaksandar Lukašenka illegally dissolved Parliament in 1996, the media-conscious public knows relatively little about Belarusan current events. Thorough analyses of post-Soviet change in Belarus are therefore scarce. Lukašenka's recent attempts at reunification with Russia have generated some coverage of Belarus. However, analyses tend towards incredulous criticism of Belarusans who are depicted

"Žyvie Bielaruś!": Nationalism, Critiques, and Cultural Responses 9

as lacking cultural and political backbone.[13] As a result Belarus is represented according to what are described as "national attitudes" or failures, through media coverage that overlooks the social and cultural climate of the country. What media sources outside Belarus fail to address is the lack of a free press in Belarus and the banning of political demonstrations (which when held in defiance of Lukašenka's government result in beatings and illegal imprisonment).[14] There is little coverage given to popular sentiment. The lack of long-term investigation and the continuing focus on Moscow as the epicenter of political change ignore the nature of political and social processes in nations that are trying to define their post-Soviet identities according to practical and perceptual separation from Russia.

Russian print media and television sources suggest that attitudes towards the break-up of the Soviet Union and the independence of neighboring states are defined by a lack of comprehension about why "their neighbors" would want to leave. The expression of this attitude was not always overt. During fieldwork in 1993, two years after the declaration of sovereignty, news segments from Moscow often included such statements as "the Belarusan province" or "the Belarusan territory," suggesting a lack of recognition of Belarusan independence. Further, Russian academics generally articulated the attitude that Belarusans were provincial through masked phrases such as, "we will always consider Belarus as our **little** neighbor."[15] Such subtle expressions are a contemporary extension of cultural colonialism whereby the acknowledgment of the nation, as well as the value of Belarusan culture are downplayed in contrast to the perpetuation of a "mother" Russia. A brief Moscow-based article illustrates the dismissal of Belarus by the media. The article, which lists the recent disappearances of Lukašenka's opponents ends as follows: ". . . Last month the authorities closed a newspaper. On October 4th, police, accompanied—it is said—by a deputy interior minister, confiscated a human-rights group's office equipment. All this has barely been noted outside Belarus. Russian journalists, among the few outsiders watching poor Belarus, must have been busy elsewhere."[16]

The lack of attention in North American media as well as the perceptual legacy of a Russian-centered Soviet Union have influenced attitudes towards post-Soviet nations. Conversely, British and French journalists have contributed much to the understanding of Western interpretations about Belarus and other post-Soviet republics. One explanation for the Russian tendency to minimize their neighbors emphasizes the difficult process of changing the definition of Russian identity. In "L'improbabilité de l'identité russe," Daniel Vernet writes that, for Russia, the celebrated sovereignty of the former Soviet republics also indicates a tremendous loss in territory that forces a shift in the definition of identity — a shift that can no longer embrace the notion of Russia as the colonizer, nor Soviet Russia as the center of an acquired empire.[17] Belarusan writer, Vasil Bykau supports Vernet's analysis by suggesting that the emerging character of Russian democracy is still defined by imperialism: "We see how Russian democracy, which liberated itself from Communism perhaps the most, has now found itself under the spell of an imperial mentality."[18]

The Russian writer Alexander Soljenitsyne, also contributes to the discourse on a newly-defined Eastern Europe. Soljenitsyne comments on world policy and the independence of the former Soviet republics of Belarus and Ukraine. He sees American intervention to secure independence in these nations as hypocrisy, since he assumes, as do many Russians, that these nations should naturally want, and be allowed to return to the Russian fold. He does not explore the strategies used to ensure reunification nor the political and social processes at work outside of a Russian-defined view of neighboring nations.[19] The ways in which Belarus is considered in the media can affect the practical and symbolic acknowledgement of a nation by the world community. The tone of reportage can also affect internal responses to a national identity where the support and validation of national reconstruction can contribute to political and cultural confidence.

The Soviet experience, Lukašenka's policies, and continuing pressures from the east [Moscow] have had a definite impact on the Belarusan people's perception of their political empowerment. The loss of a politically mandated belief system and the absence of a clear all-encompassing alternative emphasize the uncertainty of personal and national futures. In the five years after the declaration of sovereignty Belarus has, to Western eyes, returned full circle from defining its independent status from Russia to the April 1996 return to *sovereignty association* with its historical colonizer.[20]

To assume that Belarusans are indifferent to their nationhood denies contemporary attempts to articulate identity and place in a new Europe. As a result, the question *who do we want to be?* sits at the fulcrum of defining nation identity in Belarus. In addition to the inconsistent access to historical and cultural information,[21] one of the major dilemmas affecting identity definition is the ability to react to and indeed to recognize the effects of past sovietization and of the present government without fear of retribution.

Belarus is a country that culturally, socially, economically, and politically is being deconstructed and reconstructed at an accelerated pace. As in other Eastern European nations, part of the reconstruction process includes the confrontation of cultural sovietization. In Belarus the evaluation of the cultural experience that defined much of the twentieth century is complicated by the lack of a *commonly* accepted indigenous model for the future.[22] Therefore, the term reconstruction is somewhat of an anachronism because it suggests the rebuilding of a remembered, pre-existing model. Instead, like many eastern European nations, Belarus is undergoing self-imposed experiments that publicly and privately highlight issues of identity, of language choice, and of national definition. In 1993 these experiments included the reintegration of an indigenous national language, the revamping of educational systems and materials, and the construction of a positive cultural image in the media.

* * *

The mediators of Belarusan identity, such as the musicians and academicians in this study, contribute to a contemporary definition of Belarusan, whether within a subculture, within their village or urban community, or on a national level. With such a complex historiography, and with so many voices competing for dominance in the acceptance of their definition of nation and identity, how are Belarusans being presented with a foundation for cultural and political identities?

In Belarus, the search for cultural definition is primarily based on the persistent exploration of traditional forms of expression. In television and print media, language and music have become central to the process of locating a Belarusan self. The media, academicians, musicians, and to some extent politicians draw upon traditional resources in this process. By 1993, television and radio programming originating in the national studios was in the Belarusan language, Belarusan-language rock music was favored for broadcast, and politicians often piggy-backed their speeches after rock concerts and other cultural performances. The Belarusan language as well as musical expression seem to function as references for a national definition that is separate from the Soviet experience and represent the opportunity to bring Belarusan-specific expression into the public sphere.

Performances ultimately reach the public through radio, television, and sponsored live performance. For example, audiences are offered performances of rural musical repertoires from traditional calendrical rituals. Such programming attempts to give value to the Belarusan language and to Belarusan cultural practices unknown to those generations that were born into a Soviet conception of the B.S.S.R. [Byelorussian Socialist Soviet Republic]. The focus on tradition is only one of many variables affecting music making in Belarus. Other issues include,

1. the impact of World Music and Western popular cultures,
2. conflicts generated in the comparisons between new urban music and rural practice,
3. whose definition of 'traditional' and 'authentic' will have the most impact on the construction of a national identity?

For the cultural scholar this means trying to make sense of an ever-evolving question mark. In Belarus, some search for a *Belarusaness* and some look elsewhere for their understanding of cultural and political change.[23] Belarusans experience the impact of such changes on many fronts. New political figures criticize the well-established familiar doctrines that were nur-

12   *Of Mermaids and Rock Singers*

tured by the Soviet system. Changes in the economy not only reflect the success or failure of new politics but force many families to live in poverty. New education policies, tied to the reintegration of the Belarusan language, also have an impact on language expectations in the work place. In conjunction with such profound and accelerated change, Belarusans are involved in the examination and construction of a national identity. Though cultural choice is a significant aspect of a rapidly changing Belarus, the possibility to make choices does not negate the continuing impact of fear, conflict, persecution, and the negative official attitudes towards indigenous cultural practices.

With the election of populist president Lukašenka in 1994 and a renewed political instability in Belarus, many non-Belarusan scholars began to take interest in political developments in Belarus.[24] And yet Belarus represents a cultural and political enigma. Little has been written about the cultural explorations that emerged in the mid-1980s, defined the public media in the early 1990s, and that continue fervently today despite the new Moscow-linked administration.

The following section serves as a general introduction to Belarus. It places Belarus geographically and historically at the eastern threshold of Europe while considering attitudes towards the Belarusan language, culture, and national consciousness. These issues necessarily shape the study of music making in Belarus and highlight the fervent pace of self-exploration that characterized cultural and musical life in post-Soviet (1991) and pre-Lukašenka (1994) Belarus.

NOTES

[1] Franz Fanon, *A Dying Colonialism* (New York: Grove Weidensfeld, 1965; 1992), 151.

[2] Western blueprints for political change, once considered universally applicable, produce varied and complex results in non-Western countries. Charles C. Lemert writes: "Dreams of normality fashioned out of the daily residue of the West's unfinished business are common throughout East Central Europe, as they are in the Baltic, Central America and Asia" ("Intellectuals and Politics: Social Theory in a Changing World," in vol. 5 of *Key Issues in Sociological Theory* [London: Sage Publications, 1991], vii).

[3] Post-sovereignty (1991) treatments of Belarusan history and political life include the impact of political and cultural choice in the new Belarus, and of how historical colonization and the Soviet experience affects the politics of culture in this nation. The most recent historical treatments of Belarus consider the impact of history and cultural experiences on Belarusans. See Jan Zaprudnik, *Belarus at a Crossroads in History*, (Boulder: Westview Press, 1993); hereafter cited in text, and David Marples, *Belarus: From Soviet Rule to Nuclear Catastrophe* (Edmonton: University of Alberta Press, 1996); hereafter cited in text. Zaprudnik offers a broad exploration of Belarusan history and explains how writings on Belarus have been bound to the conceptual shadow of Russia. He provides a detailed his-

"Żyvie Bielaruś!": Nationalism, Critiques, and Cultural Responses   13

tory of this area and an analysis of the attitudes that have defined perceptions about Belarus by scholars and by historical experience. Additional sources include evaluations of writings on Belarus in the international press. The most comprehensive English language source is *Belarusan Review* (Torrence, California: Belarusan-American Association), and in French, *Perspectives Bielorussiennes* (Paris: Association pour le développement de la recherche, de l'information et de la culture sur la Biélorussie).

[4] James Clifford, *The Predicament of Culture: Twentieth Century Ethnography, Literature, and Art* (Cambridge: Harvard University Press, 1988), 97. In his analysis "Soviet Documentation of Byelorussia's History (1902–1919)," Jan Zaprudnik outlines the consistent omission of Belarusan culture in such publications (in *Zapisy 17: Proceedings of the Twenty-fifth Anniversary Symposium of the Byelorussian Institute of Arts and Sciences February 1977* [New York: St. Sophia Press, 1983], 132–141); hereafter cited in text. Instead, political, military, and economic aspects are the focus of Soviet attention. Zaprudnik describes cultural discrimination through omission as an "offensive" weapon of historical scholarship: "silence, turning events into non-events, persons into non-persons, and documents into dead pieces of paper buried deep in archival vaults" (138). The absence of Belarusan-based documents and publications illustrates the completeness of this silence and the lack of reference to a non-Russian cultural past. This facilitates the elimination of individual Belarusan cultural identity. Belarus was not part of the official political equation, it was instead, ". . . primarily a cultural phenomenon. To be Byelorussian was to speak the language, to have an awareness of ethnic distinctiveness and of a separate historical past" (139). In his contribution to a 1977 symposium on nationalism in the USSR and Eastern Europe, Zaprudnik includes the following excerpt from *Kommunist Belorussii*: "One must not close his eyes to the fact that certain of our people sometimes fall under the influence of bourgeois propaganda and become bearers of nationalistic and chauvinistic tendencies. This is why the very first obligation of party organizations is to conduct an unflinching struggle against manifestations of remnants of any form of nationalism and national limitation and exclusiveness" ("Developments in Belorussia Since 1964," in *Nationalism in the U.S.S.R. in the Era of Brezhnev & Kosygin*, ed. George W. Simmonds [Detroit: University of Detroit Press, 1977], 106; hereafter cited in text). The negative treatment of nationalism as well as the suggestion that it is dwindling, construct as well as support assumptions of the totality of Russian assimilation. However, Zaprudnik logically argues that the need for the critique of nationalism implies its continued existence. This was clearly illustrated in the decade preceding the break-up of the Soviet Union with the political strengthening of grassroots independence movements in many Soviet republics.

[5] Royce writes that conscious identity switching can be used as a power/protection strategy. The success of such a switch requires knowledge of the ethnic style of the alternative group (1982).

[6] The ownership of historical achievements as defining political and social development is central to the study of history and identity. Benedict Anderson suggests that it is not only a question of how a nation sees itself, but of how other nations see it. He writes: "nation is partly tied to an agreement by outsiders to

honor boundaries and national identities" (*Imagined Communities: Reflections on the Origin and Spread of Nationalism* [London: Verso, 1983], 13; hereafter cited in text). Writing history cannot escape the impact of the ideological and necessarily subjective lenses of the historian and of his sources. Such subjectivity has become apparent in the many post-colonial explorations of culture in the late twentieth century. Present trends in historical deconstruction and post-colonialism strive to balance the voices of history with the experiences of history, and spark debates amongst scholars who themselves are bound by the tradition of their disciplines. For Belarusan scholars this means making sense of political rhetoric and cultural commentary that Russifies or Polonizes Belarus.

[7] Other criteria for differentiation, for a national *raison d'être*, include the equally problematic concept of ethnicity. Talcott Parsons expresses the connection between ethnicity and nation. He writes that in the complexity of criteria that have defined the *ethnic* element of group identity, the concept of national origin is "the most accurate designation for most groups" ("Some Theoretical Considerations on the Nature and Trends of Change of Ethnicity" in *Ethnicity: Theory and Experience*, ed. Nathan Glazer and Daniel P. Moynihan [Cambridge: Harvard, 1975], 56).

[8] Michael Ignatieff, *Blood and Belonging* (New York: Farrar, Straus, and Giroux, 1993), 8–11; hereafter cited in text. Ignatieff opposes this "ethnic nationalism" to a "civic nationalism" which manifests itself in democratic systems that embrace diverse cultural environments and promotes the co-existence of various cultural identities. Cultures that have histories based on migration and immigration to new countries therefore share in a civic nationalism, where they reorganize their cultural identities as members of another nation group. Analysis stresses that nationalism, including the definition of territory, is not necessarily a natural evolutionary end to the definition of an ethnic identity. However, if considered as a catalyst for action, ethnic nationalism is often manifested as asserting exclusivity according to blood ties, often to the detriment of those outside a particular group (11).

[9] The lack of a violent assertion of nation in Belarusan history might add to the perception that Belarusans are passive about their nation identity or that they have, as Ralph S. Clem describes, "a propensity to acculturate and assimilate" ("Belorussians," in *The Nationalities Question in the Soviet Union*, ed. Graham Smith [London: Longman, 1990], 113); hereafter cited in text. Such perceived passivity is explained as a reaction to memories of war and their continued impact on family histories.

[10] Partha Chatterjee, "Nationalism as a Problem," in *Nationalist Thought and the Colonial World: A Derivative Discourse* (Japan and London: Zeb Books for United Nations University, 1986).

[11] Joseph Stalin, "The Nation," in *Nationalism*, ed. John Hutchison and Anthony Smith (Oxford: Oxford University Press, 1994), 18–21.

[12] See Valentyna Pashkievich, *Fundamental Byelorussian* (Toronto: Harmony, 1974), iv-v; Jan Zaprudnick (1993: 88); David Marples (24–39); Maria Paula Survilla (1992: 46–47).

"Žyvie Bielaruś!": Nationalism, Critiques, and Cultural Responses   *15*

[13] With Lukašenka's Union Treaty with Yeltsin's administration in December 1999, Belarus has been criticized for not upholding the process towards democracy and independence. The non-democratic means by which Lukašenka achieved this Treaty are seldom covered in media sources.

[14] The backlash against anti-Lukašenka demonstrations has increased in recent months. Also see Geoffrey York "Lukašenka tightens his grip on Belarus : Towards Totalitarianism," *Globe and Mail* , 4 April 1997; "Shadows of Soviet era again cast pall on Belarus," *Globe and Mail*, 5 August 1997.

[15] Fieldwork observations of the nightly news from Moscow (Miensk, June 1993).

[16] "St. Sasha of Minsk," *Economist*, 8 October 1999, 61.

[17] Daniel Vernet, "L'improbable indentité russe," *Le Monde*, 1 August 1995, 2–4.

[18] Quoted in Zaprudnik (1994: 214) as published in *Literatura i Mastatstva*, 7 February 1992.

[19] "Soljenitsyne: l'hypocrisie du XXe siècle finissant," *L'Express* 2407(August 1997), 50–52.

[20] The legislation that began *sovereignty association* with Russia was signed by President Lukašenka on April 5, 1996 in Moscow.

[21] For the Diaspora, knowledge of historic and personal conflict has resulted in a continued conscious definition of identity. The Diaspora has had the option to define being Belarusan in both private and public arenas. While a qualitative comparison of these environments is not the aim of this document, qualitative judgments are a part of how Diaspora and homeland communities have begun to evaluate each other. On the basis of these notions, each has made choices about how they might become involved in defining and addressing the concept of nation. See Survilla 1990.

[22] It is clear that the existence of one ideal national model is unrealistic. Max Weber makes this clear in his definition of nation where he outlines that the construction of nation is never based upon a universally accepted model. Instead, responses to the construction of a nation vary greatly from within a group: from affirmation, to negation, or even indifference. The process of defining that nation can reflect internal power struggles that attempt to articulate cultural values either in tandem with, or in contrast with existing politics. See Max Weber, "The Nation," in *Nationalism*, ed. John Hutchison and Anthony Smith (Oxford: Oxford University Press, 1994), 21–25.

[23] Understanding the idea of cultural choice affects every participant culture in the process of *decolonization*. Bill Ashcroft writes: "but the binarism of one ethnic group at the center and all others at the margin overlooks the actual overlap between the multiplicity of ethnic groups and the dynamic process and multifaceted institution of power" (Introduction to *The Post-Colonial Studies Reader*, ed. Bill Ashcroft, Gareth Griffiths, Helen Tiffin [London: Routledge, 1995], 10).

[24] Lukašenka represents a return to Soviet-style political oligarchy in a nation at the edge of Western Europe. His policies negating human rights, free elections,

and a free press, and de-legalizing Belarusan language, education, and culture have also tied Belarus politically to Russia.

2.

Terminology, Controversy, and the Interpretation of History

THE MODERN-DAY REPUBLIC OF BELARUS[1] LIES AT THE EASTERN THRESHOLD OF Europe. Its area of 80,154 square miles is bordered by Russia to the east, Lithuania to the northwest, Latvia to the north, Ukraine to the south, and Poland to the west (see Figure 2.1). Sitting at the crossroads between eastern and western Europe, Belarus has consistently felt the impact of its strategic placement; first as a crossroads for trade routes[2] and subsequently as the battleground for conflict. This territorial position has also determined the make-up and distribution[3] of the population. The ethnographic make-up of Belarus has changed most dramatically in the twentieth century through war losses, border changes due to post-war treaties, and politically-controlled migration.[4]

Such a provocative geographic location has defined Belarus' historical relationship with its closest neighbors and, as a result, has affected how Belarusans locate their cultural and political identities. The following sections consider defining events in Belarusan history. These pivotal moments are part of a cycle of cultural and political change that reflects three kinds of historical experience:

1. self-government, growth, and cultural and political definition [represented by the "Golden Era" of the Grand Duchy of Litva],
2. colonization and political and cultural subjugation [Imperial Russia, Stalinism, Sovietization],
3. national renewal through political assertion and cultural exploration [political uprisings and literary movements in the nineteenth century, cultural and national renaissance in the early twentieth century, activity of the intelligentsia, and cultural and political assertion in the 1980s–1990s].

17

In the last decade of the twentieth century such movements towards national renewal have culminated in independence and the opportunity of political self-determination. Initial reactions to independence as well as long term projections about the significance of new freedoms reveal much about how Belarusans evaluate their nation, their culture, and the importance of regional, generational, and linguistic belonging.

Figure 2.1: Miensk, Belarus and General View of Eastern Europe outlining present boundaries and ethnographic territories. The administrative divisions within Belarus are called regions (voblaść): Brest, Homiel, Hrodna, Miensk, Mahiloŭ, and Viciebsk (Map Designed by Joseph Arciuch, Courtesy of *Belarusian Review*).

STEPS TOWARDS INDEPENDENCE

On August 25, 1991 Belarus declared its independence. This official secession from the Soviet Union was part of a mass movement of political and social change that had already seen the declarations of independence by Lithuania, Russia, Latvia, Estonia, and Ukraine since March of the same year.[5] While these steps towards independence were driven by internal movements in each Republic, the direction of change in Eastern Europe and the Soviet block was given impetus by the policies of then Soviet president Mikhail Gorbachev.

Terminology, Controversy, and Interpretation of History 19

For the Soviet republics, Gorbachev's policies of *perestroika* (restructuring) and *glasnost* (openness) acquired a different meaning than was first envisioned by the Soviet administration: "He [Gorbachev] became like the Sorcerer's Apprentice, unable to control what he started because he misunderstood what he was experimenting with. He wanted reform socialism, even transformed socialism. He got democracy, however unsure and faltering" (Brown 1991, 4–5). The Gorbachev period served to foster new and pre-existing national movements by highlighting the potential for change amongst dissatisfied populations, and by announcing this potential and desire to the rest of the world.[6]

In Belarus, political, cultural, and language-based reform movements had been emerging from the underground since the early 1980s. By the end of the decade the intelligentsia as well as youth groups were publicly and aggressively expressing expectations for change.[7] Such groups had a significant impact on the process of sovereignty in many Eastern European and Soviet contexts. As Brown writes, "it was the intellectuals, in company with the young, who finally pushed through to liberty."[8]

Activism in Belarus drew upon the exploration of pre-Soviet culture and history and the renaissance of the Belarusan language. Language was a significant issue because the Belarusan language had been either outlawed or manipulated as a means to ensure Russification. Taking back control of a national language was both a symbolic and a practical move towards independence. By January 26, 1991 the Supreme Council of the Belarusan SSR passed the "Law About Languages of the BSSR," making Belarusan the official language of the republic.[9] In September of the same year, the Supreme Council of Belarus replaced the Soviet flag and coat of arms with pre-Soviet national symbols (see Figure 2.2), and reinstated the historical name of the republic. As an icon for Belarus' historical identity, the *Pahonia*[10] has served as the emblem of Belarusan freedom movements since the mid-nineteenth century. The crest has generated controversy about the ownership of the history associated with the Grand Duchy of Litva. The latter is seen by some scholars as the historical name for the Belarusan territory and as an indicator of Belarusan history. Opposing views see the Duchy and the crest as part of the history of modern-day Lithuania (see National Origins and the "Golden Era," p. 22–27).

The restoration of these national symbols reflected efforts to accentuate Belarusan culture as a fulcrum for a contemporary national identity. Academicians, artists, writers, and musicians were finally free to ask Belarusan-specific historical and cultural questions. As one student said: "We were unaware that we had a Belarusan history, we were told that history began in 1918" [with the Bolshevik revolution].[11]

National consciousness and the articulation of a Belarusan identity have been central to public debates and media activity, including music production, since the mid-1980s. That is, many of the movements for change that seemed to emerge after 1991 existed at the grass-roots level in the preceding decade. The initial steps towards independence opened a practical and conceptual threshold for Belarusans. This doorway served to expand the possibilities for national redefinition and exposed the continuing effects of Tsarist, Stalinist, and Soviet experience on contemporary Belarusan cultural identities. The public celebration of Belarus by intelligentsia and youth groups was in direct contrast to the frustration of a population that has felt the repercussions of colonization over the last three centuries.[12]

Figure 2.2: The Belarusan Flag and the Belarusan Coat of Arms Pahonia. The Belarusan flag (white-red-white) was officially adopted as the national flag in 1918 as a result of the March 25th proclamation of independence of the Belarusan Democratic Republic. It replaced the Soviet flag in 1991, and was outlawed by Lukašenka's administration in 1995.

Haunted by a cultural inferiority complex, many Belarusans are perplexed by the re-valuing of a culture that was ridiculed by Russian expansionist, Stalinist, and Soviet policies. The strategies of the process of colonization have left many Belarusans with cultural scars and damaged self-perceptions. As Paget Henry writes: "it [colonization] also uproots cultural institutions, whose transformation uproots and reorganizes, in turn, the consciousness of the colonized."[13] According to historian Jan Zaprudnik this is most evident in government bureaucracy: "Russification was an organic outgrowth of Stalinist policies. It became an additional psychological barrier to change. "Change" now meant a return to, or at least a tolerance of, Belarusian culture; but this culture was alien to the Russified bureaucracy" (1993, 124). Zaprudnik further theorizes that the Russified bureaucracy, now members of a New Class, were responding negatively to *perestroika* because this restructuring included the re-valuing of a language which they had abandoned. These negative responses often were and still are manifested as violence

Terminology, Controversy, and Interpretation of History

against those that demonstrated a willingness to explore Belarusan themes and traditional practices in the public sphere.[14]

Belarusan history reflects one thousand years of complex politics, of territorial change, and of expressive ritual life that continue to have an impact on the elaboration of Belarusan identity. The principal factors that contribute to the interpretation of Belarusan history include:

1. terminology: how it shapes territorial and historical perceptions.
2. origins: how they are defined in order to establish difference or belonging.
3. differentiation: how it is illustrated in cultural production and language.
4. assimilation and colonization: its effects on religion, education, language, and terminology.

The following sections consider these factors in relation to several significant events in Belarusan history. These events not only defined the scope of the Belarusan territory, they determined the breadth and nature of Belarusan cultural life. Today these historical moments have specific relevance as reference points for understanding past and present trends in Belarusan cultural and linguistic self-perception.

TERMINOLOGY

> To rob people and countries of their name is to set in motion a psychic disturbance which can in turn create a permanent crisis of identity
> Jan Carew (1985)[15]

The history of the Belarus resonates with a long list of labels that were established, then replaced according to peaceful unions and forcible colonization. The term Belarus (f. Bełaya Ruś: biełaja from biały meaning "white") has been applied in the modern sense for the past one hundred years.[16] Although many interpretations exist explaining the relevance of the word "white," prevalent theories reflect religious and political events in the Middle Ages, especially the repelling of Tartar invaders between 1240 and 1480.[17] Here, as in this country's contemporary literature and folklore, the term "biały" symbolizes freedom (Kipel 1983, 14). Additional designations and their spellings are outlined below:[18]

Historical terms:

Polack Rús—Polaččyna
Smalensk Rús—Smalenščyna
Litva

The Grand Duchy of Litva
North Western Territory
West Russia

Contemporary designations:

Belarus
Belorussia
White Ruthenia
Bielarus
White Russia
Beloruthenia
Byelorussia

The lack of a consistent label has generated many controversies in the historical placement of Belarus, as well as in contemporary perceptions of this nation. As with the name *Belarus*, many debates are based on terminology. The two main terminological disputes center upon the interpretation of the terms Ruś and Litva.

Historian Jan Zaprudnik (1993, xix; 1–13) compares past associations of the term Ruś with modern usage. He addresses the assumption in much eastern European scholarship that Ruś designates Russia.[19] The term first indicated the territory outlined by Kiev, Chernigov and Pereyslavl, now part of Ukraine. The scope of the name changed with the expansion of Kievan Ruś in the tenth century and included Novgorod, Pskov, Połacak, and Muscovy. In the fourteenth century, the term signaled the establishment of Christian Orthodoxy as defined by the Byzantine and Kievan Empires. More recently, Ruś has been used to package Ukrainian and Belarusan histories through Tsarist, Stalinist, and Soviet pan-Slavist policy that supported the "existence of [a] unified Old-Ruśian nationality"(9).

NATIONAL ORIGINS AND THE "GOLDEN ERA"

Studies of medieval eastern Europe emphasize the differentiation of territories according to tribal, religious, and political loyalties. Tribal migration and economic trade routes were key to the development of early city centers and principalities. The names Połacak, Turaŭ, and Navahradak refer to the three cities and their principalities associated with the historical genesis of modern Belarus.[20] The largest of these, the Połacak principality, encapsulated the lands that had been settled by members of the Kryvichan tribe as early as the sixth century AD (Smalensk, Viciebsk, Orša, Miensk, and Druck). The city of Połacak, established in 862 AD by the Scandinavian Prince Rurik, lay between Kiev and Novgorod as a central link in the route between Scandinavia and Byzantium. Political ties between Połacak, Kiev, and Novgorod reflect the intrigues, territorial expansions, and changing loyalties of a feudal era.

Połacak quickly developed a thriving economy. Conquered by Kievan Vladimir (d. 1015) in 980, it regained its independence by the end of the eleventh century under Usiasłaŭ Bračysłavič (d. 1101). Turaŭ, a smaller city and principality positioned nearer to Kiev, achieved independence in 1162 under Jury Jarasłavič (Zaprudnik 1993, 9–24). By the thirteenth century, three principalities had been defined according to territory and to ruling princes independent from Kiev.[21] These principalities, Smalensk, Turaŭ-Pinsk, and Połacak-Viciebsk eventually form the boundaries of the Belarusan territory (Figure 2.3).

Figure 2.3: The Grand Duchy of Lithuania, Ruś, and Samogitia (According to Zaprudnik 1993, 31). The bold line outlines the territory of post-sovereignty Belarus.

The late Middle Ages and Renaissance are especially significant for Belarusan historians. Politics and the division of territory are presented as the foundation of Belarusan statehood (Kipel and Kipel, 1988), while examples from the arts, literature, and law suggest a stable economy, good social conditions, and consistent connections to Western Europe. Belarusan historians refer to this period as "The Golden Era," suggesting a peak in development, growth, and quality of life. The territorial and political events that define this period are also at the crux of a debate about historical and terminological ownership. The focus of the debate centers upon the development of the Grand Duchy of Litva (1240s–1795), and the Duchy's subsequent significance in the histories of Belarus and modern-day Lithuania.

24   *Of Mermaids and Rock Singers*

In the early thirteenth century agreements amongst the ruling principalities were influenced by a succession of religious and economic affiliations. The stresses in this period were defined by the advancement of German missionaries from the west (Knights of the Sword and Knights of the Cross or Teutonic Knights) and the Tartars from the east. Over the span of several decades they forced economic trade agreements and engaged in the Christianization of the population. Eventually the Teutonic Knights extended their activities amongst the Baltic tribes to the north. Pressures from east and west added another element to the warring amongst regional principalities and influenced the consolidation of territories into the Grand Duchy of Litva in the middle of the thirteenth century. As a historical marker, the Grand Duchy has generated several interpretations about its significance in the developmental histories of this area (Zaprudnik 1993, 18–19).

The Grand Duchy was consolidated under Mindoŭh (1200–1263), a Lithuanian Prince who had relocated to the Belarusan town of Navahradak. According to Zaprudnik, Mindoŭh brought together ". . . east Lithuanian and west Belarusan territories—namely, the Grand Duchy of Lithuania and Ruś (Samogitia, the area now known as Western Lithuania, was added in the mid-fifteenth century to the name of the state.)" (18). Writing in the early twentieth century, historian Dovnar-Zapolsky describes the consolidation of the Grand Duchy as the result of inter-marriage and the breakdown of power in the once-powerful Belarusan principality of Turaŭ-Pinsk due to a lack of male heirs in the ruling families (1988, 40). Both Dovnar-Zapolsky and Zaprudnik address the notion that the Grand Duchy of Litva conquered the Belarusan principalities. Dovnar-Zapolsky writes: "The grand duke concluded treaties with the principalities of Polotzk, Smolensk, and Vitebsk and delivered them special constitutional charters, whereas in those principalities where the dynasties had not become extinct , the local Princes acknowledged themselves as vassals of the grand duke of Lithuania. And so the annals of history refute most decidedly all symptoms of a conquest of White Russian lands by the Princes of Lithuania" (40).

Zaprudnik responds to the issue of conquest and its use in histories produced during then Soviet period: "Contrary to the claims of some authors (including those of the old Soviet school of history) about the conquest of Belarusans and their domination by Lithuanians in the Grand Duchy, history has recorded neither any major battles between the two neighboring peoples nor any facts of ethnic oppression. On the contrary, the formation of the Grand Duchy was accomplished largely through voluntary arrangements, including marriages, and occurred as a consequence of centuries-long interspersed cohabitation of Slavic and Baltic tribes before the rise of the common state" (1993, 19). The independence of Belarusan principalities is of foremost importance in the historical evaluation of the "Golden Era" because it vali-

Terminology, Controversy, and Interpretation of History   25

dates a Belarusan presence in a significant period of development in Eastern Europe.

The Belarusan presence is described according to the cultural and linguistic contributions to life in the Duchy. Historian John Sadouski writes that Byelorussian became the official language of the Duchy and was used in "official business and legal procedures, as well as [. . .] literary works and religious polemics" (1981, 22). By 1517 the Bible was translated into Belarusan by Dr. Frančišak Skaryna, making Belarusan the second Slavic language group to produce the Bible in the vernacular.[22] The Statute of the Grand Duchy of Litva [Statut Vialikaha Kniastva Litoŭskaha] was published in 1529. Written in the Belarusan language, this document was considered "one of the most complete handwritten codes of the Middle Ages" (23) containing a legal system which declared that freedom of religion was the right of every resident in the Duchy.[23] According to Belarusan historians, the importance of the Belarusan language emphasizes the central role of Belarusan influence in the Duchy's infrastructure.[24] Zaprudnik concludes: "to speak of the Grand Duchy of Lithuania, Ruś and Samogitia as purely or even predominantly a Lithuanian state, then, is to distort the past by investing it with terms and concepts from an entirely different era" (1993, 19). Instead, The Duchy's "Golden Era" is a historical reference point which supports the Belarusan national idea. Conversely, the Duchy's decline has come to reflect a loss of political power and cultural position due to campaigns of expansion from the east and from the west.

Historian Vitaŭt Siučyk[25] identifies several aspects of the period which contributed to the eventual decline of the Grand Duchy. Searching to strengthen its borders against Muscovite invasion, the Grand Duchy of Litva entered into a commonwealth with the Kingdom of Poland in 1569, known as the Union of Lublin.[26] The basis of this union was the "principle of complete equality" (Łuckievič [1919] 1988, 125). Both territories remained essentially autonomous but relied on each other for military strength. However, differing political ideologies eventually placed the Duchy at a disadvantage. Poland was considered more attractive to the aristocracy and this period saw the exodus of the Duchy's elite into Poland.[27] Jan Zaprudnik writes that the exodus of the upper classes had linguistic, political, and religious repercussions: ". . . following Polonization of the upper strata, conditions for the development of Belarusan culture deteriorated severely. In 1696, by decision of the General Confederation in Warsaw, the Belarusan language in the Grand Duchy lost its official status and was replaced by Polish. Moreover, Catholicism became increasingly identified as the "Polish Creed, . . ." (1993, 38–39).

Religious tensions eventually defined divisions and loyalties amongst the ruling classes. The Union of Brest which formed the Uniate Church in 1596 "undermined the position of the Orthodox Church" [and] "hastened the

Polonization of the nobility whose members perceived political advantages in accepting Polish culture."[28] Polish historian Juliusz Bardach writes: "The loss from the assimilation of the upper social strata certainly had negative results for the peoples of Lithuania and Western Ruś by depriving them of leaders, natural for those times."[29]

According to Siŭčyk, the exodus of the aristocracy served as a capstone for events which had been undermining the Duchy since the 13th century. In *The Unknown War Against Belarus* (1993), Siŭčyk describes the continued threat to the Duchy from the east, first from Mongolian invaders (Kiev was conquered in 1240) and subsequently from their successors in Moscow. The success of these long term actions resulted in, ". . . degradation of the national consciousness of magnate and gentry estates and town dwellers, leaving [. . .] a politically passive peasantry without leadership" (9). In the eighteenth century Poland attempted to take advantage of the weakened infrastructure and gain cultural and political control of the Grand Duchy by imposing Polish as its official language.[30]

The creation of the Grand Duchy represents the consolidation of territories and power in the late Middle Ages. It became a constituent member of the Commonwealth with Poland (1569), and gradually lost its political and cultural sovereignty due to pressures from the east and from the west. Empress Catherine II with support from Prussia and Austria divided the Commonwealth and, by 1795, The Grand Duchy became a part of the Muscovite (Russian) Empire (Łuckievič [1919]1988, 126; Zaprudnik 1999, 12).

The Grand Duchy of Litva is treated by Belarusan historians as a significant developmental period in Belarusan history. It is considered pivotal in both the elaboration of a historical Belarusan identity and in the definition and growth of an independent state. The Grand Duchy continues to have relevance in present-day explorations of the historical origins of Belarusan culture through the celebration of historical icons [Francišak Skaryna, for example], and the enduring interest in the linguistic developments, political philosophies, education, arts, and architecture of this period. Presently The Grand Duchy serves as the standard against which the subsequent experiences and the consequences of colonization and sovietization might be compared. It is significant that in contemporary interpretations the Duchy serves as a historical fulcrum for both Belarus and for modern-day Lithuanians, who consider The Grand Duchy of Litva as part of Lithuanian national history. Litva is a prime example of contestation of the ownership of history. Belarusan historians most often consider the Duchy as the first manifestation of Belarusan statehood, and see its association with Lithuanian history as the result of Polish and Russian campaigns to amputate Belarus' independent history and ease the annexation of the Belarusan territory. Presently, the issue of historical origins is debated in scholarly writing and centers upon the ownership of the present capital city of Lithuania, Vilnia (Bel.) or Vilnius (Lith.).

Terminology, Controversy, and Interpretation of History 27

The city became the capital of the Grand Duchy in 1323. It was part of the Byelorussian S.S.R. when it was given to Lithuania by Stalin on October 10, 1939. (Figure 2.4).

Figure 2.4: Vilnia region given to Lithuania in 1939 (According to Zaprudnik 1993, 90).

AGGRESSIVE COLONIZATION

By the end of the eighteenth century Belarus had lost its upper classes (gentry) to the Polish territory and to the Polish language. The population was experiencing the early application of *official nationalism* through the appropriation of historical labels, the manipulation of terminology, and the control of religious affiliations. In addition Belarusans were experiencing the degradation of their national identities through the lack of language rights and the distortion and/or denial of Belarusan cultural and political history.

After the last[31] partition of the Commonwealth of Poland and Litva in 1795, Tsarist Russia tried to construct the perception of a united empire. Terminology, the manipulation of historical developments, and categorization through religious affiliation were central to strategies of colonization (Figure 2.5).

Figure 2.5: Annexation of Belarusan Territories in the eighteenth century (According to Zaprudnik 1993, 38).

Categorization according to religion was applied as a means of nationalizing religious practice and therefore justifying political assimilation: "denominations were used to advantage by both the Russian and Polish governments: Greek Orthodox Belarusans were regarded as Russians and Roman Catholic Belarusans as Poles" (Sadouski 1981, 48; also see Kipel 1983, 114; Zaprudnik 1993, 45–46) with the third major faith, Uniatism[32] as the faith of the peasantry. This categorization was supported by language use; Catholic services were controlled by Polish clergy and Orthodox services by Russian clergy. In 1839 the Belarusan-speaking Uniates were absorbed into the Orthodox Church (1993, 40).

In order to secure Belarus and its people to the Muscovite State, Russia implemented several other strategies of assimilation including the manipulation of terminology. By 1803, the only officially recognized language was Russian, education was limited to the grade-school level, textbooks were censored, and regional agrarian belief systems were systematically ridiculed in official publications (Kipel 1983, 114).[33] Belarus was stamped with a generic label: *Severo-Zapadnyi Krai* (North-Western Territory) and by 1823 the former Commonwealth of Poland and Litva were designated as Western Russia. The terms Belarus and Litva were officially banned in 1840 (Zaprudnik 1993, 49–50). Through such methods Belarusans "were stripped of their ethnic consciousness" (Kipel 1983, 116) and, if they did not call themselves Russian,

Terminology, Controversy, and Interpretation of History 29

they lost that sense of national unity that comes with a sense of territorial continuity.[34]

REBELLION

National definition, revolution, and Romanticism were key in the Europe of the nineteenth century. Despite the outlawing of the Belarusan language, writers were clandestinely rediscovering their vernacular and circulating their literature in manuscript form.[35] Political change and rebellion also defined the latter part of the century.

In 1861 the Tsar attempted to placate an increasingly frustrated population by abolishing slavery. However, the Tsar's edict served to generate rebellion because landowners still owned 60 percent of the land, thus frustrating the peasantry who expected to own their own farmland. The frustration resulted in 379 peasant uprisings in Belarus in 1861. This climate of protest climaxed in 1863.[36]

Between 1861–1863 approximately 150,000 Russian troops battled Belarusan forces in 1,500 locations (Kipel 1982, 6). Kastuś Kalinoŭski (1838–1864) became the leader of the anti-Russian peasant uprisings between 1863–1864. Publisher of the newspaper *Peasant's Truth* [Mužyckaja Praŭda], he led the Belarus uprising in March 1863. Kalinoŭski was hanged in Vilna in 1864 at the age of twenty-six, another 127 were executed. In retaliation Belarus was "inundated with teachers, priests and landlords from Russia" (Zaprudnik 1993, 57). Kalinoŭski's attempts to organize against and defeat the Muscovites made him an inspirational figure for those struggling to establish a free Belarus. In addition to his leadership role, and to the impact of his execution, Kalinoŭski left his mark through a final statement written before his execution. Known as "From Under the Gallows," Kalinoŭski's testament illustrates the tone of rebellion at the end of the nineteenth century.

> There is no greater happiness in this world than when a man has wisdom and education. Because only then may he live in prosperity and deserve the heavens, when he enriches his heart and his mind and sincerely loves his people. But as day and night do not exist together, so true education cannot be obtained in Moscow's slavery. And while it remains there, we will have nothing [. . .] we will continue to be treated as cattle, doomed to perdition. Fight for your rights as humans and as a people, for your faith, for your native land. For I am telling you from under the gallows that only then you will live happily when the Muscovite will not rule you anymore. (Excerpted in Kreŭski, 13–14).

Moscow's response to the freedom movement was to exile twelve thousand supporters of the rebellion to Siberia. Russia and Poland began campaigns to lay claim to the Belarusan territory and identity. These campaigns are most evident in Russian and Polish publications from this period which

30   *Of Mermaids and Rock Singers*

lay claim to Belarus. The last three decades of the nineteenth century are also characterized by a growing Belarusan national intelligentsia linked to students attending four teachers' seminaries, the only institutions of higher education allowed during this period in Belarus (Zaprudnik 1999, 13).

The 1905 Revolution lead to the establishment of the Russian parliament (The State Duma), to the relaxation of policies against national minorities, and to the lifting of the ban on non-Russian languages (63). After 1905 Belarus enjoyed the reinstatement of the Belarusan language, the name Belarus was officially allowed, and Belarusan-language books and newspapers appeared in many cities, most notably *Our Soil* [Naša Niva] published between 1906 and 1915 (Kipel 1982, 14). Many of Belarus' most important literary figures were active in this period giving impetus to the twentieth-century Belarusan literary movement.[37] Poetic literature is especially indicative of the climate of those times:

> What is it, lords, that you are seeking?
> And what compels you to the need
> To sound the tocsin at the speaking
> A Byelorussian Voice had freed?
>
> What terrifies you in his speaking?
> Believe me, he steals not from you.
> Only his own words he is seeking,
> Those with which he was born and grew.
>
> And now to 'guard' us you are coming,
> As if sprung from the earth, unseen;
> And what, till now, have you accomplished?
> And where, until now, have you been?
>
> [...]
>
> The Byelorussian – he affrights you
> Because he dares to say, to do?
> Ah, much the learning that awaits you
> To pay your brother honour due!
>
> [. . .]
>
> Why crust the bread with harsh callouses,
> – Abuse and onslaught combative?
> The brilliant truth – you will not dowse it:
> The Byelorussian lives, will live!
>
> Excerpted from *To the Enemies of Things Byelorussian* by Janka Kupala (1907). Translation by Vera Rich (1977, 44). Used by permission.

In these verses Kupala addresses the colonizer 's uneasiness with the exploration of Belarusan identity and language. The poem is openly critical of Moscow's intervention and presence in Belarus and emphasizes the need for a respect of Belarus [To pay your brother honour due].

Terminology, Controversy, and Interpretation of History 31

Pro-Belarusan literary and political movements from the early decades of the 20th-century gained added significance in the years prior to independence in 1991. The literary movement was referred to by members of the intelligentsia as a model for a literary and cultural renaissance. The literary basis for the movement was also seen as evidence of the artistic and intellectual value of the Belarusan language. Rock musicians embraced the ideas of cultural and linguistic ownership that characterizes the poetry from this early period. In 1991 the newspaper Naša Niva reappeared on Belarusan newsstands. The paper clearly acknowledges its connection with the turn-of-the-century newspaper. On the first page underneath the newspaper name publishers have added the following: "The First Belarusan Newspaper/Created in 1906./Re-established in 1991." Supporters of the new renaissance were clearly trying to recreate the momentum of the earlier movement. Even the popular post-sovereignty exclamation/toast "Belarus Lives!" can be traced to the poetry of the period [The Byelorussian lives, will live].

Twentieth-century Belarusan experience did much to define post-independence attitudes towards national consciousness and cultural identities. Pivotal events include the declaration of the Belarusan Democratic Republic in 1918, Stalinist policies and purges of the 1930s, the Chernobyl disaster of 1986, sovereignty in 1991, and finally the impact of the present Lukašenka administration.

THE TWENTIETH CENTURY

The modern Belarusan State was conceptualized in 1917 during the All-Belarusan Congress in Miensk. Despite the dispersal of the meeting by Russian Bolshevik soldiers the delegates managed to elect a council [Rada] who articulated three Charters for the new independent state. In February of 1918 the Russian troops retreated from Miensk under German threat. By March 25, 1918 the Executive Council of the First All Belarusan Congress proclaimed Belarus' independence. The Council also rejected the March 3, 1918 Brest-Litovsk treaty between Russia and Germany. Independence lasted less than one year due to the strategic placement of Belarus, claims to its territory by Russia and Poland, and the presence of Russian, German, and Polish armies. The Bolsheviks recognized the need to satisfy the national expectations as outlined by the Rada and subsequently created the BSSR [Byelorussian Soviet Socialist Republic] on January 1st, 1919.[38]

Following the Treaty of Riga in 1921 Belarus was divided between Poland and the new Soviet state. Territories in Western Belarus were added to the new Polish state which did not "recognize any autonomous status in its Belarusan territories" (Marples 1996, 22). The Belarusan minority lost all representation in parliament and was officially described as a non-historical entity in Polish political rhetoric. In Eastern Belarus, Soviet policies attempted to institutionalize the idea of a Belarusan nation in association with the

32   *Of Mermaids and Rock Singers*

desire to "Bolshevize the Belarusan masses" (Ihnatouski in Zaprudnik 1993, 76). The success of the Bolsheviks during the 1920s was based upon their liberal treatment of Belarusian culture and education. As a result Belarus saw the "revival of ethnic culture, literature, and science [. . .], international relations, [and] the use of the Belarusan language in the administration" (Kipel 1977, 91).

The appropriation of territory by Poland and by the Bolsheviks had enormous impact on the formation of Belarusian national identities. Belarusian national movements persisted in response to cultural persecutions in Poland. According to Zaprudnik, in Soviet Belarus Belarusan-language education encouraged the definition of a Belarusan "national idea," through "artistic pluralism and creative diversity" (1993, 80–81). Literary societies were devoted to the creation of a contemporary literature that embraced a Belarusan cultural heritage. Despite these cultural movements, Soviet life in Belarus was already defined by the practice of surveillance and censorship which culminated in cultural and political persecution and ultimately in Stalin's purges. As a result, the national revival of the 1920s was short-lived and, by 1930, "tens of thousands of leaders, educators, researchers, and students were deported to Siberia" (Kipel 1977, 92).

By the end of the 1920s, key supporters of Belarusan nationalism in public life were regularly interrogated by the secret police, imprisoned, and executed if they were deemed enemies of the state. This process had a direct impact on the membership of Belarusan literary movements: "Of the 238 writers arrested during the years of repression, only about 20 survived and were released from captivity by the time of Stalin's death in March 1953. The Institute of Belarusan Culture, established in 1922 and transformed into the Belarusan Academy of Sciences in 1928 lost nearly 90 percent of its members; "the vast majority of them were shot" (Zaprudnik 1993, 87).[39] The elimination of the national intelligentsia was paralleled by cultural and linguistic assimilation or Russification. The Belarusan language was altered (see Chapter One, p. 7), and Belarusan history was deconstructed with key figures denounced and replaced by "Russian Tsars, generals, and writers [who became] models to be studied and emulated by Belarusan youth" (88). As a result, the decades including and following the Stalinist period produced generations of Belarusans who either were unaware of their cultural heritage and history, or who dismissed it under pressure of official ridicule. Now in their sixties and seventies, these Belarusans cannot understand the resurgence of a Belarusan national consciousness nor the post-independence interest in the Belarusan language.[40]

The 1930s have become an infamous decade defined by Stalin's Great Terror. Three periods of arrests and purges (1930; 1933; 1937–1938) saw the systematic murder and deportation of hundreds of thousands of Belarusans. Ironically, it was the rediscovery in 1988 of the scope of Stalin's ethnocide that

Terminology, Controversy, and Interpretation of History 33

encouraged a public reevaluation of Belarusan historical experience and gave credence and momentum to Belarusan independence movements. When mass graves were discovered in the Kurapaty forest near Miensk, Belarusans faced the realization that victims had been executed daily in their own backyard. The staggering estimates of three-hundred-thousand victims in that site alone emphasized the potential scope of Stalin's purges, now estimated at 2.2 million Belarusans.[41]

The archeologist heading the Kurapaty excavation, Zianon Paźniak became one of the founders and the leader of the Belarusan Popular Front, eventually becoming the leader of the opposition in the Belarusan parliament. His work at Kurapaty provided a tangible frame for his criticisms of Communism and his pro-democracy political platform. Kurapaty has become a symbol of the independence movement in Belarus providing a pilgrimage site for supporters of Belarusan change.

The effect of Kurapaty on public sentiment came on the heels of one of the worst ecological disasters of the twentieth century. On April 26, 1986 the accident at the Chernobyl nuclear power plant in northern Ukraine released 50 million curies of radioactive fallout into the environment, 70 percent of which landed in Belarus (Marples, 42).[42] The medical and environmental consequences of the disaster have redefined the lives of those who have lost family and friends from fallout related cancers and/or who were relocated to instant communities away from the contamination zone. The psychological impact of the relocation alone has prompted many aging Belarusans to return to their ancestral villages despite the danger.

Such relocations, as well as first-hand experiences with the consequences of living in or near contaminated zones, are not limited to communities found in close proximity to Chernobyl. The fallout was distributed in higher concentrations than those measured beside the reactor in areas farremoved from the immediate zone around Chernobyl.[43]

Public access to any information about the disaster was not part of the Soviet government's response to the Chernobyl accident. The administration chose to cover-up the extent of the disaster, not only from the world community, but also from their own populations. Three years after the explosion, Belarusans were first discovering the true extent of the contamination and the subsequent risks to their health through exposure and through the food supply. The lack of financial, moral, and environmental action from Moscow's bureaucrats cemented the growing mistrust of the Soviet administration and nurtured support for independence from the Soviet Union.[44]

The initial cover-up also had an impact on the population's response to the disaster. Belarusans who, for three years, had been told that the radiation was not harmful, were now being asked to believe that their lives were at risk. Presently, those that realize the full impact of the disaster often point to Chernobyl as the last straw in the country's long list of negative experiences.

Figure 2.6: Contaminated fields in the Vietkoŭskaja region are still used for pasture despite the posted warnings. The sign reads: "Radioactive Danger. It is prohibited to grow and harvest agricultural products, to graze, or to hay." Note the cattle grazing in the background. Photo by the author.

Many Belarusans identify Chernobyl as the reason for the political complacency of the population, describing themselves as a disabled population who, facing territorial damage, physical illness and psychological fallout, are unable to confidently define their national future.

With the declaration of independence, the aspirations, and expectations of Belarusans continue to fluctuate from guarded optimism to deep frustration. The realization that Chernobyl is a permanent fixture in their nation's future can be added to a long list of contemporary discoveries about historical experience, loss, and efforts at restoration. Present attempts to define Belarus as a modern independent nation either emphasize or de-emphasize the new perspectives on the country's history and the consequences of Chernobyl. Some political players, such as the present president Alaksandar Lukašenka, ridicules attempts at educating Belarusans about their historical experience. He is in direct opposition to national movements that look to the past as a source for Belarus' modern identity.

It is obvious that the debate over nation, which has become increasingly violent, will not be settled quickly. Defining a modern Belarus requires a change of public perception by targeting and addressing the cultural infe-

Terminology, Controversy, and Interpretation of History 35

riority complex that evolved out of pre-Soviet and Soviet experience. The campaign to explore and to educate faces a distracted audience overwhelmed by rapid change and economic instability. As a result, nothing about this process is straightforward, neither for those attempting to initiate change, nor for those studying the efficacy of those attempts.

Belarusan history, like the path towards national definition, does not lend itself to a clear untroubled narrative. The moments outlined in the preceding sections emphasize the positive, the negative, the forgotten, and the resurrected aspects of that history. The battles fought for national definition reflect the relationship between a nation's historical experience and its effect on the contemporary lives of its citizens.

NOTES

[1] The official name change of the Byelorussian Socialist Soviet Republic (BSSR) was decided by parliament (Supreme Soviet) on September 19, 1991 and was recognized in October 1991 at an official ceremony at the United Nations. The new designation is the indigenous term for this nation "Belarus." The preferred adjective form (biełaruski) is Belarusan, pronounced *Be-la-roo-san*. Other place names are also undergoing a transition back to the indigenous form and/or spellings. For example Minsk is now Miensk.

[2] For example, the route from Warsaw through Vilnia and Miensk to Moscow placed Belarus at the center of trading activity (Clem 1990, 111). Jan Zaprudnik writes that the Dźvina and Dniepr rivers are also significant in that they provided a path between Scandinavia and Byzantium (1993, 5).

[3] Of the 10,400,000 inhabitants, 1,800,000 reside in the capital city of Miensk. Major urban centers comprise 67 percent of the total population, with 33 percent living in rural areas, villages, and small towns. For population statistics outlining post WW II urbanization see Marples (1–23).

[4] Ethnic Divisions in Belarus according to the 1989 Soviet census: Belarusans 77.9 percent/Russian 13.2 percent/Poles 4.1 percent/Ukrainian 2.9 percent/Jews 1.1 percent/Other 0.9 percent (as listed in Zaprudnik [1993, xix]).

[5] The declarations of independence of the Soviet republics were preceded in 1989 by the independence of Poland, Hungary, GDR, Czechoslovakia, Bulgaria, and Romania. J.F. Brown provides an analysis of the movement towards independence in the non-Soviet communist eastern Europe, *Surge to Freedom: the End of Communist Rule in Eastern Europe* (Durham: Duke University Press, 1991), 4–5; hereafter cited in the text. He lists the elements that contributed to the breakdown of communist systems as: (1) incompatibility between Soviet interests and national aspirations, (2) economic failure, (3) the growth of societal opposition, (4) recognition of impending change by Soviet administrations, (5) détente, and (6) Gorbachev's policies.

[6] Gorbachev tried to relate movements towards change as a means to redefine socialism. Tatyana Zaslavskaya emphasizes the eventual efforts to equate openness with a new socialism. She quotes Gorbachev: "If openness, criticism and

36 *Of Mermaids and Rock Singers*

democracy are in the interests of socialism, in the people's interests, they have no litmus" (*The Second Socialist Revolution: An Alternative Soviet Strategy* [Bloomington: Indiana University Press, 1990], 205).

[7] For example: *December 1987*: Over thirty independent Belarusan youth groups participate in their first "General Diet" exploring how to bring about national renewal; *October 1988*: Establishment of the Martyrology of Belarus in order to commemorate the victims of Communism. Organizing Committee for the establishment of the BPF (Belarusan Popular Front Movement and Party). The Party was officially established on June 24–25 1990 and became the official opposition; *January 1989*: Because their convention is not allowed in Miensk, sixty-six Belarusan youth groups hold a convention in Vilnia (Lithuania), in support of Belarusan renewal. (Chronicled in Zaprudnik 1993, 229–245).

[8] Brown makes this statement with reference to Hungary, Czechoslovakia, and the GDR. It is equally applicable to processes in Belarus (1; xx). Also see Sabrina P. Ramet *Social Currents in Eastern Europe: The Sources and Meaning of the Great Transformation* (Durham: Duke University Press, 1991).

[9] Official language legislation was preceded by several key events including: (1) The organized lobbying for language reform by Belarusan intelligentsia in 1986 through a petition presented to Gorbachev. In the "Letter of the Twenty-Eight" Belarusan intellectuals appealed to Gorbachev to change anti-Belarusan Soviet language policy (*Letters to Gorbachev: New Documents from Soviet Byelorussia*. Second Edition. London: The Association of Byelorussians in Great Britain: 1987). According to Zaprudnik, those who signed the letter were subsequently blacklisted, harassed, or lost their jobs (1993, 125–128). (2) The 1990 establishment of the Belarusan Language Society. Many artists, musicians, and writers also included commentaries on the language issue in their work and continued to highlight the issue in the public sphere.

[10] Pahonia meaning *pursuit* is symbolic of the chasing away of the enemy. The symbol reflects the combination of the pre-Christian Belarusan sun god *Jaryla* with the image of the twelfth century knight who fought invasions from Tartar armies to the east and German Teutonic Knights to the west. Sixteenth century sources describe the crest as an emblem for the cities of Miensk, Navahradak, Mscislau, Viciebsk, Smalensk, Vilnia, Troki and Drahichyn; the palatines of Brest and Miensk, Vilnia, and Navahradak; and the counties of Połacak and Rechyca (*Bielaruskaja Savieckaja Encyklapedyja* 7, 595).

[11] Conversations with students from the Institute of Culture, Miensk, May 22, 1993.

[12] Some would argue that such a prolonged colonization process indicates the loss of national consciousness. In his analysis of national identity in post-Soviet Belarus, Richard Clem connects geographic location, outside political aggression, and population losses with present-day trends towards Belarusan national/ethnic identity. Clem hints at the connection between the psychological impact of cultural stress and the "propensity of Belarusans to acculturate and assimilate" (113). He adds that forced urbanization and migration into other then-Soviet states equally contributes to the level of acculturation in Belarus. Written in the

Terminology, Controversy, and Interpretation of History 37

early 1990s, Clem's article provides a brief analysis of the historical and social contexts that have affected Belarusan self-perception and identity choice. While Clem predicted the continued assimilation of Belarus' younger population through intermarriage and migration, post-Gorbachev Belarus reflects an enormous variety of attitudes about cultural and national self-perception. One of the prevailing arguments for Belarusan statehood emphasizes the repeated assertions of differentiation and support for independence.

[13] Paget Henry, *The Newer Caribbean: decolonization, democracy, and development*, ed. Paget Henry and Carl Stone (Philadelphia: Institute for the Study of Human Issues, 1983), 95.

[14] Since Lukašenka's election in 1994 negative responses to Belarusan self-definition and self-determination have been encouraged by the government, which has made clear its own intent to re-unify Belarus to Russia. Cultural and political conflicts have become increasingly public and violent as the administration turns to detaining, imprisoning, and beating those identified with a pro-Belarusan movement.

[15] Jan Carew, "The African and Indian Presence: some Aspects of Historical Distortion," *Race and Class*, 27(1): 36.

[16] Vitaut Kipel (1983, 114); Zaprudnik (1993, 2–3).

[17] Jan Zaprudnik provides a detailed discussion of the usage and meaning of the terms "white" and "Ruś." The name Biełaja Ruś originated in the twelfth century. The term was used by Prince Andrei Bogolubski who after sacking Kiev in 1169 proclaimed himself Prince *beloruski* and used the label to underline the true orthodox faith (1993, 2–5). The earliest reference to the term Biełaja Ruś dates back to the late thirteenth century when it first appeared in written sources (Sadouski, 2–3). In the mid- thirteenth century the term "white" designated those areas that had repelled Tartar invasions: Smalensk until 1267, and later Połacak, Viciebsk, and Mahiloŭ to the west and south (Zaprudnik 1993, 2–5).

[18] Vitaut Kipel, *Byelorussian Americans and Their Communities in Cleveland* (Cleveland Ethnic Heritage Studies, Cleveland State University, 1982), 8; hereafter cited in the text.

[19] Zaprudnik adds: "Moscow, which by the end of the fifteenth century had proclaimed itself the "Third and Last Rome," took upon itself the imperial program of gathering "all the Rušias" (1993, 2).

[20] Anton Łuckievič, "A Summary Glance into the History and the Situation of White Russia" in *Byelorussian Statehood : Reader and Bibliography*, ed. Vitaut and Zora Kipel (Byelorussian Institute of Arts and Sciences, [1919] reprint 1988), 125; hereafter cited in text.

[21] These principalities, Smalensk, Turaŭ-Pinsk, and Połacak-Viciebsk were ruled by princes from the Rahvałodavičy and Rurykavičy lines. M. Dovnar-Zapolsky, "The basis of White-Russia's State Individuality" in *Byelorussian Statehood: Reader and Bibliography*, ed. Vitaut and Zora Kipel (New York: Byelorussian Institute of Arts and Sciences, [1911] reprint 1988), 39.

38 *Of Mermaids and Rock Singers*

[22] The first Byelorussian Bible was translated and published by Dr. Francišak Skaryna (Prague 1517–1519, Vilnia 1522). Born in Połacak, Skaryna received his doctoral degree from the University of Padua in 1512. The first Bible to be published in a Slavic vernacular was in the Czech language.

[23] The *Statute of the Grand Duchy of Litva* appeared in two hand-written editions in 1529 and 1566. It was first printed by the Mamonic Brothers Printing House in Vilna in 1588. All three editions were in the Belarusan language. (Lecture given by Alice Kipel at the Biennial Convention of Byelorussians in North America, Toronto 1988). Additional information can be found in Kipel (1982: 12). See also *Statut Vialikaha Kniastva Litouskaha* part 3, article 3 (1588; reprint Minsk: Bielaruskaja Savieckaja Encyklapedyja, 1989), 112–113.

[24] In addition, increased ties with Western Europe established strong trading relationships with the West, including cultural exchanges which brought humanism and the Renaissance to the Grand Duchy, as well as an interest in and pursuit of education abroad (Zaprudnik 1993, 36–37).

[25] Victar Siučyk, *The Unknown War Against Belarus: A Secret Page of Modern History* (Minsk: Navukova-Papularnaje Vydannie, 1993), 9–10; hereafter cited in text.

[26] In 1385 Grand Duke Jahaila (baptized Wladyslaw 1385–1434), married the Polish queen, Jadwiga. Despite this personal union, principalities and cities of the Grand Duchy were granted self-rule: Vilnia in 1387; Bierascie in 1390, Hrodna in 1391. In 1392 the ruler of the Grand Duchy, grand Duke Vitaut was recognized as the independent ruler of the Duchy of Litva (Zaprudnik 1993, 230–231; Sadouski, 22).

[27] Arnold McMillin writes that while weakening the nation as a whole, the elimination of patrons for the high arts and of the contexts for courtly performance created an ideal climate for the growth and continuity of folk arts and traditions (123).

[28] Jan Zaprudnik, *Historical Dictionary of Belarus*, No. 28 of *European Historical Dictionaries* (Metuchin, New Jersey: Scarecrow Press, 1999).

[29] Cited in Zaprudnik (1993, 30).

[30] In 1791 the May 3rd Constitution of the Commonwealth merged the Polish Crown with the Grand Duchy of Litva, Ruś, and Samogitia into a unitary state. This constitution does not reflect the merging of a federated state, and ignores all participants except the Polish. The constitution was abolished in 1793.

[31] The Commonwealth was partitioned in 1772, 1793, 1795 among Russia, Prussia, and Austria (as chronicled in Zaprudnik 1993, 234).

[32] Also known as Greek Catholics.

[33] Those Belarusans that emigrated prior to 1914 carried the effects of Russification into their North American environments. A primary obstacle to the recognition of Belarusan identity lay in the mislabeling of incoming Belarusans by American and Canadian immigration officials. Belarusan immigrants were labeled according to the regions from which they originated: *Miensk, Grodno, Viciebsk, Vilna,* and *Mogilev.* The authorities lacked an "official" knowledge of

Terminology, Controversy, and Interpretation of History 39

Belarus. If incoming Belarusans were recognized as White Russian they were not considered a separate group because nationality was assigned according to an immigrant's former citizenship. For their part, immigrating Belarusans reacted to the negative treatment of their culture in their homeland and simply identified themselves as tutejšyja, the natives. See Vitaut Kipel, 1983, 21; 116). Furthermore, these immigrants often accepted the labels as Polish (*polskaja viera*) and Russian (*ruskaja viera*), according to religious affiliation.

[34] Harold R. Isaacs emphasizes the necessary relationship between territory and nation. He writes that territory is a critical factor in maintaining group separateness. Without it a nationality has difficulty becoming a nation and a nation cannot become a state ("Basic Group Identity: The Idols of the Tribe" in *Ethnicity: Theory and Experience*, edited by Nathan Glazer and Daniel P. Moynihan [Cambridge: Harvard University Press, 1975], 44).

[35] The birth of modern Belarusan literature is part of such movements in the nineteenth century. Early writers, Jan Čačot, Vincuk Dunin-Marcinkievič, as well as the anonymous epic poem *Taras on Parnassus* (1840–44), are representative of literary production (Rich, 14–15).

[36] J. Kreüski, "Kastuś Kalinoŭski: Anti-Russian Uprising of 1863," *Belarusian Review* (spring 1993): 13–14.

[37] Important figures include Janka Kupała (1882–1942); Jakub Kołas (1882–1956); Ciotka (1876–1916); Maksim Harecki (1893–1939); Maksim Bahdanovič (1891–1917); Žmitrok Biadula (1886–1941); Aleś Harun (1887–1920); Vacłaŭ Łastoŭski (1883–1938).

[38] Nevertheless the Council [Rada] retained its mandate as an exiled parliament and continues to uphold the original Charter. The Rada has had six chairmen in exile since its creation and continues to be active in response to the latest developments in Belarus as defined by Lukašenka's present administration.

[39] See Zianon Paźniak's description of his 1980s excavation of the Kurapaty forest near Miensk where Belarusans were executed daily between 1937 and 1941. Paźniak estimates that 250,000 to 300,000 victims are buried there (*Kurapaty* [Miensk: Niezaležnaja vydavieckaja kampanija "Technalohija", 1994]); Zaprudnik (1993, 88–89; 131–132).

[40] Asked to partake in a family dinner in Miensk, I sat across from the family patriarch who wore his Soviet military dress uniform and medals. He was openly suspicious of my language use, and spent the evening defending and recalling the glory days of his Soviet-defined youth (Miensk, June 14, 1993).

[41] Five additional sites await excavation around Miensk, with additional sites near other major cities (Zaprudnik 1993, 88).

[42] Marples writes that an estimated 40,400 square kilometers of Belarusan territory were contaminated with more than one curie per square kilometer, which amounts to 19.5 percent of the country holding a population of 1.8–2.2 million people including 440,000 children (43).

40 *Of Mermaids and Rock Singers*

[43] For example, areas west and northwest of the city of Miensk (Marples, 43–44). By 1993 one could buy a road-map of Belarus which was color-coded according to the kinds of and levels of radioisotopes found in each contaminated location.

[44] One initial rumor described how the fall-out was contained in a weather system that was making its way towards Moscow. The Soviet administration sent aircraft to seed the clouds as they traveled over Belarusan territory and therefore guaranteed the contamination of Belarus instead of Russian territories. The story was later confirmed by the scientific community.

3.

"Stand in the doorway": Entrances And Exits In Urban Belarus

Stand in the doorway
Take a look what's going on
Stand in the doorway
That's the place where you belong

[. . .]

Walk through the doorway
See the world behind the wall
Walk through the doorway
Feel your heart and feel your soul
It doesn't matter where I go

But the real thing I know
I will be there
I will be there
I will be there
I will be there

Excerpt from Krama, "Stand in the Doorway" from *Vodka on Ice*, REX
Records, 1993. Used by permission.

IN 1993 THE MIENSK-BASED ROCK GROUP KRAMA RELEASED "VODKA ON ICE"
through the British firm REX Records. The songs, originally sung in
Belarusan, were translated by the company into English for this release.
One of these, "Stand in the Doorway," evokes the essence of change and
the spirit of expectation in Belarus. The "doorway" represents a moment of
transition and a moment of hesitation.[1] As Krama offered their new releases
to the public, Belarus reverberated with the various sounds of political, economic, and cultural exploration. Political debates publicly suggested efforts
towards a new democracy, urban construction signaled new living conditions and access to new consumer goods, and the media offered new domes-

41

42   *Of Mermaids and Rock Singers*

tic and international programming. All of these indicators of change emphasized that Belarusans were poised on a momentous threshold—trying to establish the practical and ideological details of Belarusan life after the Soviet experience.

As the primary stage for political and cultural debate, Belarus' capital city offers clues to popular expectations and subsequent responses to change. Miensk reveals the accelerated nature of change in many ways. Commuters crowd the public transit system and can literally watch economic expansion and capitalistic experiments unfold as they travel to their old jobs and stand in a bread line at the end of the day. They are reminded that the passage from old to new is identifiable but not necessarily accessible. Drawing on the image of the threshold as a point of transition, the following sections explore everyday life in urban Miensk. Some of the practical and philosophical considerations that influence the shaping of contemporary Belarusan culture include:

1. the management of, and the symbolism in, old and new construction;
2. the treatment of public and private spaces;
3. frustrations with the practical results of a Belarusan democracy;
4. attitudes towards Belarusan-language legislation;
5. the increased visibility of Western products, including television programming;
6. the continuing impact of the Chernobyl explosion.

SINGULAR VISIONS AND MULTIPLE DIRECTIONS IN URBAN BELARUS

Cityscapes do much to explain histories and legacies by outlining the dynamics between diverse city-dwellers and announcing urban change and current trends.[2] Identical suburban apartment block communities in Miensk are connected to the city center by bus and metro lines. These fabricated neighborhoods were originally conceptualized as complete microcosms including schools and day care facilities, grocery stores, and medical clinics.[3] Small neighborhoods of traditional private homes contrast with such new construction. Nestled between contemporary high-rises these older structures are ancient architectural islands, the old limbs of their long-abandoned orchards reaching over the border between old and new.[4] The high-rises and old private homes comprise the most immediate visual contrast in this capital city, where asphalt and cement circumvent the cobblestone lanes that lead to ginger-bread houses.

It seems doubtful that the survival of these small village neighborhoods has anything to do with preservation. Miensk lost much of its architectural

"Stand in the doorway": Entrances and Exits in Modern Belarus   43

legacy in the twentieth century.[5] Presently the "old city" comprises four blocks of buildings in differing stages of disrepair and restoration. The already restored quarter in view of the Intourist Hotel is used for tourism shops and restaurants. Across *Niamiha* street, north of the Orthodox Cathedral of the Holy Spirit,[6] lie a few additional blocks, historic remnants of this architectural history. New construction has been replacing the old town for the better part of the century. There is little evidence of the historical wealth of this region before Stalin's "wedding cake" architecture, the destruction of W.W. II, and the massive socialist-style buildings that overcame much of the old city in the 1960s. One philosophy offered in explanation for this destruction is that in order to create a sense of historical community, the Bolsheviks felt that the slate of historical legacy had to be wiped clean. That is, that visually the population had to be reminded that their history began in 1917.

The traditional intimate setting of older neighborhoods beside the concrete "packaged" new ones become symbols of the opposites evident in this process of urban change. Opposites also provide views into either side of a moveable threshold—a threshold that, like Wells' time machine,[7] brings pasts and presents, and hoped-for futures into simultaneous existence. The observable physical duality of the city (old–new; wealth–poverty) shapes the understanding of this urban Belarusan culture in a time of transition.

The threshold is also a turning point for expression, and equally a position from which cultural actors find resources and significance for that expression. Miensk-based artist Ryhor Sitnica concentrates on the detail of architecture in the historic quarter of the city. Sketching every brick in a yet unrestored facade, or concentrating on the shape and shadow of a chain-link fence, he gives scattered elements of the past a formal cohesion, an iconic significance. His precisionist approach provides a visual statement of the importance and symbolism of detail. It is at once a comment on the importance of, and on the mistreatment of the past. He sees a parallel between his own interest in recontextualizing traditional historical detail with the independently established Belarusan *folk-modern* movement.

During my visit to his studio with members of the Belarusan folk-modern rock group Pałac (July 1995), he expressed an enthusiasm in the connections between his approach to architectural symbolism and Pałac's own uses of traditional Belarusan musical elements as sonic frameworks in their contemporary music (See Chapter Five). As introspective resources for these artists, visual and sonic architectures are sources of cultural exploration and commentary. Their creative control of the threshold is a dynamic and a positive one, moving and valuing past into present. This is in many ways an uneasy task. Whatever the motivation of the artist/musician, and there are many, these individuals are forcing the acknowledgment of the past, not as archeology, but as viable elements of contemporary art and music.

44 *Of Mermaids and Rock Singers*

Recontextualization does not produce any predictable response from audiences and the viewing public. In reaching through the threshold, these individuals are forcing questions about who Belarusans are, and who they want to be. They are valuing a past that many are either unfamiliar with and/or have chosen not to value because of colonial and especially Soviet experience. The threshold therefore holds many psychological implications about choice, about action, and about the positive reconstruction of a modern cultural memory.

THE PUBLIC AND THE PRIVATE

Despite the number of high-rises under construction, Miensk populations, like those in other post-Soviet cities, are faced with a shortage of housing. An apartment is cause for celebration for any resident. Typically, married couples have priority in the bureaucratic lottery for living space.[8] Moreover, dynamics within extended families are often defined by the nature of living arrangements because families with apartments are necessarily multigenerational.[9] Communal living has generated a very specific definition of the personal space, and has considerably raised the value of privacy. This privacy means more than peaceful retreat from noisy neighbors. The space provides an escape from communal living, a haven for expression, a symbol of ownership, and for many, it represents status that differentiates them from others.

It is around the apartment that the lines of public and private are most obvious. Entering the foyer of my first apartment I was struck by the lack of maintenance, the staleness of the air, the lack of light (there had apparently been a rash of light bulb thefts during a recent bulb shortage), the dirty elevators, and the overall abandoned character of this shared private space. In sharp contrast to the entrance of the building, the threshold of the private apartment has a strikingly different effect: it is spotless, warm, and inviting. Everything has its place and is obviously carefully managed. It is paradoxical that in a context where communal living was a dogmatic philosophy for almost three generations, people seem to value the private but they do not recognize the responsibility of creating a mechanism to manage the public. While delineating ownership and responsibility in terms of the one bedroom apartment, the point of transition between the foyer and the private apartment, as the threshold between the public and private, remains undefined.

Ironically, those urban areas open to general public scrutiny are still managed by city workers and some private citizens. The summer dust is swept off *Skaryna Boulevard* by women in orange ponchos, park benches in front of the Miensk Opera are painted in the Spring, and the *metro* resembles a spotless museum. These spaces are municipal and as such are officially managed by city workers. By contrast, the maintenance of the apartment foyer, stairway, elevator, and hall require that the residents cooperate in order to maintain their own "backyard." It is clear that this kind of community

"Stand in the doorway": Entrances and Exits in Modern Belarus   45

responsibility, which parallels the notion that one can act to effectively alter their environment, is **not** considered a part of the formula for change.

The threshold is an appropriate symbol for change in this environment. It not only mirrors a general hope for instantaneous change (from a dark foyer to an inviting apartment), but in terms of points of departure and destination, the threshold suggests that change is perceived as immediate and dualistic. That is, that the transition from old to new is absolute.[10] Ownership, empowerment, and social responsibility also function according to this dualism. The apartment is mine but the foyer is no one's. This dualism touches upon the psychology of this environment and is openly discussed in relation to the communist experience. The lack of conviction in the power of the individual is recognized by some as a national deficit that contrasts popular expectations for change with an unwillingness to become involved in that change.

EXPECTATIONS FOR CHANGE IN BELARUS

> By 1993, three years after the collapse of Communist regimes in Eastern Europe, more and more analysts had arrived at the conclusion that the greatest damage done by the old order was to human nature.
>
> (Zaprudnik 1993, 136)

With little optimism about the future, present political and economic contexts provide little comfort for a population that in many ways waits breathlessly for change. Change in the short term brings dissatisfaction, home life has not improved, products are expensive and harder to find, and realities about capitalism and economic growth do not begin to match the expectations of the population.

As the field of choices for this new "national" environment broadens, so does the absorption and criticism of Western concepts and philosophies. On one level, it is clear that expectations of the new system were abstract at best. Such abstract hopes were based on a concept of the quality of life in the West that was **universally** better than in present-day Belarus. This universal expectation was also predicted by Western analysts who based their projections about Eastern Europe on the theoretical assumptions that democracy was a natural end for nations who had evolved out of traditionalism into modernity. Jeffery Alexander writes: "Non democratic societies were understood simply as not yet modern enough. Democracy was adaptive because it was flexible. Because it was flexible it would survive." [and] "In the postwar world, democracy was formally introduced into other nations by the Allies; constitutions were put into place, legal guidelines established. These normative expectations, it was believed, would be cherished and followed in due course."[11]

It was clear however, that such concepts as freedom and democracy could not be instantaneously understood nor applied. In Belarus, when the outlook on economic change was analyzed as positive, democracy was carefully praised. Most often however, the word democracy was used with derogatory references to capitalism, and both terms became strategic labels through which political and media commentators could question and criticize the impact of Western ideologies (See Figure 3.1).[12]

Belarusan assumptions regarding democracy and capitalism reflected a dissatisfaction with the growth of a rich class of elite referred to with envy and suspicion as *businessmen* [biznizmen]. The presence of this new class was most obvious in the luxury *Ferraris* that stood out amongst the *Ladas* on Miensk boulevards. However, for the population that had not and could not have benefited from initial investments in the early years of sovereignty, the contrasts in economic opportunity were constantly underlined by the appearance of new shops with expensive luxury merchandise that the average citizen could only dream of buying. For the majority of these city dwellers, the new order had only served to shatter the expectation that with a Western system all would live comfortably and have access to the same wealth. As a result, the word democracy [demakracyja . . .], understood as "There's democracy for you," became a private and public slogan reflecting a growing climate of disappointment. It could be heard in reference to all sorts of situations, when commenting on the number of beggars on the street, or when monthly salaries were delayed because of a shortage in paper currency.

Figure 3.1: "The Face of Contemporary Democracy" Photograph by Victor Stavera (Courtesy of *Holas Radzimy* [Voice of the Homeland] 41/233, June 14, 1993).

Such expectations cannot be criticized as naïve. Belarusans were trying to adjust from a system where practical and ideological boundaries had been articulated through communism and had defined public policy as well as pri-

"Stand in the doorway": Entrances and Exits in Modern Belarus 47

vate mechanisms of circumvention, i.e., buying and/or returning "favors." Beyond the theoretical dialogue of politicians and academicians, the prospect of replacing overnight the expectations of the old system with "ideological choice" posed new problems. For the average citizen this had many repercussions. A doctoral candidate in ethnographic studies at the Belarusan Institute of Culture articulated the challenge of conceptual change. In describing the educational system, she mentioned that most students no longer had a sense of what was expected from them ideologically: "Before the political changes, students knew that to write a passable thesis they had to quote Lenin. Now it is not clear what is expected."[13]

Such statements are clear contrasts to those made by members of the intelligentsia, journalists, politicians, and popular artists who were trying to consciously and publicly explore the state of the nation. Their active professional and private lives are defined by conscious exploration of a national future and with it the support of a Belarusan identity. Through both public and private dialogues these figures analyze the national struggle to embrace a new order and consider the options for a national identity. Valancina Tryhubovič, then a member of the BNF (Democratic Opposition: Belarusan Popular Front), and the editor of the leading fine arts publication "Art" [Mastactva], described a story that explained the Belarusan climate for change.

> There was a man who had spent his entire life behind bars. He knew his jail keepers and knew exactly what was expected from him on a day to day basis. One day, when he was already an old man, his jail term was over, and he was ceremoniously shown the gate to freedom. A few days later he was back. He had committed a petty crime in order to return to what he knew. When asked why he had sacrificed his freedom he replied: "In jail I knew the exact nature of what I was fearing. Out there, I knew I was afraid but I did not know what to expect. I am better off here, better off knowing."[14]

This story offers clues to a national predicament. On one level it depicts how those that choose to become involved in the definition of Belarus' future might interpret those that do not. The choices made by the old man also serve to explain the fear of becoming involved in one's destiny, the need to justify the reasons for everyday experience, and the importance of identifying the *nature* of fear. Subsequently the fear and the cause could be made tangible and one could understand who or what was to blame for life conditions.

Current change includes a re-establishment of a Belarusan cultural consciousness in a general climate of economic and political instability. The public is being asked to adapt to economic hardship, political uncertainty, and to overcome the negative attitudes about Belarusan language and Belarusan identity that were characteristic of Soviet ideology. The renaissance, the process of cultural *re-invention* (Clifford, 15–16), generates various responses.

48   *Of Mermaids and Rock Singers*

As part of the media, of cultural production, and of political platforms it has become a consistent presence in public consciousness. However, to propose a clear theory about the effects of present efforts would require the false suggestion that a unifying uni-directional process for cultural change simply needs to be identified. One of the most effective examples of contrasting attitudes is the variety of reactions to language.

"AND WHAT PLEASE, IS A PLEASE . . . ?"

In early 1993, I had the opportunity to meet Alexander Krudastoŭ, the English professor employed by the Belarusan Lycée in Hajnaŭka (Biełastoččyna, Eastern Poland). While he worked in Biełastoččyna during the school term, his family stayed at home in Miensk. In discussing attitudes towards the Belarusan language, he had this to say: "Not so long ago you could go into a store and say: Chleba kali łaska [Bread please]. They would hand you a loaf and say: "And what please is kali łaska? [What please is a please?]."[15] His anecdote emphasized that Belarusans were so removed from the everyday use of the Belarusan language that they did not even understand the term for "please." Language choice was constantly debated in post-sovereignty Belarus. Language was debated in intimate circles, at social gatherings, in the work place, and on the street. The media, academia, and government bureaucracies continuously announced that language use would define the new Belarus.

I arrived in Miensk in early Spring. The city held the promise of warmth, and for me, cultural renewal, and I looked expectantly at the budding trees and the growing strength of the new season. My metaphoric revelry did not reflect the reality around me. People still huddled around bus stops outside my apartment on *Surhanava*. The stubborn winter wind had them holding their hats and tightening their coats with gloved hands. Except for some brave moments, the sun kept receding behind the clouds. From my apartment window I could see the pattern of daily activity. Cars and citizens alike leaving their breaths in the air as they went to work and then came home again. It was striking that the volume of cars was quite small (one car for every five people in Miensk).

In the cool air of a May night my roommate Rita and I slowly walked towards our apartment and I marveled at the stillness of the city. The streets were almost empty, and except for a few loud gatherings around apartment blocks, the walk was peaceful. Two stops from the apartment we hopped on a trolley. People getting off the late afternoon shift were sitting exhausted on the bus, would-be pick-pockets were eyeing their prospects, children were asleep against their mother's shoulders, and inevitably, the remnants of a party, or of a private celebration would stumble into the vehicle and weave about as we headed towards our destinations. One such gentleman had placed himself beside the rear doors. He had the air of a Dickens character,

"Stand in the doorway": Entrances and Exits in Modern Belarus   49

bright eyes, red cheeks, and a sense of purpose. He watched and listened to his fellow passengers for a while and I recall that Rita and I were both caught by his movements. His first exclamation came as someone offered a new passenger a seat saying "please" in Russian. "Pozhalsta?" he lamented out loud, "tell me sometin'," he continued, "can you tell me why no one says "kali łaska?" ["please" in Belarusan]. He continued to ask everyone and no one in particular. Needless to say, the usual protective silence characteristic of public transport was shattered. The passengers didn't know what to say, and the man's questions got louder and louder. I looked at Rita and tried not to smile, but eventually the entire group at the back of the trolley began to smile. The man shrugged his shoulders and continued to mutter as he got off the bus.

Such public exclamations by a private citizen were rare. In fact, at the beginning of 1993 speaking Belarusan on the public urban street was an oddity. Before the declaration of sovereignty in July of 1991,[16] official means were slowly emerging for the support of Belarusan as the national language. Official documents were being translated, the media was mandated to offer Belarusan-language programming and, starting at the pre-school level, education was being reformatted to teach Belarusan.[17] Some of the greater challenges faced by this cultural reform (dubbed the cultural renaissance) had to do with cultural psychology, identity definition, generation, and professional practicality.

The public response to the Belarusan culture and language, the practical basis for the cultural renaissance, was driven by an inferiority complex that reflected attitudes towards Belarusan expression during the eras of the Russian Empire and the Soviet Union. The Belarusan language was loaded with associations based upon cultural comparisons between Belarusan and Russian. In the nineteenth century and throughout the Soviet period much effort was made to depict all things Belarusan as inferior to Russian/Soviet "alternatives." The contrasts were based on the idea that the rural/urban comparison necessarily included qualitative judgements about education, social culture, and sophistication. One Russian-speaking woman in her thirties epitomized this attitude. I began a conversation speaking Belarusan with her at a birthday party. She exclaimed, "Well, I'm Belarusan but I speak Russian. I just don't like the way Belarusan **sounds**. It's not as refined as Russian."[18] When I asked her how she had come to that aesthetic conclusion she answered that Belarusan was the language of her village-dwelling grandparents, and that everyone in the *city* spoke Russian. Rather than representing a singular experience, this commentary exemplifies many similar opinions on language choice heard throughout 1993—comments reflecting cultural value judgements based on the refinement and urban superiority of Russian over Belarusan.

This leads into the second aspect of language change, the role of identity in language choice. One of the overwhelming attitudes expressed by

Belarusans contrasts a clearer articulation of geographic identity over cultural identity. Overwhelmingly Belarusans have a clear sense that they are regionally-bound. That is, they are from Miensk, they are from this village which differentiates them substantially from the village two kilometers away, and that Belarus, as a geographic entity is definitely different from Russia. This "movement at differentiation" somewhat reflects Horowitz's model based on cultural uniqueness.[19] However, the parameters of that differentiation often exclude a connection to native language. Belarusans also acknowledge cultural distinctions, but the reflection of identity in language choice is not necessarily clear. This is particularly true for the generation that is now middle-aged. This generation, raised in the middle of the Soviet period, reflects the effect of the Russification process in Belarus during the twentieth century. In addition to questions of identity, the change of official language has a practical impact in education, in the media, and amongst professionals.

For many professionals in Belarus changing the practical impact of a language is frightening. I often heard presenters at official cultural concerts apologize for their lack of knowledge in Belarusan and state that in order not to embarrass themselves or to "bastardize" the Belarusan language they would continue their duties in Russian. The insecurity felt by these individuals was palpable. In most cases their attitudes were sincerely apologetic.

Together with these statements are those that express a frustration at the new linguistic expectations for professionals. Belarusan had been excluded from the academic arena, and professionals deeply resented that they had to learn a new language in order to function in the "new" Belarus. In conversations with Belarusan ethnomusicologist Zinajda Mažejka, I understood how the past system established clear Russian-language venues for publication and career advancement. In reviewing her many publications with her I asked why Russian had often been her language of choice. She responded that it was easier to be published in Russian, and anyway "hardly anyone would read your work if it was in Belarusan."[20] Belarusan was therefore considered too isolated, or perhaps not scholarly enough to be used in academic works for an international audience.[21] The irony of Belarusan academics writing about their own cultures, from within that culture but in another language was reflected in other areas.

The Institute of Culture (now part of the State University of Belarus, BDU) caters to students from all over Belarus who pursue an education in the performing arts. The majority of the curriculum reflects an education in traditional forms of Belarusan theater, music (instrumental and vocal), and dance, as well as ethnographic scholarship. Traditional performance genres are differentiated as the *authentic* performance genres, in contrast to stylized performance in the Soviet cultural style. Individual performers and groups perform an institutional style, reflected in a nasal vocal style and the balletic choreography framing traditional dances. All lessons were read in Russian,

"Stand in the doorway": Entrances and Exits in Modern Belarus

repertoire was translated into Russian but performed in Belarusan. The Belarusan linguistic and cultural elements were learned but not lived in this academic process. The overall effect was that of teaching a foreign culture.

The musicians and cultural mediators treated in the following chapters contribute to the exploration and definition of a Belarusan identity in the public sphere. It is a process of exploration that challenges existing cultural assumptions, and most immediately, challenges the practical issues involved in making a language change.

The issue of language is both a symbolic and a practical qualifier for change in Belarus because it is the most publicly mediated aspect of Belarusan cultural reform. Language reflects the complexity of a threshold that does not provide an instantaneous passageway. As Zaprudnik has remarked, "Belarusization—which entails the rebuilding of the national consciousness of the Belarusian people, healing the spirit, and instilling self-esteem—is a generational process. It requires not only material means and political support but time as well"(1993, 141).

POPULAR CULTURE WITHOUT A MARKETPLACE: PERFUME, LIPSTICK, AND THE SOAPS

The cultural debates and the efforts towards language reform that defined Belarus in 1993 were often eclipsed by access to Western products through imported consumer goods and through media programming. In Miensk, the choice of imported products increased daily as did the number of private kiosks, and dollar stores.[22] These new businesses encouraged the curious browser rather than the consumer since most products had an asking price that far exceeded the average monthly wage. Belarusans were consistently reminded that their economic means would not grant them instantaneous access to Western comforts and luxuries.

Behind the Miensk Opera House on the ground floor of a small residential building sit two stores side by side. Visually they represent the collision of two social histories. On the left, the Soviet Military Book Shop boasts utilitarian wooden shelves and polished linoleum floors that click against the boots of the occasional uniformed customer. On the right marble floors and glassed-in displays suggest wealth and luxury, and frame the products in a museum-like ceremonial space. This new establishment, selling the products of French and Swiss cosmetics companies, initially drew quite an audience. Under the glow of directed spotlights the salesgirls looked as though they might be in any cosmetics boutique in a Western city. Their refined hairstyles, black dresses, and polite yet somehow snobby expressions completed the ambiance of this new shopping experience. However, the similarity with a high-end Western boutique ended here. Bouncer-like guards stood menacingly on either side of the cashier underlining the relative wealth that the customer must have in order to acquire the imported merchandise.[23] Prices were

52 *Of Mermaids and Rock Singers*

marked both in American dollars and in comparable ruble amounts that changed daily with the erratic zajćyk (Belarusan ruble).[24] Only the few nouveau-riche could afford to buy the products behind glass. Others moved through as though in a museum, observers not participants in a new economic age.

Despite such obvious contrasts, Belarusan interest in Western products is evident. After decades of non-access, everything from Italian shoes to French lingerie is available for a price. The method of display is not always straightforward however. One can find shoes at the Bazaar, cassettes in the kiosks, and cigarettes at open air tables that appear and disappear with startling speed. While the range of products has grown, the systematic retailing of the merchandise has not. If a buyer wants to find something there are few *logical* places to look. As such the idea of shopping all day to find what you need has been extended from food products to other goods. The idea of marketing, or targeting a certain consumer is unimportant as long as the merchandise moves. The effect is jarring: an audience motivated by want and need and a supplier focused on creating an instantaneous market, any kind of market.

Product dumping adds to the confusing panorama of choices. Overstocks suited to other world markets are displayed in Belarusan department stores and suggest that the retailer and the customer alike are interested in any kind of goods as long as they are imported. When Miensk's newest department store (*Niamiha*) first opened, merchandise was spread across departments to give the impression of a wealth of choice. Walking through one day I caught a glimpse of a new display of T-shirts, most with non-specific logos. One however was particularly memorable. In bright orange letters the shirt boldly declared: "The hardest thing to be in the world is an African-American woman." Not only are there very few people of color in Belarus, but the still dominantly patriarchal society would balk at such a fashion statement. The image of Belarusan men and women wearing such a T-shirt served to highlight the mismatch between retailer and consumer.

The growing number of television advertisements also suggested a new access to a Western quality of life. Far from the streets of Miensk these messages also reach the rural town and village where acquiring a foreign product not only reflects a connection to the exotic but for some functions as a status symbol. On the televisions of many village homes one can find empty aerosol cans of perfume and deodorant displayed as trophies of acquisition. What these products partially represent is a closeness to what is perceived by many as a quasi-utopian Western lifestyle. While this does not mean a rejection of traditional values, it does imply a desire for a quality of life that equals what is seen in magazines, movies, and on the television screen. The adage is "why can't we have what they have?"

"Stand in the doorway": Entrances and Exits in Modern Belarus 53

Most Belarusans are unaware of the variety of economic classes and the multicultural diversity found in North America and in Western Europe.[25] Indeed they get their repertoire of images, of ideal standards through Moscow– from imported American television, voiced-over or dubbed into Russian. The fascination with these programs is evident in both rural and urban settings. While waiting for a friend in a Miensk salon I sat in the waiting room with a few customers watching television. The customers were arriving steadily and keeping the staff busy satisfying an obviously full appointment schedule. In an instant, exactly at eight o'clock, the ambiance of this business environment changed into that of a friend's living room. Customers and servers alike congregated in the waiting room and for a hushed forty minutes watched *Santa Barbara* on the screen (without commercials). This American soap, full of moral intrigue, wealth, and beautiful people, offered a powerful glimpse of *the* American lifestyle and suggested a better life for Belarusan audiences.

The fascination with the West is partly the result of this new media access. A previously forbidden resource has become a consistent presence for the stores and in the media. However, the West not only reflects the desire for economic prosperity. In 1993 it was symbolic of a better future, of a national potential, and for many provided a practical resource for change. The importance of this "West" is most evident in responses to another characteristic of Belarusan life, the continuing impact of Chernobyl.

RED WINE AND RADIATION: CHERNOBYL IN EVERYDAY LIFE

In 1993 the nuclear catastrophe at Chernobyl marked its seventh anniversary. The reactor explosion in Chernobyl, a border town on the north central tip of Ukraine produced enough fallout to release 50 million curies of radioactive material affecting 17 million people of the former Soviet Union. Belarus was contaminated by 70% of the total fallout.[26]

Adding to the complexity of the after-event, the Soviet government used its own scientific community to deny the immensity of the catastrophe. The degree of knowledge about the aftermath of the disaster has been the subject of many critiques in books and articles since the late 1980s.[27] The academic community continues to explore and discover the physical and psychological effects of radiation on the human condition. Amongst the published works on the subject it is clear that the search for information has required dialogues between many parties with differing agendas: the media, scientists, atomic energy advocates, politicians, and members of many immigrant communities with vested interests in the homeland. While debates based on statistical data will continue to fuel the evaluation of the disaster, the cultural, political, and psychological impact of the aftermath permeates public consciousness. The disaster remains tangible, somewhat like a malevolent creature from legend barring the threshold to a positive national future.

54 *Of Mermaids and Rock Singers*

The legacy of Chernobyl disaster was a consistent aspect of life and work in both rural and urban Belarus. In Miensk, the environmental after-effects were evident in the choice of produce, in the number of sick children, the number of benefit concerts and Chernobyl conferences, and the conspicuous absence of pregnant women. Discussions about the effects of Chernobyl on daily life included narratives about government attempts to dilute the extent of the contamination. I was told the government had ordered the replacement of the labels on milk originating in highly contaminated southern regions with labels from the other milk processing plant in northern Belarus, and that contaminated meat was regularly mixed with other meats in order to seemingly weaken the potency of the radiation and to use up contaminated stock. Lastly, I heard stories about tampering with imported Geiger counters so that the public would assume the tested produce was safe to consume. While the urban public seemed somewhat aware of the potential risks and the existing problems caused by Chernobyl, rural populations were less willing to accept the extent of the health risks. The main crisis for these populations is that of resettlement and the physical loss of a regional connection with land and community.[28]

After three years of denial following the explosion, rural communities are hard-pressed to change attitudes about the ecological danger in which they live. Despite the relocation of several villages, many older generation Belarusans do not believe in the health risks. Most cannot justify giving up their roots to land and community. They do however acknowledge the impact of the disaster. In late August of 1993 I visited the village of Bukča in southern Belarus. The village was trying to save its crops from the extensive flooding of the Prypiac River. The waters had reached the back doors of the village community and farmers were busy bringing in wet hay by boat from their flooded fields. Many of the vegetable gardens had also flooded. One woman lamented that all their food for winter was lost. Her desperation was evident as she said: First Chernobyl, now this . . ."[29]

Acknowledgment of Chernobyl's impact does not guarantee that these rural populations act to protect themselves from contamination. On one expedition in early June we had the opportunity to share a meal with the resident singers of Janava, a small village on the eastern border with Russia which sits on the edge of a contaminated pocket of land. Our hostess offered us bread and eggs and a plate full of local mushrooms. My friends and I passed the plate knowing that mushrooms readily absorbed the radiation in the environment and should be avoided. Our hostess innocently remarked that she was so pleased with how large the mushrooms were this year and how surprised she was that they were now appearing before the normal berry harvest (May 1993). It was clear that the connection between environmental anomalies and the danger of radiation were not evident in this rural context. In addition to mushrooms, those foods that naturally absorb radia-

"Stand in the doorway": Entrances and Exits in Modern Belarus 55

tion are berries, cucumbers, and tomatoes, all staples of the Belarusan rural diet. Alarmingly many stories circulated regarding the effect of radiation on crop size and the cover-ups on the dangers of the fallout. In one such report local populations who were alarmed at the enormous size of their tomatoes were told that this was a positive result of Chernobyl (conversations Miensk, 1993).

Some artists choose to make Chernobyl the theme of their work. However, whether it is overtly expressed or publicly suppressed, Chernobyl has produced an entirely new genre of Belarusan expression (See Chapter Eight). It has equally generated a kind of black humor that both recognizes and attempts to absorb the implications of the disaster. Chernobyl has entered everyday language, for example, at the dinner table: "have some red wine, it is good for radiation" or "be careful, radiation is good for fertility" (field work, 1993). These are not naïve remarks, they are simply dark ones.

Chernobyl has certainly changed the face of the nation and as Marples (1996) has outlined, forced some primary questions about Belarusan national confidence and national resources. He writes: "The revelations of early 1989, which indicated widespread radioactive fallout in the Homel', Mahiloŭ, and Brest regions, caused great consternation in Belarus, and within three years, the dissolution of the Soviet Union left the republic of 10.3 million alone to deal with its problems" (38).

In addition to forcing an evaluation of national competence in the face of a catastrophe, Marples points out that Chernobyl also has had an impact on the resources for defining that nation. He emphasizes the difference between rural and urban conceptions of Belarus. In rural villages where Miensk and its bureaucrats seem a country away, Belarusans of an older generation have retained the Belarusan language and a more consistent concept of a Belarusan identity. Miensk, the center of operations for the relocation out of the contaminated zones was "a city in which the Belarusan language and culture had never been permitted to dominate, [that housed] politicians who were by no means all committed to the independence of their republic or its future" (39). Marples concludes that, as a rural catastrophe, Chernobyl would affect the nature of a renewed nation by destroying or rendering inaccessible rural lifestyles and ideas, as well as many historical places that could have symbolized a national history and identity.

CONCLUSION

> Walk through the doorway
> See the world behind the wall
> Walk through the doorway
> Feel your heart and feel your soul

As Krama's song encourages a conscious *walk through the doorway*, Belarusans confront change as the transition from the familiar to the unfamiliar. Whether one is immersed in the transition or attempting to observe the process, grasping such accelerated political, cultural, and national experiences is somewhat like trying to analyze an explosion without slow-motion replay. While making sense of the state of the nation may be accomplished through theory and abstraction, such analysis cannot begin to reflect that the individual, the generation, the family, and the community, the artist, the musician, the bureaucrat, the laborer, the professional, the revolutionary, the intelligent, the staunch communist– that all of this citizenry continuously projects what that doorway and its threshold should provide. In Miensk, the world *behind the wall* is accessible through a series of thresholds, each representing an aspect of national, urban, and personal experience. These include,

1. the response to civil and cultural choices in a post-soviet context through
   a. the psychology of inaction;
   b. an emphasis on the artifacts of transition and their recontextualization in modern expression;
   c. the cultural and social implications of language choice in both the public and private sphere;
2. political, economic, and environmental limitations and challenges as
   a. the challenge of shaping and selling a model of democracy;
   b. the frustration with the lack of economic progress;
   c. the Chernobyl legacy as physical, territorial, and psychological in scope
3. the expectations for personal and national futures as defined by
   a. interpretations of Western lifestyles from imported products and
   b. media programming;
   c. the various often conflicting blueprints for a national renaissance.

"Stand in the doorway": Entrances and Exits in Modern Belarus 57

The simultaneity of these various thresholds makes the doorway a difficult transition point. Bombarded by possibilities, by potential, and by limitation, most Belarusans know that this is a key moment in their social and national histories. There are those that approach these thresholds with an eye on consciously transforming or manipulating the passageway. They are the mediators of future visions. The determination of cultural meanings, *Belarusan* meanings, is a powerful aspect of this passageway. What Belarus should mean is publicly manipulated and privately debated, it responds to Western styles as well as to the demands of a rapidly redefining society.

It is in this complex urban environment that the designs of *Belarusaness* are transformed into a presence in popular culture. The following chapters examine the intent, the styles, the impact, and the artistic and practical resources of contemporary urban musicians who by chance, or by their own design, reflect and influence the cultural mood of the nation.

NOTES

[1] In this chapter I examine those images and sentiments that served to guide my ethnographic inquiry and that reveal my efforts to conceptualize and/or recognize the nature of *cultural cohesion* within this environment, what Judith Becker and A.L. Becker describe as a "few deep metaphors [that] bind various things together, make them resonate and mutually reinforce each other." See "An Essay on Translating the Art of Music" in *Karawitan: Source Readings in Javanese Gamelan and Vocal Music*, vol. 2 , ed. Judith Becker (Ann Arbor: University of Michigan Press, 1984). *Cohesion* can include elegantly-linked elements from within a culture. Equally as often it can evolve out of the researcher's attempts to develop an explanatory ethnography for a culture system. Cohesion is therefore a marriage of ideas originating in both subject (systemic) and researcher (interpretive) that provide metanarratives for cultural interpretation and ultimately for ethnographic writing. James Clifford sees the current metanarratives in ethnography as shifts between homogenization and emergence. That is, a past reliance on the authority of tradition faces the reality of culture change (1988, 16–17). The "depth" of systemic or interpretive metaphors can always be questioned especially since one single metaphor rarely satisfies every aspect of a complex cultural environment. However, metaphors can serve to describe the relationships between cultural contexts and cultural actors. In "Art as a Culture System," Clifford Geertz explores our need to talk about art (visual, sonic, and performance) as human expression (*Local Knowledge* [New York: Basic Books, 1983], 95–120; hereafter cited in text).The breathless list of approaches he offers reveals the struggle and ingenuity through which we try to grasp the significance and impact of the creative act: ". . . we reach for scientific metaphors, spiritual ones, technological ones, political ones; and if all else fails we string dark sayings together and hope someone else will elucidate them for us" (95). I reach for several metaphors to provide reference in this study of contemporary Belarusan culture in Belarus. The metaphors are connected to the nature of change in this envi-

58   *Of Mermaids and Rock Singers*

ronment—change that is infused with the interplay between authenticity, cultural authority, and the definition of Belarusan identity.

[2] In his Charles Seeger Lecture given for the Society for Ethnomusicology conference held in Seattle in 1992, James Clifford saw the city as a metaphor for mobility between and amongst cultures in New York City. His description of movement through communities, and of cultural adaptation and appropriation by these communities provided a tangible "picture" of culture processes in a highly dynamic and diverse urban environment.

[3] Despite the similarity in construction and design, these communities were not considered equal. An apartment near Maŝerava, close to the city center, was considered to be an "uptown" address housing prominent figures in academia, sports, and politics.

[4] Since 1991, some of Miensk's population has migrated farther than the outer boundaries of the outlying suburban regions, to build "luxurious" monolithic private homes. Most remain in various stages of construction and habitation. Those that are complete are still not occupied because the city has yet to provide plumbing and electricity to these new suburbia. They are strange looking monuments, out of place in what are still farmer's fields. They are also indicators of the uneven distribution in wealth. One friend remarked that the necessary loans for construction were only available to the "well-connected," and that with the fluctuating ruble and interest rates, inside traders could borrow three-hundred-thousand rubles to build (when 1000 rubles = $1 US) and when the ruble fell to 10,000 to the dollar, they paid the bank back $30.00 US and stood back while the tax-payers paid for their houses.

[5] For the history of architectural change in the city of Miensk see Kipel and Kipel 1988; Zaprudnik 1993; Marples; Guy Picarda, *Minsk : a historical guide and short administrative, professional and commercial directory* (Minsk : Technalohija, 1994).

[6] Built in the seventeenth century and formerly the Catholic Church of Women Bernardines.

[7] See H.G. Wells, *The Time Machine/The War of the Worlds*, ed. Frank D. McConnell, New York: Oxford, 1977.

[8] Some private entrepreneurs and private companies are building/managing apartment complexes that circumvent the allotment system. However these apartments are for the diplomatic and economic elite or are especially built for company employees, for example the Belarus Bank.

[9] The favored trend however is not towards this familial living arrangement. For example, many young women rate suitors according to whether or not they own their own apartment.

[10] My friend Rita had recently converted to Orthodoxy and was in the process of fasting for Lent. Her literal devotion to the doctrines of her new church was affecting her health. In voicing my concern we entered into a discussion about the interpretation of dogma and how interpretation affects our understanding of meaning and our subsequent actions. Her initial surprise at the possibility of interpretation made her uncomfortable and we dropped the subject. A few days

"Stand in the doorway": Entrances and Exits in Modern Belarus 59

later she offered a parallel with the communist experience. She said, "In the past you were either a communist or you weren't, you were either black or white, there was no middle, no gray area. I suppose that we see many things that way" (conversations June, 1993).

[11] Jeffery C. Alexander, "Bringing Democracy Back In: Universalistic Solidarity and the Civic Sphere," in *Intellectuals and Politics: Social Theory in a Changing World*, vol 5 of *Key Issues in Sociological Theory*, ed. Charles C. Lemert (Newberry Park: Sage, 1991), 157.

[12] Eventually the poor economic climate, the falling ruble, and the lack of salary payments would be associated with the "failings" of Western capitalism. Lukašenka seized such associations and made them part of his platform for a return to a Soviet-style state.

[13] Field work interviews with student group at the Institute of Culture, Miensk, May 26, 1993.

[14] Interview with Valancina Tryhubovič at Kurapaty (outside Miensk), June 22, 1995.

[15] Interview with Aleksandar Krudastoŭ, 1993 Hajnaŭka, Biełastoččynna, Poland, February 19.

[16] Implementation of language change was legislated on September 20, 1991.

[17] "The Law About Culture" (passed on June 4, 1991), which stipulates that language policy is determined by "The Law About Languages" was followed by the "Law About Education" (passed on October 29, 1991). This law defines the goal of education as, among other things, (1) forming and re-strengthening the national consciousness of the citizen of the Republic of Belarus as well as feelings of respect towards other countries and peoples of the world; (2) securing knowledge of the state language as the principle means of communication among the citizens of the Republic of Belarus; (3) preserving and multiplying intellectual property and cultural treasures of the Belarusan people and other national communities of the republic" (Zaprudnik 1993, 137–140).

[18] Conversations, House of L. Šymaniec, Miensk, Belarus, May 29, 1993.

[19] Often, reaction to cultural stress (colonization; Russification) manifests itself in a cultural effort to establish distinction. Donald Horowitz describes this reaction as a *movement of differentiation* recalling historic glories and "emphasizing cultural uniqueness" (71).

[20] Interview with Zinajda Mažejka, Miensk, September 10, 1993; hereafter cited in text.

[21] This had as much to do with the diminishing production of Belarusan-language publications in the Republic. Between 1960 and 1985 the total number of Belarusan-language books published in Belarus declined from 50 percent to 9 percent. For publication statistics see Zaprudnik (1993, 107).

[22] By the summer of 1995, exchanging currency into American dollars had become public and practical. New exchange kiosks had popped up all over the city. In 1993, one could exchange money at official booths beside government-sanctioned tourist shops, or on the black market where individuals with different

60   *Of Mermaids and Rock Singers*

currencies paper-clipped onto their lapels would stroll along looking for buyers and sellers.

[23] With the fluctuating Belarusan ruble, monthly salaries steadily diminish in value while prices for even basic products continued to grow closer to or even exceed prices in the West.

[24] Slang for the 1000 ruble note of the Belarusan currency that began circulation on May 25, 1992. Each denomination (up to the ten thousand ruble note) is represented by a native animal. The zajčyk (diminutive form of zajac) refers to the rabbit or bunny on this bill.

[25] It was increasingly clear that the West was considered to be a kind of magical Oz. There seemed to be comfort in the idea that somewhere there exists a place where money and opportunity are within easy reach, if not given away. I recall many conversations where I was challenged to prove that Western (here American) life was in any way stressful. When I explained the need for mortgages, educational loans, medical coverage, and credit cards, etc., I was confronted with angry disbelief. The West, as the model of not only a better life, but a perfect life was held up as the grand prize, perhaps the compensation for difficult cultural and political histories. In the general climate of frustration, many Belarusans were ignoring the importance of historical and economic process in the definition of a Western prosperity.

[26] 19.5 percent of the population absorbed cesium-137 and 80 percent of the affected population absorbed iodine-131 (Marples, 42).

[27] Notably Murray Feshbach and Alfred Friendly, *Ecocide in the USSR* (New York: Basic Books, 1992); Grigori Medvedev, *No Breathing Room: The Aftermath of Chernobyl* (New York: Basic Books, 1993); Marples (1996).

[28] While my research dealt primarily with contemporary music, I was able to meet with Belarusian researchers who have focused upon the Chernobyl legacy in their own work. Zinajda Mažejka, ethnomusicologist, has worked with the changes in what she calls 'authentic repertoires' due to the resettlement of populations from contaminated areas. For statistics on relocation strategies and actual population moved, see Marples (54–55).

[29] Field work, Bukča, Palešsie (May-June, 1993).

4.
From Legislation to the Renaissance: Belarusan Rock and Urban Folklore

THE MIENSK LIVE MUSIC SCENE IS AT ONCE DYNAMIC, SPORADIC, AND VARIED. Classical music, stage band jazz, institutionally-trained cultural ensembles [kalektyvy], and variety show crooners [estradnaja muzyka or stage music] can all be heard in the auspicious surroundings of the Miensk Philharmonia, a building whose imposing neo-Classical architecture hints at the art music and classical dance that had originally been intended for its stage. In the lounges of the *Intourist* hotels, bands perform covers of Western hits or Russian popular ballads, as the waitress tells you which part of the menu is really available that day.

Hotel performers are directly tied to the tourist market. Special hotels were built during the Soviet era as Western-style lodgings for visitors from outside the Soviet Union. The facilities also allowed government officials to control the movements of tourists and businessmen. All passports were given to the front desk at check-in and were returned when a visitor left. Rumors of surveillance cameras and bugged telephone lines were common. With sovereignty, these facilities were busy housing a new generation of business people and tourists. The restaurants were some of the best stocked in the city, and the nightlife focused on dancing and a successful bar scene. When live music was provided, the bands (often comprising a lead singer, bass, keyboard, drummer) focused on Western covers or light musical fare, i.e., synthesized arrangements of Russian ballads, or stage music repertoires. These musicians could boast regular salaries and what was considered good pay for their work. However, musicians who tried to succeed with their own repertoires in varied rock venues often described hotel musicians as sell-outs, adding that if they "gave up" they could always make a living as part of a lounge band.[1] Many musicians that have not "given up" play in the walkways beneath

61

62   Of Mermaids and Rock Singers

Victory Square. These underground passages that lead to the city metro resound with the eerie echo of a saxophone or violin. Down the street in the House of Literature bards with guitar in hand sing of love and of politics. And, at the occasional concert or song competition, audiences are treated to the sounds of Belarusan rock.

In addition to live performance venues, Miensk audiences, as well as those in other parts of the country, listen to Miensk Radio and watch television programs that range from explorations of cutting-edge popular genres to the affirmation of authentic rural repertoires and performers. In 1993, Western European and North American music videos were rarely broadcast although some pirated copies were being passed amongst enthusiasts. Access to foreign music, though still a challenge, was not impossible. Pirated cassette copies of the latest Western hits could be bought for 2000 zajcyki[2] at certain city kiosks or could be heard on American Bandstand which was broadcast every Sunday on Radio Moscow. Local Miensk musicians, members of the Belarusan music scene, were disconnected from the benefits of, and infringements from, the Western music industry. Cassette-albums by local rock bands, bards, and new traditional music groups were often acquired through networks of musicians, journalists, and fans, from the rare promoter, or from the bands themselves.

Throughout 1993 the urban music scene reflected an increasing variety of musical styles. The lack of industry-generated publicity and of consistent performance venues created the impression of a scattered musical menu, unconnected concerts, and sporadic musical events. Yet performers were clearly establishing their signature sounds. Radio and television programs designed to highlight specific aspects of musical culture were becoming a consistent resource for audiences. Performers and audiences had access to more live and televised concerts as well as media attention. Urban Belarusan music was at once being celebrated, criticized, and dismissed while being recognized as a consistent proponent of contemporary Belarusan culture.

The genres and performance styles heard in Belarusan contemporary music-making include rural repertoires, Classical music, variety performance [estradnaja muzyka], staged folklore, bardic performance, popular music, and rock music. Responses to these genres vary according to attitudes towards traditional culture, responses to institutionally-defined performance, and reactions to the appropriation of Western styles.

Rural musical tradition comprises a vast repertoire of songs and dances including songs belonging to the calendrical song cycle (spring, harvest, and summer solstice songs), family ritual songs such as wedding songs, non-ritual songs on themes of love and daily life including male epic songs, and a vast repertoire of instrumental music. The musical characteristics and performance styles vary by region, can differ according to the estimated age of the repertoire and according to the function of the song.[3] Rural music-mak-

From Legislation to the Renaissance   *63*

ing is a part of contemporary village life, is the basis of ethnographic research, and is recorded, mediated, and broadcast as examples of "authentic" Belarusan expression. Rural practice is also mediated through educational institutions where the songs and styles learned in the field are transposed onto the urban stage.

Institutions, such as the Institute of Culture in Miensk, produce performance ensembles specializing in the recontextualization of Belarusan musical tradition. The repertoire is most often presented through musical theater where rural and village vignettes provide the scene for the interaction between characters within the story lines described in many songs. The most popular scene is that of the marketplace or kirmaš. Despite the suggestion of a rural setting, these performances are highly stylized. Traditional songs are given a musical accompaniment (comprising of cymbalom [hammered dulcimer], bayan [accordion], and string bass), dance movements are ballet-inspired, and vocal projection has a more nasal quality compared to village practice. These mediated characteristics of staged folklore reflect the urban attempt to "standardize" and "elevate" varied rural musical traditions. This genre of the urban-traditional remains an active part of the urban music scene. Ensembles specializing in this staged folklore, such as Sviata [Celebration], were the leading touring companies of the Soviet era and still perform in formal performance spaces such as the Miensk Philharmonia.

Responses to this staged style vary according to notions of Belarusan tradition and its role in current cultural exploration. That is, whether performance practice should be based on rural authenticity or urban mediation. Ethnographer and television personality Vasil Lićvinka commented that there was room for both urban and rural manifestations of tradition. He saw the staged folklore as another means to expose Belarusans to their musical culture.[4] Lićvinka was the host and producer of a weekly television show "Viačorki." The show alternated venues from the television studio to the rural setting and highlighted calendrical ritual songs performed by village ensembles. Criticisms of the show were based on what was perceived as the staging of cultural practice. Ethnomusicologist Zinajda Mažejka and radio producer Rehina Hamzovič, both interested in researching what they consider to be non-mediated rural performance, were critical of the show which they saw as a misrepresentation of Belarusan tradition. Aware of such criticism, Lićvinka supports his approach saying that: "it is more important to expose Belarusans to their expression in as many ways as possible" (1993). While current media trends clearly concentrate on depictions and transpositions of traditional Belarusan culture, several contemporary genres have not become part of the mainstream media.

The urban bard is the modern version of the poet-musician. These singing poets [pl. bardy] base their performance on texts taken from literary works or on literary newly–composed texts set to strophic musical form and

64 *Of Mermaids and Rock Singers*

performed with guitar accompaniment. Nadzia Kudrejka, a journalist with the music desk at National Youth Radio described the development of the bard genre in Belarus: "Earlier bards as such didn't exist in Belarus. In Russia, understood as the Soviet Union, there were bards, such as Visotsky. . . . Russian-language bards in Belarus were started as an organization and with time Belarusian bards became very well known. This is especially evident in Bard festivals. At the latest held in Kiev, four Belarusans received prizes, and in Talinn, two out of the four winners were from Miensk."[5]

Bards such as Aleś Kamotski, Valżyna Ciareśčanka, and Siarżuk Sokalau-Vojuš were public advocates for the Belarusan language and the Renaissance movement. These performers are highly respected by the literary community. They perform in the Miensk House of Literature and are evaluated according to their social commentary, humor, and quality of their texts.[6] As an intellectual genre, bard music is not considered a viable commercial style and suffers from a lack of sponsorship often found in popular and rock music.

As a category, popular music refers to various styles in urban Belarus. An official brand of popular music can be heard on the variety stage [estradnaja muzyka]. Male and female ballad-style crooners perform with full orchestral backup, black-tie glamour costumes, and stage presence reminiscent of Vegas-style showmanship. This brand of performance is mediated in several ways. Rising stars are associated with musical directors and institutions who guide their training and provide performance venues. Performers gain reputations and exposure by participating in a series of juried, nationally-televised music festivals such as the pan-Slavic Sławianski Bazar [Slavic Bazar] held in Viciebsk in 1993, and the national music festival held in Maładečna.

The term "popular music" is also used to differentiate a variety of musical styles from "rock." The application of "popular" varies considerably according to the perspective of the musician. The members of the rock band Ulis (Chapter 6) used the term to contrast what they describe as the artistry and sincerity of rock with the less aggressive, more casual and commercial definition of popular music. For example, popular music was more suited to female performance because: "they can't play guitar, drums, bass like a man, they don't have the same life experiences . . . they're not suited to rock, but pop—yes."[7]

Belarusan rock has been an aspect of urban culture since the early 1980s. As the black sheep of contemporary music in Belarus, rock has played a significant role in the movements towards cultural and political change. Belarusan-language groups that emerged in the early part of the decade adapted to the oppositional conditions of the period. While they found inspiration and support in the political and cultural momentum of the time, they still had to contend with the powerful cultural bureaucracy of the Soviet sys-

From Legislation to the Renaissance   65

tem. In Belarus, rockers were not only choosing to perform in the Belarusan language but, as in other republics, they were also part of a music movement that was heavily criticized by Soviet cultural policy. As a result, rock groups were immediately considered anti-establishment. Nevertheless, Belarusan-language rock has had a powerful impact upon cultural and linguistic awareness. The genre introduced the Belarusan language as well as Belarusan-specific themes to a generation that had had little contact with traditional cultural histories.

GENERALITIES AND SPECIFICS OF THE SOVIET ROCK SCENE

The development of the Soviet rock music movement in general, what Timothy Ryback calls bloc rock (1991),[8] was influenced by several common factors across the republics. The evolution of rock music in the Soviet Union is characterized by attempts to officially control interest in Western popular music and subsequently to police the development of non-Soviet, indigenous popular music styles.

The most far-reaching agent which affected the general "Soviet" rock movement was government legislation.[9] The distrust of rockers and their followers in political rhetoric was linked to the notion that the music reflected Western, and therefore anti-Soviet ideas. Since rock was seen to have emerged out of a curiosity with Western trends, it was immediately suspect. The speed with which musicians and audiences became aware of new artists, acquired underground recordings, or appropriated rock and roll styles signaled the power of this infiltration by popular culture. By the time youth audiences in the Soviet Union had converted to the Beatles in 1964, Soviet authorities were forced to recognize the power of the rock movement and were busy devising the means for idealistic and aesthetic control (1990, 181–191).

In the transfer of power from Kruschev to Breznev and Kosygyn,[10] rock music went from being banned to being state controlled—a shift of policy which signals the increasing strength of the rock movement at the grass roots level. Subsequent legislation, control of repertoire, of band membership, and of approved performance spaces defined the means of production for state-approved music. The 1960s saw the development of official bands that contradicted the rebellious, youth revolution, coming-of-age themes of Western rock, and instead preached a passive view of a stable and happy world. These bands were formed with the blessing of the Ministry of Culture after 1966 and were viewed as an official compromise in the face of a growing youth and rock movement: "Musicians willing to cut their hair, moderate their decibel levels, and purge their repertoires of offensive Western songs, could enjoy the benefits of state sponsorship—national concert tours, appearances on radio and television, recording opportunities . . ." (Ryback, 106).

66   *Of Mermaids and Rock Singers*

These groups gained healthy followings in the 1960s and 1970s, although their official approval, their regimented repertoires, and their performance styles drew criticism from rock enthusiasts who had pledged an intellectual, philosophical, and aesthetic commitment to the rock produced outside the sanctioned system. Russian rock critic Artemy Troitsky describes their music as "limp Russian-language covers of melodies from American hits and Russian pop tunes with soft-electric sound."[11] The best known were the "Happy Guys" who emerged in 1968 and represented through their lyrics the epitome of the Soviet aesthetic for popular culture. (Ryback, 106; Ramet 1994, 183; 192). In addition to attempting absolute control of this new popular music, from the mid-sixties Soviet authorities tried to prescribe the locations for dance clubs and rock clubs. The growing trend to gather in private apartments, restaurants, and cafes brought about the renovation of Komsomol Youth clubs where new dance styles such as the Twist were banned, often with the threat of incarceration (Ryback, 107).

This regulation generated different levels of reaction. Essential to the rock movement was the development of a sophisticated black market system through which Western popular music and the music of non-official bands could be produced and distributed. Rock music enthusiasts found the means to listen to, and to acquire a variety of different kinds of Western music. Private one-night dance clubs continued to appear whether in an apartment or the more visible rented hall. Local bands were emerging from the underground and, at least in Moscow, taking over those performance venues that had once highlighted Soviet jazz. It was clear that there was a growing appetite for rock music and a growing roster of unofficial local bands who were seminal to the development of a Soviet rock culture (107). The practical needs of these unofficial bands, finding performance venues, practice studios, and recording opportunities, gaining media exposure, and receiving adequate payment came to define the professional frustrations and personal challenges of life as a rock musician. With the lack of an industry infrastructure, these challenges continue to define rock life in post-Soviet context.

Despite the enormous energy expended on the control of popular youth culture, the Soviet government's response to change in popular culture was not always consistent. Officials would reject and harass independently-formed bands but might eventually recognize the same bands when they reached a certain level of popularity, seemingly hoping to maintain a semblance of control by appropriating such groups into the official fold.

By the 1980s discos were registered, DJ's were required to have gone through ideological training, groups were forced to register with the Association of Musical Groups, and the Komsomol had established youth patrols to monitor and control the quality of music in public places, as well as commandos to control black-market distribution of forbidden recordings (Ramet, Zamascikov, and Bird 1994, 185). Those groups that were active in

From Legislation to the Renaissance

67

the early 1980s lived under the danger of constant harassment, including KGB interrogation, for creating outside the boundaries of sanctioned expression. Siarhiej Krauĉanka, a former member of the Belarusan band Ulis, dismissed the hardships of bands emerging in Belarus in the 1990s. He emphasized the rocker experiences of veteran Belarusan bands who had emerged despite the Soviet system saying that: "if you survived what they did to you in the 1980s, then this [present economic hardships] is nothing."[12] Overall, criticism of unofficial groups continued to be based upon the perceived philosophical defection towards Western popular culture. Unofficial groups challenged Soviet policy by constructing a style, choosing a language, or communicating a message that might reflect generational, political, and national concerns.

According to Alexander Dugin, a freelance journalist and self-ascribed expert of avant-garde youth culture, the Gorbachev era allowed for a reevaluation of rock and of the West.[13] He considers that the new access to the West, as a result of glasnost, disputed the negative images of Western culture that had been characteristic of Soviet-era rhetoric. This new world view encouraged a sense of commonality because both sides of the iron curtain could engage in the same ideals which he identifies as: "honesty, struggle, protest, and rebellion" (66). Followers of the rock movement felt a powerful fellowship with Western rock that was defined by the perceived sincerity of the musical message. Sincerity was linked to an emphasis on social rebellion and an anti-establishment expression of "the truth." Dugin writes: "But it was Rebellion that had always been the inspiration of true rock. It was rebellion against alienation and loneliness, against the dogmas, against the fatigue brought on by civilization" [. . .], and "Soviet rock fans have no doubt at all that rock is a social phenomenon, one hundred percent, and that it is a clear sign of rebellion against sloppy songs about things that do not exist in real life, against vulgar sentimentality and undue optimism, against the imitation of folk music never accepted by the people, and against marches that evoke no desire to march (67).[14]

Sincerity, truth, and rebellion are key words in the passionate description of rock by rock critics and rock enthusiasts that explore the construction of meaning in local and in imported Western rock music. The importance of artistic integrity is also prominent in Belarusan rock criticism of the early 1990s (Martynienka and Mialhuj, 1991). Such analysis reveals the view that the rock movement has social power because of its potential influence on youth audiences. By extension, "good" rockers could be recognized according to their demonstration of social responsibility.

The analysis of the rock movement has produced other attempts to define Soviet rock. Geydar Jemal (1991) offers three general criteria that attempt to assign a gestalt for the Soviet rock movement. The first of these reflects the underground rock movement and garage-style bands that

68   *Of Mermaids and Rock Singers*

emerged despite Soviet sanctions. The result is an emphasis on the amateur hero-musicians that Jemal describes as having spontaneity and sincerity over professionalism. That is, if you were state-approved, and by implication a professional, your message could not be trustworthy.[15] The second characteristic, lyrics over music, highlights the importance of text in much Eastern European expression. Eastern European rock texts are often heavy with introspection, a Slavic tragic-comedic world view, expressed through a high level of poetic skill. The third criteria is simply described as an energy level fueled by the rejection of conformity which, as Jemal emphasizes, is achieved through gutsy rock and shaped by an intellectual personality (12–14). These three broad characteristics, sincerity, lyrics, and energy, can easily be applied to rock outside the Russian sphere, including rock music in Belarus.

Beyond such general analysis, post-Soviet writing on rock music often ascribes a Russo-centric character to the rock movement. The development of rock music in the Soviet Union is therefore represented as a Russian cultural phenomenon. The resulting perception of post-Soviet rock movements are, by extension, defined largely as Russian-language rock derived from Moscow- and St. Petersburg–based sub-cultures: "The 20–year pregnancy of Soviet rock [. . .] can hardly be grasped without an acquaintance with its parents and godparents, without unearthing its cultural roots, without getting immersed in Soviet mentality, and finally without grasping the **Russian aesthetic tradition** [my emphasis] that gave birth to Soviet rock of the 80s" (12).

Non-Russian rock movements, many of which gained strength in the mid-1980s were inspired by another kind of rebellion. Rock was not only about the empowerment of youth, or stretching one's world view in the context of an overbearing political parent. Rebellion was also about exercising one's non-Russianess, discovering pre-Soviet roots, and exploring the notion of distinct cultural identities. This revolution would predict the advent of cultural rebirths that contributed to the eventual call for cultural and political independence. Prior to the emergence of Belarusan rock in the years leading up to and following the fall of the Soviet Union, Belarusan popular music was defined by the music of the Pieśniary [Songsters]. Their signature style, their language choice, and the construction of their public image served to define a Belarusan-specific popular music that would eventually influence emerging rock groups in the 1980s.

THE PIEŚNIARY [SONGSTERS]: FROM VIA TO "PIEŚNIAROK"

It is not without irony that the first group to develop a definitive Belarusan popular music style appeared in Miensk in the late 1960s and that this group was the Belarusan version of the official VIA (vocal instrumental ensemble) band.[16] In 1969, a group of ten conservatory musicians formed The Pieśniary (the Songsters) under the direction of composer Uładzimir Muljavin. They would eventually define a style based on Belarusan traditional repertoires

From Legislation to the Renaissance

which they performed in the Belarusan language. Their official status, which afforded them a recording contract with Melodiya, a private recording studio, instruments, and domestic and foreign tours, allowed them to reach an enormous Soviet audience who in 1977 voted them the most popular vocal instrumental ensemble in the Soviet Union (Ryback 1991, 150).

The Pieśniary were the model VIA ensemble. Physically they were well-groomed, their stage performance was passive, they could incorporate Pagannini-esque variations and quote Bach as well as they played electric guitar and psychedelic keyboard. In fact, they diffused the Western image of the corrupt cacophonous rock band, and according to official bureaucratic strategies, were successfully distracting Soviet youth with acceptable music and non-Western role models.

Despite criticism of the band as another counterfeit VIA ensemble, particularly by underground rock critics,[17] the Pieśniary were well-respected by their public. By 1977, Melodiya had produced 10 million albums. Their success with audiences and their simultaneous adherence to official dogma suggests that this group of musicians was managing an official image while they were shaping a definite musical style. Timothy Ryback writes, "The VIA Pesniary [sic] from the city of Minsk also cultivated official favor. In 1973, as part of their effort to woo cultural officials, Pesniary publicly renounced its origins as a Beatles band. "We might as well admit it," Pesniary stated in the Soviet magazine Ogonyok in October 1973, "At first we tried to sing like the Beatles [. . .] but before long we started to feel that it wasn't us" (151).[18]

Instead the group began to sing arrangements of traditional Belarusan folk songs in an eclectic mix of musical styles using traditional instruments along with electric guitar, bass, and electronic keyboard. Their perceived rejection of a Western style in favor of an indigenous musical tradition was on the surface a coup for cultural officials.[19] The Pieśniary's style may have suggested the institutionalizing of the folk repertoire through "rock," but their music, and their public statements suggested a focus on a Belarusan, as opposed to pan-Slavic, musical style.

What the Pieśniary began on a mass-media scale was the association of contemporary music performance with cultural assertion. Music was a means through which language and culture could be introduced into the public sphere. Lavon Bartkievič, lead tenor with the group, emphasized a connection between language choice and cultural identity that precluded the Soviet philosophy: "As far as I am concerned I am Belarusan and I will sing Belarusan songs both traditional and modern."[20]

The Pieśniary were mediating two polarized cultural and political messages. As much as they were emphasizing a national culture, they were satisfying a system that had given them their raison d'être as a VIA band. The fact that the band was mediating between two sides of the cultural and political fence was not lost on their fans:[21] "Pesniary had two faces, there was the official band you could see on television, but they also played covers to western hits, and wrote great songs like "Alesia." At their best they sounded a lot like Jethro Tull"[22] (quoted in Ryback, 151).

The visual image of the group also contained a mixture of the traditional and the official. Their album covers offered the public an image of the group and their style. They often stood in rural settings, wearing watered-down versions of traditional dress while holding examples of traditional instruments. Figure 4.1, from an album dating from 1988, places the group in the middle of a hay field. The design of their costumes, at once generic Slavic and 1970s chic, reflect costumes used by traditional folk ensembles linked to official cultural institutes and cultural centers or Damy Kultury. Their clothing borrows the geometry of traditional ornament, but it is exaggerated and displaced on the clothes.

Figure 4.1: Front cover design from the album *Pesniary* (Melodiya 60–11287–88). Used by permission.

From Legislation to the Renaissance 71

Figure 4.2: Back cover design from the album *Pesniary* (Melodiya 60–11287–88) Used by permission.

Six members hold instruments: two traditional flutes, two lyras [hurdy-gurdies], a skrypka [fiddle], and an acoustic guitar. While these instruments suggest the group's use of traditional resources, they do not announce the band's true style, which relies heavily on electric guitar, bass, drum set, and electronic keyboard. It is only on the back of the album (Figure 4.2) that one sees the band at work in the studio using instruments that were borrowed from the Western rock genre. Black and white journalistic photographs now depict a group in leather jackets, Jean jackets, and turtlenecks. The album juggles the image of the rural/accessible/authentic with that of the successful/urbanite/professional. It is as though the images try to satisfy every possible expectation of a potential audience as well as of the official onlooker.

The ambiguity of these images is as much a reflection of the official conditions under which the group recorded and performed, as it is a reflection of their eclectic musical style. The Pieśniary manipulate existing repertoire

72   *Of Mermaids and Rock Singers*

through the 'plugging in' of characteristics from other genres. The construct a new musical text through a convincing fusion of styles that would be considered polarized in Western practice. For example, the incorporation of flute cadenzas and classical violin variations, rock ballad vocals, and jazz-style improvisation within the same arrangement. Wooden flutes, violin, cymbalom, and hurdy-gurdy share a *soundscape* with electric bass, guitars, keyboards, and drum sets. The combination of these sounds and the expansion of musical texture suggest a specific musical agenda in which the listener is guided through traditional repertoire towards contemporary music idioms. As a result the Pieśniary suggest that their traditional repertoire choices be considered as contemporary music and not as folk artifacts.

The folk song "Pierapiołačka" (The Little Quail)[23] is an allegorical lament that describes the life condition of a Belarusan woman during the period of serfdom. The Pieśniary 's lengthy arrangement provides one of the most comprehensive examples of their reworking of traditional resources. The Pieśniary explore the piece through a complex treatment of the melody and text that eventually focuses upon instrumental improvisation. The arrangement sustains the structure of the folk melody which is repeatedly emphasized through the use of a significant pause between each verse/chorus group. The effect is that of a theme and variation form, where the variations are based on stylistic experimentation. The traditional two-line verse, two line refrain structure remains intact for sections with text (see Example 4.1). Instrumental sections, separated from the formal needs of the text, include the most exaggerated rhythmic manipulation of the melodic material (Example 4.2).

"Pierapiołačka" [The Little Quail] (Transcriptions and translation by the author)

A ŭ pierapiołki dy hałouka balić.	The little quail's head aches.
A ŭ pierapiołki rućki balać.	The little quail's hands ache.
(kalency)	(knees)
Ty-ž maja, ty-ž maja pierapiołačka.	You are my, You are my little quail.
Ty-ž maja, ty-ž maja nievialičkaja.	You are my, You are my little one.
A što pierapiołka rana ŭstaje.	The little quail wakes early.
A što pierapiołka rana ŭstaje.	The little quail wakes early.
A ŭ pierapiołki dy stareńki muž	The quail's husband is old.
A ŭ pierapiołki dzietki małyja	The quail's children are young.
Dzietački płačuč, jeściejki prosiać,	The children cry, they ask to eat,
Dzietački płačuč, jeściejki prosiać,	The children cry, they ask to eat,
A ŭ pierapiołki chleba niama.	The little quail has no bread to give.
A ŭ pierapiołki chleba niama.	The little quail has no bread to give.

Note: In Belarusan the diminutive form is used as both an expression of affection and to describe the young. In this song, pierapiołka occurs as pierapiołačka; the adjective 'old' or stary becomes stareńki; children or 'dzieci' becomes dzietački etc.

From Legislation to the Renaissance

Example 4.1: Melodic Basis for "Pierapiołačka" (verse refrain structure). Transcribed by the author.

Example 4.2: Introductory segment of "Pierapiołačka." Transcribed by the author.

The first two statements of the melody do not include text. The group emphasizes the traditional roots of the melody through the use of traditional instruments, flute, cymbalom, and violin. As an underlying drone supports the echoing treatment of the two-part verse-refrain melody, the listener is pre-

74 *Of Mermaids and Rock Singers*

pared for the textural layering to come. The drone is consistently used at the beginning of each verse/chorus pair and provides a stable characteristic as the music becomes more improvisatory in character. The drone also evolves through various devices: it is first heard as a trill on the interval of a fourth, is eventually embedded in arpeggiated patterns (Example 4.3) or, in the most energetic part of the arrangement, replaced entirely by ostinato patterns played by electric bass (Example 4.4). Although the underlying vamp-like ostinato is a common element of contemporary popular music and especially jazz performance, in this context the repeated pattern functions as an echo of the drone, adding a sense of continuity to each new stylistic statement of the melody. Example Two also illustrates,

1. the rhythmic variance on beat 3 of each statement of the melody,
2. the placement of each statement along the bar-line: an "out of phase" positioning where the melody begins on beats one, four, and three of the bar line,
3. the layering effect initiated by this introduction where, after each melodic statement is complete, the instrument continues on a sustained note. This sustained note also reflects a typical aspect of Belarusan vocal performance, where the last note of a melodic phrase is held and typically ended with a punctuated aspiration, or with a fade-out that descends in pitch.

In most cases, once the melodic structure has been presented, the group adds an improvisatory section that also replaces the function of the drawn-out final note, and allows for additional genre and style combinations. Schema 4.1 provides a mapping of the typical treatment of each verse-chorus pair,

The arrangement of "Pierapiołačka" by the Pieśniary gains momentum through an increase in texture, instrumental innovation (within the treatment of folk songs), and the fusion of styles. In the most elaborate section, melodic improvisation is paramount. The drone/ostinato relationship is manifested as a repetition of the textual refrain by the 'choir' while, using the same text, a solo voice 'wails' an improvisational line on Ty-ž maja, tyž maja, pierapiołačka (You are my little quail). The textural tension and improvisational fury of this section grows in intensity as the number of voices increases and they become denser and more active. As the musical energy peaks, the texture suddenly cuts off to silence offering a dramatic simultaneous release of the accumulated sonic tension. It is at this point that the final statement of the melody is played on a solo flute, recalling the traditional style and sound of the very first statement of the melody.

From Legislation to the Renaissance   75

Example 4.3: "Pierapiołačka." First manifestation of layering as the drone is replaced by arpeggiated ostinato patterns. Transcribed by the author.

Example 4.4: "Pierapiołačka." Ostinato transformed into bass line heard under the most improvisational segment of the arrangement. Transcribed by the author.

Schema 4.1: Melody, Chorus, and Drone elaborations in Pierapiołačka

Each melody/chorus package is introduced through an increasingly elaborate musical statement that functions as a drone at the beginning of the piece: the end of melodic statements can include a lengthy melodic, usually soloistic tag (X).

For each statement of the melody/chorus (A B [X]) :

INSTRUMENTAL INTRODUCTION	VERSE MELODY A	CHORUS MELODY B	X—
[drone —› ostinato]			expansion of material through improvisation

First and Second melodic statements/non-texted:

| 1. tremollo; violin | staggered entries flute hurdy-gurdy cymbalom | flute; hurdy-gurdy and cymbalom | extended flute cadenza |
| 2. tremollo; cymbalom, flute hurdy-gurdycymbalom | | | A' Paganini-esque variations of verse melody - double stopped violin |

76   *Of Mermaids and Rock Singers*

This song illustrates some of the style manipulation heard in the Pieśniary's construction of a Belarusan-defined urban genre. While not all of their songs contain the level of intricate combinations of genres heard in "Pierapiołačka," this song serves to illustrate key aspects of this group's version of Belarusan urban popular music. In this, as in most of their selections, the Pieśniary maintain the melodic structure and text of a traditional song. They embellish the texture with complex Western-derived vocal harmonizations and instrumental accompaniment or, as in this example, use the song as a basis for elaboration, often drawing from genres and performance techniques from Western Classical, Jazz, or European and American popular music groups. In "Pierapiołačka" the influence of Yes and Rick Wakeman's electronic keyboard virtuosity is strongly suggested, as is the sonorous texture of Emerson Lake and Palmer.

The Pieśniary hold a unique position in Soviet and now Belarusan popular music. The VIA label under which the Pieśniary emerged in 1969 has placed them on a stylistic fence between official Soviet popular music and the music which underground rock fans associated with a sincere rock rebellion. The Pieśniary's rebellion, through the use of the Belarusan language and the prominence given to Belarusan traditional repertoires is still relevant in the styles and repertoires of contemporary Belarusan urban rock. From within the ranks of Belarusan music, the Pieśniary continue to be a respected group. For example, they perform as the guest stars of gala evenings celebrating national song contests (such as Viciebsk 1993). Most telling is the treatment of this group by current Belarusan rock groups. 1998 saw the release of *Pieśniarok* in which Belarusan rockers perform covers of the Pieśniary's greatest hits.[24] Their impact on the development of Belarusan rock is based on the consistency of their style and cultural choices, but their success is equally based on their technical facility with a variety of genres. Their technical abilities reflect the group's musical education in the Conservatory system and are highlighted in the heavy use of Classical gestures. But their successful mixture of musical styles is the result of an in-depth understanding of the mechanisms of other genres, from jazz to the Beatles, to the rock styles of Western bands in the 1970s and 1980s. While their approach illustrates the **conscious** use of musical elements borrowed from Western sources, the musical result is a syncretism of styles and a redefined, not simply rearranged, performance of the traditional.

Sitting on a political, cultural, and stylistic fence, the Pieśniary are in a unique position in Soviet and now Belarusan popular music. They are mythical in the level of their popularity within the Soviet system, and yet are considered pioneers in increasing Belarusan awareness in the public sphere. They are criticized for their VIA roots but have contributed to the model for Belarusan-language, Belarusan-inspired contemporary rock. As much as the Pieśniary have contributed to contemporary Belarusan music, the art-music

From Legislation to the Renaissance 77

connection, the clean-cut image, and passive performance style separate them from the music and image of contemporary Belarusan bands who respect the musicianship but feel divorced from the financial and public success of the Pieśniary.

Bands emerging in the 1980s would not benefit from the reputation, resources, or financial support that was enjoyed by the Pieśniary for more than two decades. The Pieśniary remain part of the official cultural establishment and are not now, nor were they ever, a marginalized part of a Belarusan rocker sub-culture.

DEFINING THE ELEMENTS OF "GOOD?" BELARUSAN ROCK

> We make our own steps in rock [. . .] that *all* [my emphasis] the people can dance.[25]

In 1986 rock music in Belarus became Belarusan rock. 1986, the year of the Chernobyl disaster, marks the time when the Belarusan renaissance became a significant and recognized social movement in the public sphere. This renaissance motivated many to learn the Belarusan language and to base contemporary expression on cultural rediscovery and their search for a pre-Soviet Belarusan identity. In the mid-1980s this Belarusan-specific aspect of the rock movement was especially dangerous. In the Soviet context Belarusan rockers were not only social rebels, they were cultural rebels as well. The choice to create and perform rock music was attacked in several ways. Those that followed the Soviet platform considered interest in non-Soviet definitions of Slavic cultures to be expressions of national chauvinism. Ironically, members of the Belarusan intelligentsia, who were also actively engaged in shaping a contemporary Belarusan identity, had difficulty accepting popular urban culture despite the congruence with their cause.[26]

Since the mid-1980s Belarusan rock groups were defining signature styles which borrowed various elements from Western rock and popular music, including heavy metal and rhythm and blues. While their musical directions were varied, their music comprised several characteristics that reflect the climate of cultural curiosity, assertion, and renewal. Belarusan rock can include some or all of the following: reference to traditional melodies, reference to historical experience, political commentary, and language choice.

Language choice was and remains a key aspect of Belarusan rock. Rockers that chose to produce Belarusan-language rock were facing several challenges. The use of the Belarusan language forced the creation of a selected audience that was ready to accept Belarusan, rather than English or Russian, as a viable language choice for this contemporary music. The rock movement also faced the cultural fallout of the Soviet period which continued to affect attitudes towards Belarusan language and culture. How receptive would audiences be to accepting this new Belarusan-language rock?

Lavon Volski a member of one of the original Belarusan-language rock bands Mroja [Dream] and Kasia Kamockaja, lead singer of one of the newer Belarusan groups Novaje Nieba [New Sky] addressed this issue in 1993. Their responses signal the development of a Belarusan rock audience, and emphasize that the rocker community makes a definite distinction between Belarusan rock and rock produced in Belarus. I asked them how, after seven years of Belarusan rock, they compared their popularity with that of groups who perform in Russian.[27]

> **Kamockaja:**
> I don't know. I have been to Russian concerts, but I can say that more people show up at our concerts. But these Russian-singing Belarusan groups should only be compared to Russian groups because they have access to an established industry there, to proper recording facilities. They don't feel their roots. Of course they have overall a larger audience because of language, but I could fairly say that we have more fans.
>
> **Volski:**
> Well for example, when Mroja started, we had a small audience. But our music is seen as more original, partly because of language choice. Our audience has been steadily growing.

Kamockaja makes a significant distinction between audience and fan. The implication is that the former exists by default and that the latter consciously pursues this language-specific musical choice. Both musicians also emphasize the different resources available to rock bands and how evaluations of popularity differ according to Russian- English-, and Belarusan-language bands. Kamockaja explains that positive public response to Belarusan-language music was not immediate and required determination and commitment from key figures in the media:

> **Kamockaja:**
> We have a resource in Belarusan Radio. They have the program Youth Radio, and there they only play Belarusan-language groups. This makes a difference. Because Simaška[28] started this work six years ago and has pounded into their heads that they need to hear Belarusan groups. So the criticism in letters has stopped. "Why don't you play Russian groups, etc. . . ." They know there is no sense in doing this.
>
> **Volski:**
> We also have to include the groups that now sing in English. These projects are there in order to go beyond our borders. For us it would be great to travel, but we are happy with our choices, it is not our aim to go, while it is theirs.

From Legislation to the Renaissance   79

Kamockaja:
These projects are really for outside of Belarus. There is nothing for
them here. There is less and less Russian awareness here. It is not a
reality for them here to find popularity in Russian. Belarusan groups
feel at home here. The others are now switching to English because
they understand that Russian gives little guarantee at airplay or at an
audience in Belarus.

Kamockaja and Volski are describing a rock music scene that was coming of age in 1993. The development of a consistent audience and of airplay
opportunities was certainly energizing the Belarusan rock community.
Nevertheless, Belarusan rock was still being criticized according to another
set of criteria that compared its position in popular culture with a value system defined by art music, literature, and intellectualism.

The movements that defined a resurgence of national identity draw
from traditional cultural resources in order to provide very definite parameters for cultural value. The result are repertoires that encourage and inform
national awareness– an indigenous and contemporary expression of cultural
pride and political commentary. In Belarusan history, the creative activity
emerging around national movements has been defined by the production of
literature and the publication of Belarusan-language newspapers. These
movements were energized by anti-establishment groups of writers, artists,
and educators who supported the revaluing of the Belarusan language as a
foundation for a renewed cultural and national consciousness. Poetic and
narrative expressions of love of country, filled with traditional symbolism
and masked political criticism have become the celebrated center of
Belarusan intellectual production.

The significance of poetry in national movements has affected contemporary urban music through the urban bard. These singing poets [pl. bardy]
base their performances on texts taken from literary works or on literary,
newly-composed texts that are performed with an acoustic guitar accompaniment. Considered a natural extension of the intellectual movement, bards
are supported by the literary intelligentsia who endorse their performances
in the auditorium of the Dom Literatarau, or House of Literature. As Nadzia
Kudrejka explained "poetry is the basis for bards, their music is a literary
mechanism; they don't consider themselves as writing music, but as writing
literature" (1993).[29]

The positive consideration of the bard genre seems to contradict the
negative consideration of texts in Belarusan-language rock. Both repertoires
are well-crafted, draw from human experience, cultural issues, politics, and
provide humorous, scathing, or sober contemporary commentary. The different evaluations of these genres emphasize the extent to which rock is often
criticized according to notions of the rocker lifestyle and of the evaluations of

80   *Of Mermaids and Rock Singers*

rock music as unlearned because of its link to the West, to youth culture, and to commercialism.[30]

While the specter of Soviet propaganda still guides such attitudes, Belarusan rock texts are considered a key aspect of "good" music from within the Belarusan-language rock movement. Amongst the five most popular Belarusan-language bands active in 1993, two bands, Krama and Ulis boasted lyricists as members, Novaje Nieba often drew texts from contemporary poets, Mroja consistently produces philosophically-charged words, and Pałac based most of their repertoire on texts from traditional rural repertoires. In 1994 the booklet *Bielaruski Rok-n-roll: Texts* (Miensk: Kovcheg) highlighted the song-texts of five Belarusan-language bands. Funded by the Belarusan Student Association in Biełastok, Poland, the book is categorized as part of a "Literature and Arts Series," emphasizing the placement of these rock texts in the same class as traditional literary, and therefore as intellectually serious, genres.

Language choice and references to Belarusan-specific repertoires are common options amongst rock groups that exhibit a wide variety of musical styles. Defining Belarusan rock in terms of musical style does not produce a single list of characteristics. Each of the five groups considered in this study boasts a different sound, and reflects the influence of very different popular music trends. Lavon Volski emphasized that this variety lessened the presence of direct competition and by extension cultivated an audience that could appreciate each group according to their unique musical choices: "We [Mroja] play traditional Heavy Metal, even by American standards, Krama plays rhythm and blues, Novaje Nieba experiments with the avant-garde, Ulis plays their own styles, so . . . there is little direct competition" (April 1993). The newest band Pałac also differed in style, playing in a self-described folk-modern style.

Aside from language, these bands share a common resource in the musical detail drawn from traditional Belarusan repertoires. However, the degree of appropriation from folk traditions differs greatly, at times defining a band's signature style (Pałac), a particular concept album (Ulis' *LONG-WHITECLOUDLAND*), or a particular song (Mroja's "Aŭstralijskaja Polka").

Another important influence on contemporary music-making are those styles copied or appropriated from Western popular music. In Belarus, as in several other republics, these Western influences began with the import of the Beatles whose music was still hitting the charts within the most popular foreign groups category into the 1990s (Ramet 1990: 2–5).[31] Most recently music from outside the Western mainstream has had an impact on the music of several bands who experiment with reggae, Afro-Cuban and Spanish rhythms, and the timbral qualities of non-Western instruments that are sampled into their electronic keyboards. Critical responses to such appropriations are often negative. Many Belarusan scholars and critics preach cultural authenticity

From Legislation to the Renaissance 81

that they define as a clear focus on Belarusan cultural elements. They perceive cross-cultural appropriation as an inappropriate mixture of styles which results in a loss of focus on Belarusan musical elements and authentic expression.[32]

The variety of stylistic labeling, as well as the evaluation of contemporary music according to the degree of cultural awareness, has resulted in a broad application of the term rock. The stylistic choices of each band, as well as the sometimes stylistic experimentation inherent even within the repertoire of one band, makes it difficult to assign a definitive style to Belarusan rock. Martynienka and Mialhuj use a phrase that at once suggests generation, continuity, and cultural authenticity by describing rock as "contemporary young urban folklore" (1990).[33]

The Belarusan rock movement is also defined by the logistics of producing recordings, getting air play, developing an audience, and generating a viable income. All of these reflect the conditions of the Belarusan urban context. Groups and ensembles who had managed to produce records under the Soviet system had done so on the Melodiya label. Veteran rock groups in Belarus had produced three records in the mid-1980s (Ulis produced "The Stranger" on Melodiya, Moscow (1991), *LONGWHITECLOUDLAND* through Polskie Nagrania, Warsaw (1991) and Mroja produced *28thStar* on Melodiya (1989)). With sovereignty, Belarusan rock groups lost any potential access to the Melodiya studios in Moscow and Riga, and began to work in the Miensk, Belarus Radio studios in after-hours recording sessions, paying out-of-pocket in American dollars.[34] Bands have had to find the means to not only produce and record their music, but they have had to cultivate a following without the benefits of industry mechanisms such as marketing, regular performance venues, recording studios, and CD production. This lack of infrastructure, and of record- and CD releases, has affected access to recordings and has subsequently shaped the scope of past research into contemporary Belarusan music.[35]

* * *

In their introduction to *Reading the Popular: Authenticity, Appropriation, Aesthetics* (1999), Kevin Dettmar and William Richey consider the theoretical approaches that have framed popular music studies over the last three decades.[36] Their historiography describes the general nature of the questions that characterize past writing on popular music. What is the nature of the institutional and cultural contexts in which the music is produced? What is the function of the music? How can we define it? How do we determine its value? While Dettmar and Richey emphasize the value of these questions, they suggest that close readings of particular songs and of particular performers allow for what they label an intertextual approach to popular music study, a consideration of how "the musical and lyrical texts [are] associative,

82   *Of Mermaids and Rock Singers*

allusive, or even quotational" (3). In this intertextual model the construction of meaning is bound to the construction of image. The source pool for such constructions and for the subsequent associations that inform the listener/fan are tied to the assumption that both performer and audience are aware of past constructions and past meanings, of the established iconographies that are part of popular music past and present or the "ongoing contribution between the tradition and the individual talent" (6). The reference to, borrowing of, and recontextualizing of musicians, styles, and songs adds to what Dettmar and Richey describe as the "multiple dimensions [of a] verbal and aural polyphony" (5) that challenge the reading of popular music.

These intertextual and dialogic approaches to popular music provide a useful theoretical focus for the study of Belarusan rock bands. The meanings that are being constructed by these bands are part of a broad spectrum of musical styles, borrowings, and appropriations. These groups recognize their membership in a Belarusan rock movement that itself is informed according to the individuality of each group, the intent of their music and, where relevant, the impact of their public image. While their intent is not consistently tied to political activism, many of the groups in this research describe themselves in relation to the backdrop of current politics and cultural movements. As a result, these musicians have had to place the self. They have had to define themselves according to the opportunities and limitations offered by their urban musical context, assert their public identity according to musical and performance styles, and they have had to decide the extent to which the national climate might define their artistic intent. That is, how might their music contribute to or reflect the shaping of the nation.

NOTES

[1] Conversations with Pałac members Juraś Vydronak and Aleh Chamenka, field work May 10, 1993; hereafter cited in text.

[2] About $1 U.S. in July 1993, although the accelerated rate of inflation continually affected the relative cost.

[3] Aleś Lozka, *Belaruski narodny kalandar* (Minsk: Polymia, 1993); Zinajda Mažejka "Belarus," in *The Garland Encyclopedia of World Music*, vol. 8., ed. Rice, Porter, Goertzen (New York: Garland, 2000), 790–799; Vasil Lićvinka, *Sviaty i Abrady* (Minsk: Belarus, 1998).

[4] Interview with Vasil Lićvinka August 4–7, 1993; hereafter cited in text.

[5] Interview with Nadzia Kudrejka, Producer with Małádziožnaje Radyjo, Miensk, April 28, 1993; hereafter cited in text.

[6] For a discussion of qualitative comparison between rock and bard texts see Chapter Seven.

[7] Interview with Viačasłaŭ Korjan, member of Ulis, Miensk, September, 1993; hereafter cited in text.

From Legislation to the Renaissance

[8] A reference to the *Soviet Block* countries. Timothy Ryback, *Rock Around the Bloc* (New York and Oxford: Oxford University Press, 1990); hereafter cited in text.

[9] In "The Soviet Rock Scene" Ramet, Zamascikov, and Bird describe the effect of political ideologies on an emerging rock culture (*Rocking the State* [Oxford: Westview Press, 1994], 181–218); hereafter cited in text.

[10] Policies on popular culture, which included jazz and rock music, often reflected the personal tastes of political leaders. Krushchev was the most conservative, making it known that he disliked both jazz and rock and remarking that the music and the dancing were "indecent." Between 1961 and 1965 the Department of Propaganda and Agitation denounced the music as "cacophonous" and dangerous to the party ideologies. It was with Breznev and Kosygin that reluctant Soviet policy-makers saw the power of the rock movement, and began to involve government mechanisms in the management of bands, performance venues, and in the surveillance of fans. The KGB was a key organism in the harassment and monitoring of rock enthusiasts and musicians (Ramet, Zamascikov, Bird, 182–183).

[11] Artemy Troitsky, *Back in the U.S.S.R.: The True Story of Rock in Russia* (London: Omnibus Press, 1987), 34; hereafter cited in text.

[12] Interview with Siarhiej Krauĉanka, member of Ulis, Miensk, June, 1993; hereafter cited in text.

[13] Alexander Dugin, "The Phenomenon of Rock in the USSR," in *Soviet Rock: 25 years in the underground +five years of freedom* (Moscow: Progress Publishers, 1990), 66–71; hereafter cited in text.

[14] There are many significant references in this quote: sloppy songs and vulgar sentimentality refer to the *happy* songs characteristic of the style of the Vocal-Instrumental Ensembles or VIA. The imitation of folk music is a reference to the Soviet-sanctioned popular music based on traditional repertoires. This was an extension of the Soviet cultural philosophy that was based on the construction of a Soviet *kinship* through the universalization of traditional repertoires.

[15] Geydar Jemal's emphasis on spontaneity over professionalism must not be understood as a comment on the musical ability of these garage bands ("The Roots," in *Soviet Rock* [Moscow: Progress Publishers, 1990], 11–28); hereafter cited in text. Since many groups learned their craft by listening and imitating styles from Western recordings, they are at ease drawing from a large repertoire of genres. The stylistic competence exhibited by many of the groups active in 1993 was impressive.

[16] The make-up of the VIA usually included ten musicians: rhythm section, two guitars, organ, some horns, a couple of singers, and a tambourine (Troitsky, 21).

[17] The association of the Pieśniary with the official vocal instrumental ensembles of the Soviet administration has prompted some critics to dismiss their music despite their obvious popularity. See comments made by Russian rock journalist Artemy Troitsky (34).

[18] The group was considered and referred to as the "Belarusan Beatles."

84 *Of Mermaids and Rock Singers*

[19] The central role of traditional repertoires is also linked to official and academic attention given to ethnographic materials throughout the twentieth century. Since the late nineteenth century, scholarly energies were geared towards the collection and documentation of musical and poetic repertoires throughout Eastern and Central Europe. In the former USSR, folk repertoires were systematically collected and interpreted on modern instruments as a contemporary musical mirror of a united 'Soviet' society– united in work as well as in folk expression. However, traditional music also provided a means for expressions of identities separate from the Soviet ideal.

[20] Lavon Bartkievič is quoted in Vitaŭt Martynienka and Anatol Mialhui, Praz rokpryzmu: zbornik artykułau i interviu (New York: Instytut Navuki i Mastactva, 1989), 182; hereafter quoted in text. The Belarusan/Russian language issue produced some interesting statements on the group's albums. The selections would be described in Russian, French, and English on the back of the album with an addendum at the end of each selection that the song was being sung in Belarusan.

[21] For a detailed discussion of how the Pieśniary were considered by Belarusan audiences in North America see Survilla, 1990; 1994.

[22] Jethro Tull was distinguished from other 1970s bands for their use of a flute amongst the traditional rock instruments. The Pieśniary also included a Western transverse flute as a key solo instrument.

[23] This example appears in part in Survilla, "Rock in Belarus," In *Rocking the State*, Ed. Sabrina Ramet (Boulder: Westview, 1994), 225–226.

[24] "The CD "Pesniarok" was released on the day of the 930th anniversary celebration of Miensk, and apparently was devoted to that event. From financial/marketing side it was a joint project of "FRELIAJS", "Panrecords", "Radio Rox", "ART Studio", and "USHI" ("Ears") magazine. And it was a joint project in terms of performers: altogether 13 bands are presented, among them such "monsters" as "Krama", "Liapis Trubetskoy", "Neyro Dzubiel", "NRM", "Troitsa", "Tornado" and others. All of the songs are from the repertoire of the legendary "Pesniary", including all-time hits "Kasiŭ Jas' kaniušynu", "Rečan'ka", "Vologda", "Aleksandryna", "Što za miesiac". Now, it is available in most of those small music kiosks in the city" (Uładzimir Katkouski, e-mail communiqué, April 1999).

[25] Lyrics by Juraś Bratčyk as quoted in *Through the Prism of Rock* (1990, 22).

[26] Many criticisms voiced by the intelligentsia reflect the impact of Soviet antirock rhetoric that described rock and rockers as amoral.

[27] Interviews with Novaje Nieba's Kasia Kamockaja and Mroja's [NRM], Lavon Volski in Miensk, Belarus Radio Studios, May 17, 1993; hereafter cited in text.

[28] Kamockaja is referring to Villi Simaška, a journalist and director of programming with the Youth Radio section administered by Belarusian State Radio and Television. Simaška has been a key promoter of Belarusan popular music and has been active not only on the air and behind the scenes, but has also been on the editorial board of *Pop*, an occasional magazine published by Kovcheg, the pro-

From Legislation to the Renaissance 85

motion firm associated with Youth Radio. The Russian-language magazine highlights Western artists, Belarusan-language groups, and Russian rock.

[29] Kudrejka is a journalist with the music desk at National Youth Radio (see p. 64).

[30] The morality of expression is central to contemporary views of arts and politics. In the most recent comprehensive publication on Belarusan rock music (Martynienka and Mialhuj, 1990), foreign artists are considered as much according to the social awareness projected by their music as by the music itself. These attitudes are derived from the importance given to the moral responsibility of the artist.

[31] While the earlier rock 'n roll movements of the United States seem not to have significantly affected notions of rock music in Belarus, they have influenced other former republics, especially the Baltic countries.

[32] In Belarusan rock music criticism, language, text quality, and traditional borrowing from indigenous Belarusan repertoires have become essential criteria in the evaluation of the renaissance rock movement. Contemporary Belarusan rock critics prescribe and describe the value of a performer and his music in 'authentic' terms. Authenticity is based on a recognition of folk roots through the use of the national language, folk metaphors and iconography, and direct musical quotations from the poetic and musical folk repertoire. In one sense, these components of authenticity represent a communality of experience that is translated into a specific national/ethnic sentiment of belonging. The language and folk devices listed above inform the variety of themes in the music: the love song, the overt 'political rebellion' song, social commentaries, and self-reflexive songs about the "belonging" of the listener. From this perspective, music not only describes but informs the community—which differs from Frith's model where the music seems to *create* the community (*Sound Effects: Youth Leisure, and the Politics of Rock 'n' Roll* [New York: Pantheon Books, 1981], 159–165); hereafter cited in text. Some Belarusan rock critics go as far as to describe the *responsible* listener and performer as being in touch with this aspect of group definition. In comparison, the Western-style fan is often criticized on the basis of the perceived control of western commercialism over musical choice. Thus, authenticity in rock expression can extend to the style of (read motivation for) rock consumption.

[33] In comparison, Simon Frith analyzes the construction of a perceived dichotomy between folk/rock and pop based on the changing definition of 'authenticity': where authenticity of expression, communal experience (kinship), and a notion of value often develop out of a critique of commercialism. Frith presents the idea of folk romanticism and community (sub-culture) solidarity as integral to the construction of folk consciousness. The folk-authenticity relationship can equally be found in rock/folk in Belarus (1981: 159–165).

[34] *Krama* is the exception. The release of *Vodka on Ice* in 1994 by British firm REX Records provides Western listeners with the first Western management of a Belarusan band.

[35] Popular music resources offer some insightful if general descriptions about world music production. One such publication, *World Music : the Rough Guide*, ed.

86 *Of Mermaids and Rock Singers*

Simon Broughton, et al. (London: Penguin, 1994), provides some interesting pre-liminary information that suits the enthusiast/collector perhaps more than the researcher. However, as a meter of available knowledge, the publication illus-trates that information on contemporary music in different cultures is uneven at best. For Belarus (pg. 101–102), three brief paragraphs mention traditional music style: "as practiced by groups of old grannies," the Pesniary Bazylki [sic] (Vasilki) a folk ensemble, and Ulis a rock group. This listing is not representative of the tra-ditional and rock music activity heard in contemporary Belarus. The reasons why these examples are included probably has to do with accessibility. The publication was compiled from available discographies. The traditional music is available through UNESCO, the Pieśniary toured the United States in 1976, Vasilki toured Europe, and Ulis recorded in Poland and have toured in Germany and Great Britain. The issue of limited accessibility (through dissemination and recording on prominent labels) must be considered when examining the popular music con-text in Belarus. The majority of the production is domestic and is disseminated on domestic airwaves, or through live performance in selected cultural and "Slavic" festivals, such as the *Slavianski Bazar* held in Viciebsk in 1993). Of the sources on Soviet and post-Soviet era popular music, consideration of Belarusan bands is sorely absent (Ryback 1990; Troitsky 1987). These sources mention only the Pieśniary.

[36] Pieśniary (New York: Columbia University Press, 1994); hereafter cited in text. The study of popular music in the West has generated many critical writings about the 'placement' of this music by its audiences, by the industry, and by the academy. Scholars offer a variety of methodologies and vocabularies in their attempts to understand the processes that define popular culture. Some of the key issues in such research include listener response, the construction and mediation of meanings, the juxtaposition of various texts [multitextuality], mass-market production, the development of musical and performance styles, appropriation, and most recently the impact of World music. These issues allow researchers to manage the enormous variety of musicians and genres, and the speed with which they enter and leave the public sphere.

5.

Of Mermaids and Rock Singers: Ethnography and Shifting Authority in Pałac's "Rusałki"

Pałac [Palace] serves to illustrate one of the central debates in the redefinition of Belarusan culture– a debate waged between supporters of authentic tradition and those who, aware of the traditional, prefer their version of cultural reinvention. The public image of this group is clearly meant to create certain cultural associations governed by the theme of urban youth rediscovering a musical practice and making it their own. In addition to providing a case study for the mediation of traditional repertoire, Pałac offers the opportunity to consider the role of ethnography in the Belarusan media and the implications of the appropriation of rural repertoire and performance styles.

This chapter considers the marriage of the mermaid to the rock singer, a metaphor borrowed from the transposition of a rural ritual song about mermaids to the urban rock scene by the group Pałac, the newest addition to Miensk rock culture in 1993. The marriage of musical styles resulted in a unique urban sound that reinvented traditional Belarusan song for the urban audience. Pałac generated much debate about the appropriate function and application of traditional culture.

By 1993 Belarusan-language programming, broadcasts of traditional Belarusan musical performance, and a growing attention given to Belarusan-language popular music worked to validate Belarusan culture for the public. Proponents of a return to "authentic"[1] Belarusan culture were fighting a conceptual war with those that considered authentic folklore as a building block for new, contemporary idioms (for example, using calendar-specific ritual song as a framework for a rock song). The impact of World Music and of Western popular culture, and comparisons between new urban music and rural practice, add to the discourse about an accepted definition of contem-

87

88   *Of Mermaids and Rock Singers*

porary Belarusan expression. The process of ethnographic collection was the starting point of the debate on the treatment of traditional repertoires, their dissemination in the media, and their redefinition by contemporary groups.

CULTURE CONTACT AND THE EXPEDITION

In Miensk, recordings of traditional songs and rituals were transcribed in scholarly publications, the songs were heard on radio programs, and performances were incorporated into a variety of cultural presentations for television, for the institutional stage, and in popular music.[2] The raw materials for this programming were collected through what is commonly referred to, amongst ethnographic researchers and students, as the "ethnographic expedition." The frequency of these expeditions varied according to the availability of funding, ethnographic curricula in educational institutions, and the projected programming for television and radio.[3] During these exercises the urban specialist travels to the rural performer to collect, archive, and learn their traditional repertoire and ritual practice.

These treks did not seem monumental in distance and scope, but they required considerable effort. The only constant in the research was that such trips underlined the outsider as the institutionally-funded urban dweller, and the cultural insider as the rural performer/specialist. Overall, these field workers shared a sincere passion for their research. They also shared their frustration because they were limited by the increased lack of sponsorship from economically-burdened institutions. In 1993 grant moneys were no longer readily available because academies, like all government agencies, were experiencing economic hardship. Finding a vehicle or even a reliable source of gasoline stopped many researchers from leaving Miensk. Under the best of circumstances, expeditions to rural Belarus were the result of:

1. student projects with the Institute of Culture, The Philology Department of Belarus University, or with the Conservatory,
2. research trips by independent but well-connected researchers,
3. documentary field trips by reporters from Belarus Radio and Television.[4]

In general, such expeditions are short, allowing for the recording of a specific calendrical event or of a particular village repertoire.[5] My first expedition revealed all the complexity inherent when popular culture and traditional culture meet head-on. In late May, I was asked to help organize an expedition with the members of the then emerging Belarusan popular group Pałac [Palace].

Although established as a group in 1992, the three original members Aleh Chamienka, Juraś Vydronak, and Dzima Karabach, had begun to play more than six years earlier, gaining experience playing diverse musical styles from jazz and rock, to the music of traditional weddings (viasielle).[6] They

Ethnography and Shifting Authority in Paɫac's "Rusaɫki"

gained further experience as students of the Institute of Culture in Miensk. In 1989 they began to experiment with what has become their signature style. Aleh Chamienka described their early influences: "When we were first beginning we needed money. We played dance tunes in discos and we were often asked to play at rural weddings. You have to understand that rural weddings are different than the city celebrations that now take place in restaurants. We would get some instruments together and play for the village celebration. It gave us a chance to perform together. It was during these weddings that we were moved by rural traditions – when at three A.M. two women would decide to sing together. We could hear that they were so much better than we were, even without instruments."[7]

Paɫac gained public attention by basing their music and their stage performance on the reworking of traditional repertoires. They recontextualized specific traditional repertoire (especially from Paleśsie in south-east Belarus) or they applied their knowledge of traditional Belarusan musical styles to new compositions. Their sound blends Belarusan regional song with appropriated elements from Western and non-Western music (for example: reggae rhythms and English-language rap segments). They sing in the Belarusan language, and have appropriated the traditional Palessian vocal style, as they combine traditional and contemporary instruments (electric guitar, saxophone, recorder, żalejka,[8] accordion, sampled sounds through a sixteen track *Roland* keyboard, and vocals based on traditional harmonies). In 1993, Paɫac's fusions were becoming a powerful part of Belarusan contemporary music. They received constant airplay on Belarusan television and radio and were invited to perform in regional, national, and more recently international music festivals. Their growing popularity did not reflect the heated criticisms about their reinvention of traditional repertoires. They were, at that time, not at all popular with my circle of authenticity-centered academic friends.

When I first met with Paɫac, their primary composer and their manager, Juraś Vydronak, expressed his frustration at the stone-walling he experienced from the various archives in Miensk.[9] His desire was to rework traditional music performance in order to produce a self-ascribed *folk-modern* genre. However, he had little access to the primary materials on which the group was hoping to base their style. They were not interested in those traditional songs that had been repeatedly mediated by other groups trained in cultural institutions, but were hoping to find an original traditional repertoire, one that would guarantee the uniqueness of their sound. They had been hoping and planning for an expedition for many months.

Transportation presented the first challenge. Even if one could get a vehicle, it was not guaranteed that there would be gasoline available. Nevertheless, after one month of inquiries a good friend arranged for me to rent a Ford.[10] With a route that eventually covered 1500 kilometers, we set out on a six day trek that took us east to the Belarusan border and south, through

90   *Of Mermaids and Rock Singers*

radioactively-contaminated Belarus to the villages of Paleśsie (south central Belarus). Four members of Pałac (Juraś Vydronak, Aleh Chamienka (lead singer), and Dzima Vajciuśkievič (singer and wind player) and a recently invited new singer, Veronika Kruhłova) navigated while I drove– since I was the only one with a license.

The route they had chosen was clearly defined by where, they had heard, we could find "good" singers. "Good," I was informed, meant women that were older and that, not only remembered older repertoires, but still actively sang them in their villages. These Miensk musicians were, in their own way, searching for authenticity as the starting point of their style. The music they heard was considered and chosen according to how it might satisfy their own music performance. They would listen repeatedly to the collected field recordings and dismiss songs that would not provide a compelling backdrop for their arrangements. They were also looking for repertoire that had not been mediated by the cultural workers or *kultrabotniki*, who managed the local Houses of Culture.[11] As they put it, "we are searching for ancient songs that were part of private village practice."[12]

When we arrived in these villages they asked to meet with the older women. We had no calling card, no pre-arranged meetings. Often we waited until these singers finished their work in their gardens or in the fields, at which time Pałac explained their projects and negotiated a performance. While waiting, often for several hours, it was clear how these Belarusans from the city looked out of place in these rural environments. This was not field work in the *participant observation* sense, it was gathering through chance meeting, "vypadkova," as is said in Belarusan (Figure 5.1).

How these various performers reacted to what I would easily label our audacity was surprising. They were thrilled to perform (partly because it was made clear by my companions that I was from America), but most importantly because we were not the first to come to their villages and demonstrate an interest in their local knowledge. Many of these women had performed for ethnographers and television producers. They had a specific body language and a performance etiquette when I videotaped them. In Stołbuny (Vietkaūskaja Region, Homiel) they sat in the living room of a traditional village house. The lean-to entrance way leads into one large room with a canopied bed in one corner, and a table and benches in the center. They sat in a row, feet together with hands on knees while they sang. If, after awhile, one singer faltered by moving her hands, she was quickly nudged by her neighbor.

Ethnography and Shifting Authority in Pałac's "Rusałki" 91

Figure 5.1 Aleh Chamienka, Dzima Vajciuškievič, and Veronika Kruhłova, wait for the local experts: May 1993 Janava, Vietkaŭskaja Region, eastern Belarus. Photographed by the author.

These women considered the interest in their work a compliment to their knowledge and expertise. They not only sang for us, but mothered us in a style that I had come to know well in Belarus. They insisted that we stay and share a meal, or as in Stołbuny, that we spend the night at their farm instead of camping out in the local fields. Their warmth was embracing.

From the perspective of these Miensk musicians, it was a great honor to hear these women sing. The members of Pałac treated them with great respect and emotion, at times overcome by what they heard in conversation and in song. While their interest in these performers was sincere, I was troubled at how we could compensate them for their time and their expertise. The members of Pałac had brought ritual bottles of vodka as gifts for, as these women put it, "warming their throats." When we tried to pay with money, they responded as though insulted, and when we could we would send one of our expedition to hide money in the cardigans that usually hung just inside their front doors. When I asked other researchers how these traditional performers were compensated for their work, they seemed surprised. It was clear that ownership of this Belarusan music was considered a public issue. The music belonged to everyone, and the return for these rural performers was in publicizing expertise and reputation. One researcher commented: "Paying them for something they do naturally is asking for trouble—anyway how do you gauge it, how do you pay for the priceless . . ."[13] From the point of view of collection, Pałac was therefore behaving within the norms of contemporary ethnographic practice in Belarus.

92   *Of Mermaids and Rock Singers*

Perhaps the most compelling cultural issue that became obvious in this experience with Pałac was the use of the collected repertoire. That is, how the transfer of this rural musical knowledge to the contemporary urban rock studio changed the voice of cultural authority. As much as these women were generally honored for their knowledge, their female voices were drowned out by the new music that these younger musicians had begun to offer to the listening public. Pałac's appropriation of these predominantly female repertoires was generating many questions and criticisms about the place of tradition in contemporary Belarusan life.

The first "hit" by this group, a song first released in the Spring of 1991, was constantly heard on the air when I arrived in Miensk in early 1993. The song "Na Hrannoj Niadzieli" was used by this group long before they had access to first-hand expeditions. They were, at the time, exploring Belarusan traditional music mainly through ethnographic recordings and their performances with local musicians at various village celebrations. "Na Hrannoj Niadzieli" (literally *Sunday of transition*) is tied to seasonal changes in calendrical ritual and, in some regions, to the celebration of mermaids [rusałki], which is how the rock rendition came to be known.

"YOUNG GIRLS, OUR SISTERS . . ."

> "When I was young we saw them all the time. I used to play with them with the other young girls in this village. But I haven't seen them for a long time. They used to live here but then came the war and they all disappeared. . ."[14]

About 400 kilometers east of the capital city of Miensk, in a small village called Janava, I encountered first-hand accounts of the Rusałka or mermaid. Mermaids or rusałki (pl.), are a part of the pre-Christian belief systems practiced by the populations of eastern Slavic peoples (Belarus, Ukraine, and Russia). In Belarus, existing ways of celebrating these spirits, and their function in the overall ritual calendar, vary from region to region, and indeed from one village to the next.

In general, rusałki are celebrated with the coming of spring and the passing of summer. The height of the ritual time occurs in the seventh week or the 50th day after Easter. According to ethnographer Aleś Lozka, the songs associated with the rusałki were meant to encourage fertility and ensure that the community enjoy a positive future [dola or fate] (115–116). While traveling in eastern and southern Belarus, I also heard of the ritual marking the beginning of summer (Hrannaja Niadziela). During this week, villagers would use song to escort mermaid spirits out of their winter dwellings in the streams and lakes and would drive them into the forests and fields. The mermaids were represented by a young village girl dressed in greenery. The end

Ethnography and Shifting Authority in Pałac's "Rusałki"   93

of summer would reverse the process. These dates also marked the time when children were allowed to swim because mermaids were both malevolent and benevolent creatures and had been known to drown people in the streams and lakes.[15] Evoked in the spring, rusałki are strongly associated with fertility and are therefore deeply linked to female-centered social practices in village life. Apart from first-hand accounts by older-generation women of having seen or played with mermaids in their youth, songs about these creatures call to the young girls in the village to bring them water and pick flowers [both symbols of purity], and ultimately to sing with them.

The mermaid is an appropriate metaphor for the female role in the traditional ritual—a role that reflects rural beliefs and Belarusan gender relations in traditional cultural practice. The focus of the metaphor lies in the traditional empowerment of women as the keepers and mediators of ritual song and culture in general. Songs celebrating the interaction between mermaids and mortals exclusively stress activities between women and these nymphs, including the singing of songs. The present example reflects the beckoning to women by these spirits to participate and interact with them.[16]

As the music-keepers and primary music-makers, women perpetuate cultural attitudes, beliefs, and value systems. However, this gender-specific cultural role and the implied empowerment is rarely stated. The important role of the woman in familial relationships is a masked one because traditional familial relationships are articulated as paternal—they center around the male figure. The dichotomy of gender power relations is also present in the relationships between traditional music makers, who are predominantly female, and contemporary popular musicians who are predominantly male.

The power shift from women as performers to men as performers is played out in the public sphere. Women presently dominate traditional repertoires but men produce the contemporary version of a popular music. In the case of Pałac, many of their male-produced songs are based on traditional women's music, about women, or even considered an exclusive part of women's calendrical ritual. Performance practice is also reflective of this shift. Aleh Chamienka, lead singer of the group, has adopted a vocal style that is traditionally associated with Palessian women's music. All of these shifts are in evidence in their first national hit "Rusałki" which was both accepted and criticized upon its release.

From the perspective of supporting a rebirth of national culture, including the Belarusan language, the impact of Pałac and other Belarusan-language rock groups was applauded. Members of the programming staff of the Youth Radio of the Belarusan National Radio in Miensk were ecstatic at the new sound and with the fact that a connection with Belarusan tradition was implied and redefined.[17] Those producers who worked on more traditional programs considered their own programming to be a more appropriate forum for the representation of culture. For the most-part, however, the schol-

94 *Of Mermaids and Rock Singers*

ars I spoke with expressed anger that a ritual music should be 'bastardized' by a rock group, and that the sacred function of the song and the belief system it reflected was not being treated with the proper respect. I did not hear criticism related to the shift in gender power that was implied by the urbanized performance of such songs.

The text of "Rusałki" is central to the recontextualization of the song and of its implicit cultural significance.[18] The version serving as the basis for the Pałac hit uses the text included below (Schema 5.1).[19] The original power relations of the song, and indeed the cultural roles inherent in its traditional ritual placement are greatly transformed by these urban musicians. The song becomes less about mermaids/women and more about male/female interaction. When sung by women, the song reflects the voices of the mermaids calling to the village girls with intimate, gender-connected implications. For example, Verse 3:

Dzievacki	-siastrycy,
Girls	our sisters
(diminutive/affection),	(diminutive/affection),
Padajcie	-vadzicy
bring us	some water. . . .

In singing the song with male voices the original dialogue between spirit and mortal girl shifts to that between male singers and audience, more specifically between male singers and the female members of the audience. This relationship is well supported through the group's stage presence where the audience-performer dialogue is decidedly male singing to female listener. Lead singer Chamienka controls the front of the stage and waves invitingly to the crowd as he summons their participation. Rather than implying the original playfulness of shared female experience, the song becomes a flirtation between rock star and fan.[20]

In addition to being selective about the verses they include in their version, Pałac also adds a newly composed text to the song. This text, an English language rap-style addition, is sung/spoken over what normally would function as an instrumental interlude in the middle of the song.[21] In "Rusałki" the rap text suggests several of the group's intentions:

1. an understanding that the genre of "rap" that they see and hear from pirated MTV and videotapes of the new Moscow MTV programs is specific to English languages.
2. a use of a Westernized idiom in order to internationalize their music and gain an audience outside of Belarus.
3. a clear nod to a potential English/American/Western European audience without sacrificing the Belarusan language that defines the body of their musical texts.

Ethnography and Shifting Authority in Pałac's "Rusałki"   95

4. an example of the prestige associated with the use of English as part of this urban genre, giving their Belarusan style historical and cultural authority in relation to the music industry and the development of rock as a genre.

The rap text in "Rusałki" addresses a listening audience as opposed to a participatory ritual audience. As the first hit by this group, it appeals to listeners to try this "song" and their music as something new.

"Rusałki" Rap text, Pałac. 1993. Used by permission.

Now—Here is a song you've never heard before,
And—**Here is a group that you're looking for . . .**
Well, count this music it's a piece of cake
And try and understand **it's a beautiful way.**
Put out all your problems from your **everyday life**.
You can ask: this song is in Belarusan, why?
You can say you can't only several times
But listen! only listen! to this **folk song** for awhile.

This English text performed by Dzima Vajciuškievič is difficult to understand through the layering and the Slavic accent. Nevertheless there are certain phrases that stand out in the performance and somehow manage to communicate some of the meaning of the complete text. The bold type indicates which portions of the text are emphasized and more clearly articulated in performance. Most emphatic are the last two lines where the group has incorporated a request that the audience give this "folk song" a chance. This appropriation of rap, as well as the shift in meaning resulting from the new musical context for the traditional text, do little to perpetuate the traditional significance and function of this song.

96   *Of Mermaids and Rock Singers*

Schema 5.1: Mapping of the Pałac version of "Rusałki" (text translation by the author)

Musical Episodes and Text Organization

Section One:
Free-rhythmic section followed
 by 32–beat introduction
emphasis on recorder,
acoustic keyboard, guitar

Section Two:
Verse Group 1 and 2:
1. On Hrannoi Sunday
2. The mermaids sat
3. Early, early
4. The mermaids sat

5. The mermaids sat
6. Looking at the young girls
7. Early, early
8. Looking at the young girls

Section Three:
Instrumental interlude (32–beat)
emphasizing guitar wail
and keyboard ostinato.

Section Four:
Verse Group 3 and 4.
9. Young girls, our sisters
10. Give us some water
11. Early, early
12. Give us some water

13. Give us some water
14. From the cold spring
15.Early, early
16. From the cold spring

Section Five:.
Brass punches leading into rap
segment followed by alto sax solo.
Verse 5 sung as a countermelody at
the end of rap segment:
17. From the cold spring
18. From under the willow
19. Early, early
20. From under the willow

Section Six:
Verse Group 6 through 9.
21. Give us some water
22. To clean our souls
23. To give luck to the?
24. Early, early

Ethnography and Shifting Authority in Pałac's "Rusałki"

25. To clean our souls
26. For life to return
27. Early, early
28. For life to return

29. Then we will be with you
30. Then we will pick flowers
31. Early, early
32. Then we will pick flowers

33. We will pick flowers
34. And sing songs
35. Early, early
36. And sing songs

Section Seven:
Verses 6 through 9 in succession performed antiphonally with staggered entries and divided according to each 1/2 line of the verse, with a steady bass pulse on the quarter beat.

A comparison of the musical differences between the ethnographic recording and Pałac version is also telling. Most obvious is the effect of taking an asymmetrical, polyphonic vocal song and transforming the pulse to a symmetrical 4/4 rhythm with a complex mix of acoustic and mainly sampled instrumentation (Examples 5.1 and 5.2).[22]

Example 5.1: Melody and text distribution for traditional version of "Na Hrannoj Niadzeli." Transcribed by the author.

Example 5.2: Melody and text distribution for Pałac version of "Rusałki." Chamienka's vocal performance emphasizes the bending of pitches marked by arrows in the example. Transcribed by the author.

98   *Of Mermaids and Rock Singers*

In his arrangement, Vydronak borrows from traditional group performance practice. The traditional singing technique, which is similar to *lining out*,
has a lead singer begin each verse alone. She is then joined by the rest of the
ensemble around the second syllable of the second word of text. The members of Pałac respond to Chamienka's singing of the verses by joining him on
the third line of text, somewhat like an energetic antiphonal exclamation
(Early, early). The resulting shape of the verse in each version is also different.

Verse structure in traditional version:
Na hrannoj niadzeli rusałki siadzieli
Rusałki siadzieli

Verse structure in Pałac version:
Na hrannoj niadzeli
rusałki siadzieli
Oj, rana, rana (answer)
Rusałki siadzieli

The organization of both texts creates a different rhythmic effect. The
traditional performance suggests consistent pulsations generated from the
stress on certain syllables. These stresses do not result in an implied division
of the verse into sections. Instead, the performance of each verse retains a
connected, lyrical quality. The end of one word is tied to the beginning of the
next by avoiding breath marks between words, and instead by catching staggered breaths before the second syllable of "early" or "ra'na." The Pałac version emphasizes a four-line verse structure through the inflection of the first
syllable of each "new" line as shown above. Pałac sings the verses in groups
(2/2/4/4 with the final group as a round) interspersed by instrumental interludes and the rap section, all of which play down any predictability resulting
from the four-line verse design. The one element retained in the new version
is the forecasting of the first line of each new verse by the last line of the preceding verse. Overall both versions use the same text material, but the
arrangement of the text, and the performance practice generate very different
rhythmic effects.

Pałac's version is also different because of the instrumental arrangement and because of the distribution of the verse amongst instrumental and
rap interludes (the traditional version is performed a cappella). The instrumental introduction makes use of several elements that are elaborated as the
musical texture becomes increasingly complex throughout the song.

The first few seconds of the piece are electronically generated. A synthesized low Theremin-like sound fluctuates over a bass drone and synthesized chimes that musically suggest emergence. A single wailing guitar note
slurs up a sixth and then hovers tensely until it is cut off by the first struc-
tured articulated beat on a synthesized bass drum. The next section is a 32

Ethnography and Shifting Authority in Pałac's "Rusałki"

beat-instrumental, rhythmically-stable prelude to the first texted verse. The wailing guitar returns throughout the song as a melodic response pattern based on a third and eventually turns into an upper register counter-melody to the texted melody (Example 5.3 and 5.4).[23] Two additional elements are introduced at this point, a synthesized piano melody of sixteenth notes (Example 5.5), and an improvised, at times jazz-influenced line on soprano recorder played by Vajciuškievič, vocalist and wind specialist in the group. The recorder and the acoustic-sounding keyboard pattern recur throughout the piece, most often providing a stable background to the complex texture.

The introduction offers a mixture of lyrical almost delicate elements and timbres (piano and recorder) that are combined with the aggressive qualities associated with dance club rhythms, techno, and cock rock (electric guitar, drum set - especially bass and cymbal, and the eventual use of a pattern played on low register electric bass). In fact the acoustic piano (played on an electronic keyboard) seems out of place amongst the obviously electronic sounds that initially define the texture, and the expectations of the listener.

Example 5.3: Rhythmic underpinning for Pałac version. Transcribed by the author.

Example 5.4: Guitar response pattern established in instrumental introduction. Transcribed by the author.

Example 5.5: Recurring keyboard pattern heard as acoustic piano. Transcribed by the author.

100   *Of Mermaids and Rock Singers*

When Chamienka enters with the first verse, the instrumental layers are sparse, focusing the listener on the text and on the drum pattern. The response on "Early, early" is sung by Chamienka and doubled by Karabach a fourth higher, imitating the doubling heard in traditional vocal practice. With each subsequent verse, the accompaniment becomes increasingly layered and the response is sung by more voices. The drum pattern, text melody, and background texture remain consistent except for two sections in the piece: the rap text preceded by a trio (trumpet, tenor and alto saxophones) and the final section of the piece, where the verses are sung as a round with a regular bass drum beating the quarter note. The song ends by recalling the opening sound effects and a final guitar riff.

Complex staggered layering of instrumental counter-melodies against a regularized strophic verse describes Pałac's musical style.[24] The counter-melodies are reminiscent of many different genres reflecting traditional, if altered, Belarusan performance practices, as well as jazz, classical, Beatle-esque, and other rock and popular music influences. The layering is possible primarily due to the group's access to a *Roland* keyboard that can combine up to sixteen tracks of digitized information. Vydronak composes at this instrument experimenting with an assortment of timbres and complex rhythms. The drum, acoustic piano, and brass choir (heard during the final round section) are all generated through this instrument. In performance, the musical tracks stored on a floppy disk are run through the sound system and combined with live elements.

Schema 5.2: Live and Electronically-generated elements in a Pałac performance.

Electronically-generated instruments and effects	Live performance
guitar wail	guitar riff/wail played by Chamienka
drum set (bass and cymbal) synthesized clap	often doubled by a guest drummer in live performance
acoustic piano melody	played in concert together with the *Roland* track by Vydronak
brass choir	soprano recorder saxophone: Vajciuškievič trumpet: Biełakou
electric bass	keyboard generated
vocals	Chamienka (lead) Karabach, Vydronak, Vajciuškievič

Ethnography and Shifting Authority in Pałac's "Rusałki"

It is the use of this technology that allows a five-member band to generate the degree of multi-voiced layering heard in their live performance. The mixture of these genre-specific elements, as well as the unexpected style shifts, especially once a song's musical territory has been defined, provide an energetic texture-propelled quality to this piece, and an anticipation for the unexpected in Pałac's style as a whole.

The conscious development of their *folk modern* style, the marriage of the *mermaid* to the rock singer, is also reflected in their public image. Chamienka, a long-haired rocker in Levi's, sings wearing a shirt especially designed to evoke male traditional dress, yet the traditional woven belt hangs loosely around his neck. Dzima Karabach wears a traditional straw hat, while Vajciuškievič wears a Hawaiian shirt, head band, and Belarusan flags painted on his cheeks. The visual impact of this mixture of traditional and contemporary dress codes is made evident by the cover photograph of their first cassette release Pałac - *Folkmodern* - Palace (Vigma 1995). Here the historical locale evokes tradition, longevity, and Belarusan identity, as do the long coats and the vest that Pałac members wear over their jeans and sweaters. Vajciuškievič stands out in full rapper's uniform even adopting the physical stance often used in rapper body language. While the exploration of Belarusan identity seemed evident in their approach, the stylistic mixture did not satisfy many fellow cultural mediators (Figure 5.3).

While Pałac enjoyed increasing success amongst young listeners in the mid-nineties, they were criticized because many of their musical and artistic mixtures seemed erratic and, for some, sensationalist. No one questioned their musical abilities, but rather their cultural sincerity. That is, was the use of traditional material a commercial gimmick– a result of riding the public wave of Belarusan renewal that dominated media and policy activity in 1993?

While the debate continued, Pałac worked on their style, releasing several additional songs based on some of the pieces they had recorded during our expedition. Their public interviews began to be exclusively in the Belarusan language, which was not the case before 1993. They were seen as providing the music that would connect Belarusans to their culture. Despite the attention, other rock bands who were also increasingly successful during that year did not consider Palac to be a fellow group. They were new to the scene, had not paid their dues, and were riding the wave of the traditional; that is their musical creativity was put into question.

For those mediators who were attempting to establish public awareness of Belarusan culture according to the original rural performance style and repertoire, the success of Pałac continued to be a problematic phenomenon. From the listening public's standpoint, however, it was clear that both the traditional and the rock versions of Belarusan music were part of a new listening experience. The urban public did not necessarily judge the music according to criteria of authenticity. Some of the listeners I spoke with considered traditional programming as a reflection of institutional mediation generated from academically-mediated, ethnographic recordings. Urban audiences would judge these traditional performances, which were often staged for the camera, as nostalgic, even exotic examples of their culture. Therefore, the 'power' of these traditional performances seemed marginal and specialized. By comparison, a 'rock' version, such as "Rusałki" reached a national audience through constant play on radio and television, offering performances that emphasized contemporary methods of music-making. They recontextualized the traditional into the 'here and now' and therefore seemed to have much more of an immediate impact on a Belarusan public that was unaware of, or simply not interested, in rural performance practice.

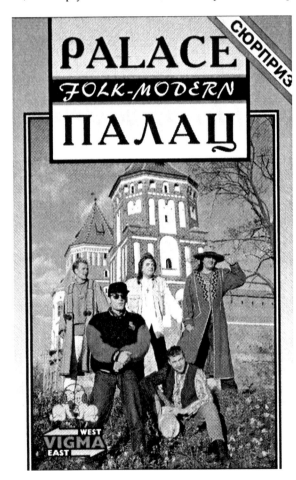

Figure 5.2: J-card photograph from Pałac - *Folkmodern* - Palace (Vigma 1995). Used by permission. Note the combination of traditional clothing (straw hats and long coats with ornamentation) and elements from urban fashion (Jean jacket, baseball cap, and jeans). The backdrop chosen for the cassette cover is also significant. The towers are part of the sixteenth-century castle of Mir in the Hrodna region. The historical significance of the castle as a remnant of sixteenth-century Belarus adds to Pałac's image as a group which values Belarus' historical legacy.

These simultaneously existing reflections of contemporary Belarusan musical culture also generate questions about authorship and cultural

Ethnography and Shifting Authority in Pałac's "Rusałki"   103

authority. The male singers are empowered by fame and eventually will reap financial benefits from this music (although they do not earn anything near the funds earned by their nationally-renowned Western counterparts). However, Pałac did not indicate that they would do anything to financially "honor" the sources of many of their songs. Their connection to the rural resources was clearly finite and not considered an extended musical and creative relationship.

While Pałac was applauded as having created a contemporary venue for traditional Belarusan musical elements, they were criticized for 'using' these traditional resources in an inappropriate manner, and introducing the sacred song into a mass media context that, despite the absence of a commercial music industry, is considered by some as inauthentic and cheap commercialism. The rural authorities of the traditional repertoire risked losing their cultural voice, their prestige, and any practical return their expertise might generate.

The shift of gender power relations in the transformation of this traditional repertoire is an aspect of Pałac's other songs. Throughout my stay they expanded their repertoire to about thirteen songs, mostly based on the repertoire that they had collected in the field. Their subsequent repertoire received more attention and eventually critical acclaim as they connected with Belarusan youth through their energetic, original, and positive explorations of contemporary Belarusan music.

NOTES

[1] See end note 13, Preface.

[2] The ethnographic collections themselves were stored in the offices of the Belarusan Academy of Arts and Sciences, or in the archives of Belarus Radio. Thousands of tapes were catalogued and shelved in a manner, that according to my guide, did not guarantee their preservation. Producing recordings on record, or ensuring archival preservation was not a realistic option because of a shortage of funds and resources. Prior to the break-up of the Soviet Union, scholarly ethnographic recordings had been funded by the state and recorded on the *Melodiya* label, although UNESCO had funded several recordings for Zinajda Mażejka. In general, ethnographers were deeply frustrated at the lack of funds for research and for the management of their field recordings. Researchers that worked with Belarus Radio could at least count on the tapes becoming part of a broadcast.

[3] The use of ethnography in television programming was most evident in the show "Viačorki" hosted by Vasil Lićvinka. This weekly program was based on rural music performance that had been filmed on-site. At times rural performers were brought to Belarus Television studios to perform on a studio reconstruction of a rural scene.

[4] Interview with H. Pieśniekievič, radio producer of ethnographic programming for Belarus Radio Studios, Miensk, April 28, 1993; hereafter cited in text.

104   *Of Mermaids and Rock Singers*

⁵ While I was puzzled at what could be learned from the almost fervent collection of songs, dances, and oral traditions, I also realized that these collecting mediators were puzzled over my interest in researching their musical traditions. That is, that even though most of these individuals were urban citizens, they had a sense of cultural ownership that extended into every corner of the Belarusan ethnographic territory. Ethnography was about studying your own music. Why would I, they asked, be studying music outside my own backyard? To complicate matters, I was engaged in exploring a music that most traditional scholars did not consider "serious." One reporter assumed that I was studying rock music because I didn't know anything about the wealth of traditional Belarusan repertoires (Conversations with radio producer and ethnographer Rehina Hamzovič, Motal, South-Western Belarus, August 19, 1993; hereafter cited in text). Partly because I was a visitor, and partly because I was being taken under a series of well-meaning wings, I was invited to participate in several expeditions throughout my research. Traveling with members of Belarus Radio, Belarus television, and one rock band, I was able to consider *traveling cultures* in a new way (Clifford, 96–116).

⁶ By 1993 Pałac also included Juraś Bielakoŭ, Dzima Vajciuškievič, and Veronika Kruhłova.

⁷ Interview with Aleh Chamienka, June 8, 1993; hereafter cited in text.

⁸ A traditional aerophone made of animal horn, wood, or paper, in a conical horn shape with an internal reed.

⁹ The implication here is that the scholarly access to these materials was tied to a certain level of privilege and only available if one were what was considered a legitimate researcher concentrating on academic projects. There was also, as in all ethnography, a suggestion that the research was owned or controlled by the collector. When I asked about such ownership I most often received anecdotal answers: "When a man is very rich, he is open and shows the wealth of the music" (interview Pieśniekievič, 1993).

¹⁰ I did have access to some other offers. The then-Mayor of Miensk, who called me for a "diplomatic" cup of coffee, asked if he could help me in my work. Frustrated by the ordeal of trying to rent a vehicle (at $30.00 US per hour in Miensk), I asked him if he had a car that I could borrow. I had to turn down his chauffeur driven official car, even though he assured me that the driver would stay out of the way.

¹¹ The House of Culture or Dom Kultury is a remnant from the Soviet era. Administered by institutionally trained ethnographers and ethnomusicologists, known as *kultrabotniki* or cultural workers, these municipal organisms were meant to manage traditional regional and/or village life including the establishment of ensembles [kalektyvy] and of repertoire. Performances and rehearsals were often held at the town community center, traditional dress was often standardized as a watered-down version of the regional dress, and repertoire could be accompanied by accordion. At their worst, these *kultrabotniki* restricted the use of certain repertoire, or preached institutional arrangements of traditional song. Often they provided resources and managed concert schedules while allowing the local experts freedom to perform in their regional styles.

Ethnography and Shifting Authority in Pałac's "Rusałki" 105

[12] Conversations with Pałac members during May-June expedition, Eastern and South-Western Belarus (1993).

[13] Rehina Hamzovič, Motal, 1993.

[14] Conversations with Janava ensemble, May 19, 1993, Vietkaŭskaja Region, Eastern Belarus.

[15] The benevolent/malevolent character of the mermaid reflects the balance of nature and the inconsistency of fate which is a central narrative in Belarusan traditional epistemology (Aleh Lozka, Biełaruski Narodny Kalandar [Miensk: Połymia, 1993], 115–116; hereafter cited in text). Lozka briefly explains the regional differences associated with this part of the ritual calendar. He writes that the celebration of the end of spring and the start of summer varies greatly. Hrannaja Week is also known as Kusty (pre-Christian worship of bushes and trees), and Trojca (the Christian celebration of the Trinity). In some areas where the rusalki are central to this calendrical period, straw effigies of the mermaids are burned. The level of adherence to traditional ritual varies and in some villages this week is a time to sing and perform the appropriate music without any implication of ritual consequence. The end of the swimming season is marked by another syncretic ritual called Spas [The Savior]. Held on the 19th of August it marks the return of the mermaids to the water ways and the end of the summer. In the Orthodox religion, Spas is a remembrance ritual for children who have died. The congregation brings baskets of apples that are blessed with holy water. After the liturgy the apples are placed on the crosses of children's graves (field work Motal, South-Western Belarus, August 1993).

[16] The relationship between mother and child, grandmother and grandchild is a foundation of family dynamics in Belarusan home life. The importance of the maternal role model as nurturer and educator is repeatedly illustrated in rural and urban settings. Often, children are raised by their grandmother in the village while the parents study and work establishing themselves in the city. The mother and grandmother are central to the cultural and linguistic education of the child. Many times my companions asked me if it was my grandmother or my mother who had taught me to speak Belarusan.

[17] The two versions of "Rusałki"reach two different kinds of public audience, the local village audience and the national public through radio and television broadcasts. In 1973, Belarus Radio began to broadcast Radio-Club Folklore directed by ethnomusicologists Z. Mažejka and C. Samalavina. It was a forum through which they could highlight "authentic folklore that hadn't been affected by outside influences or orchestration" (conversations with Zinajda Mažejka, September-October, Miensk, 1993; hereafter cited in text). The present editor of the program, H. Pieśniekievič, suggested that the primary listening audience for this music is "the village populations – this is their life, their music" (April, 1993). In addition groups interested in performing authentic styles are a consistent audience. Pieśniekievič also stressed that this programming was equally meant to inspire younger audiences because the youth "didn't understand." One advantage to the programming had been its long history on the air and the consistent time-slot: "People know that this is when the program airs, and they know they can listen

106 *Of Mermaids and Rock Singers*

to traditional music." The performers highlighted on this program are not professional groups. They are the grandmothers [babulki] and grandfathers [dziadulki] who still perform this music.

[18] Three textual versions of this song are included in A.C. Fiadosik, ed., Paezija Bielaruskaha Ziemlarodnaha Kalendara, vol 10 of Bielaruskaja Narodnaja Tvorčaśc (Miensk: Navuka i Technika, 1992), 289–290.

[19] Vydronak also led me to several ethnographic recordings that included this song and indicated that these versions had inspired the version by Pałac.

[20] The connection between the rusałki spirits and the young women is clear in the lyrics of this song. Perhaps this is one reason why the older generation of scholars reject Pałac's version or, as in the case of older female villagers, don't recognize it as the same song. During our expedition, Aleh asked villagers in Stolbuny if they had heard the song and they smiled and nodded that something like it had been on the radio (field work, Eastern Belarus, May 20, 1993).

[21] The words are usually composed by an acquaintance of the group who is comfortable enough in English and in the genre to provide these segments according to the message intended by the group. Although not always in a rap style, many of Pałac's other songs incorporate one English language verse, placed almost as a verbal interlude to the body of the song. In one case, I was asked to compose an English verse to a song they planned to release in the Summer of 1993. The text was spoken over a musical interlude, Luther Vandrose style.

[22] This use of instruments as well as this kind of rhythmic transformation is also heard in the music of the Pieśniary. In their case however, many of the traditional songs already had a symmetrical distribution of the beat, and therefore basis of their versions was on broad formal reorganization and the mixture of various musical genres (see Chapter Four).

[23] In addition to establishing the sound expectations for the song, the guitar-centered introduction connects the group to an instrument that reflects both the genre of rock and the maleness associated with the guitar itself. As Frith writes: "the electric guitar, central sound of rock , has always been treated personally; the archetypal rock image is the guitar hero– head back, face clenched, his feelings flowing visibly from his fingertips" (Frith 1981, 161). The male sexuality associated with the guitar-hero style should also be mentioned here, where: "mikes and guitars are phallic symbols (or else caressed like female bodies)" (227). More recently Robert Walser described the connection between maleness and the virtuosity of rock guitar performance. He writes: ". . . heavy metal shares with most other Western music a patriarchal context wherein power itself is construed as essentially male . . ." [and] "At least until the mid-1980s, heavy metal was made almost exclusively by male musicians for male fans [. . .] a demonstration of physical and rhetorical potency" (*Running with the Devil: Power Gender and Madness in Heavy Metal Music* [Hanover and London: Wesleyan University Press, 1993], 77). Pałac's style does not resemble the explicit male posturing of the heavy metal genre. The use of the guitar-sound (Chamienka strummed a red electric guitar for some performances) is perhaps a bow to the genre of rock. There is no question however, that Pałac saw rock music and their *folk modern* style as male-centric. It

Ethnography and Shifting Authority in Pałac's "Rusałki"

is therefore enticing to consider the guitar as an announcement of their appropriation of a female genre.

[24] I had the opportunity to watch Pałac's Vydronak compose several times during my stay. When I asked him about his inspiration, he did not refer to any particular recordings or styles. For him the question required a spiritual response and he, quite sincerely, pointed up and said that it came to him from above (conversations, Miensk, September 1993). His listening and performance experience points to a variety of favorite genres including jazz. As a listener he was trying to consider how a style "worked" musically, and how he might incorporate those qualities into his own work. In reworking a traditional Christmas tune in time for the 1993 Christmas season, Vydronak asked me to sing the "Western" carols that I knew.

6.

Ulis: "America is Where I Am"[1]

> Rock performers are never merely musicians. They are to a greater or lesser extent also actors playing characters they have invented.[2]
>
> (Shumway 1992, 122)

> Rock and roll is not a style, it is a religion.[3]
>
> (Siarhiej Kraučanka, 1993)

T HE PUBLIC IMAGE OF EACH ROCK GROUP IS DERIVED FROM A COMBINATION of elements that include: (1) how the group intentionally constructs itself in the public sphere, (2) the mediation of a music industry, and (3) subsequent public perception. Image is not only tied to the music itself, it is tied to the construction of meaning derived from behavior associated with the performers and interpreted by listeners (Shumway, 120).[4] Some performance styles reflect trends connected to the industry mediation of popular culture while others underscore the sincerity and authenticity of a specific, often marginalized artist. Whatever the context, most writers on rock agree that some interpretation of message, a sense of personal meaning, and the subsequent production of pleasure define the rock and roll music experience.[5] In Belarus, the varied dialogues between musicians, mediators, and listeners reflect different motivations and intents amongst members of the rock community.

The impact of domestic media on the construction of image of each Belarusan band has been minimal. There is instead an attempt to sell or convince the public that rock is worthy of public attention, that it is a solid aspect of contemporary culture. The absence of mediation from a music industry has certainly contributed to the individual directions taken by each group. The differing strategies of Belarusan rock groups have only recently drawn

109

Of Mermaids and Rock Singers

interest from Western European record producers. Individuality is reflected in the wide variety of musical styles and public images that are seen and heard amongst the most successful bands. Pałac's obvious appropriation of traditional repertoire, styles, and fashions is a unique phenomenon in the rock movement. Their construction of a Belarusan "sound" is overt and their stage production is full of reinterpreted traditional symbols. Pałac's public stance, obvious in their radio interviews, is an intentional construction of a specific public image: that of a sincere group of young men motivated by Belarusan tradition that they articulate in the Belarusan language.[6]

While a Belarusan folk image is part of Pałac's discourse in the public sphere, overt traditional connections are not a typical component of other Belarusan groups. The public images of these other bands are tied to other musical styles and philosophies of what it means to be a rock musician. Most have formulated their philosophies through rocker experiences that reflect certain common factors. These include struggles to secure resources and to maintain group solidarity in the face of social, economic, and political challenges. A group's image can reflect a band's identity, their personal tastes, and their evaluations of current trends. Ultimately image is directed by their definition of rock. The performance is the end product and gives the audience a role in contextualizing the music through the construction of personal meanings. In observing rock performances over the course of a year, it was clear that some bands offered the public a complete and consistent package of performance style, stage demeanor, and musical style. Other bands used the public sphere as a means to experiment, often changing their look, their stage behavior, and their music.

GROUP DYNAMICS AND THE PRACTICE SPACE

Each rock group is a complex mixture of familial and professional interaction. On the performance stage this dynamic is seldom visible, it is rather acted out and negotiated in the practice studio and in the social activities in which group members participate. The rehearsal space provided a unique view of the individuality of each band. As a resource for honing performance skills each space reflected the different types of access to resources and equipment that each group had managed to secure. Rehearsal styles were also different. While some groups spent as much time socializing as they did practicing, for others the studio was for practice and composition. A few rock groups (Mroja and Novaje Nieba) met daily, late in the afternoon, and always worked. There was nothing ambiguous about the role of this space, but also nothing ambiguous about the respect and friendship generated by the members in these groups. These musicians were not new to the rock scene. They had long established personal and professional expectations.

Pałac was housed in a three-room apartment in a local student residence [internat] tied to a local technical school. One room housed their

Ulis: "America Is Where I Am" 111

instruments and was the practice, rehearsal, and composition space for the group. The other two rooms were second living spaces. It is there that they received friends and persons interested in their music. It was there that they threw parties to celebrate birthdays and concert successes, and it was there that they could sleep when they had missed the 1:00 AM cut-off time for public transport home. The space, although large according to housing standards was definitely modest, almost primitive when it came to basic amenities, but it was central to establishing their identity as an ensemble committed to the music and at some level committed to each other. With Pałac, the social potential of the space sometimes eclipsed the regularity of their rehearsals.

Several groups had practice spaces that emphasized the rehearsal, the business at hand. Mroja and Novaje Nieba shared a room in the rear of the Miensk Philharmonia three floors up from the back stage entrance, past the ballet practice rooms on the second floor. They took turns practicing their repertoires, and because the bands had members in common, managed to work out an equitable use of the space and the time. These musicians also connected outside of the studio. They could party as hard as any other group, but this happened in people's private spaces.

The rehearsal studio provided some of the best insight into the chemistry of each ensemble. It also afforded a view into their musical and business strategies and into their frustrations. This chapter considers the image definition and rock philosophy of Ulis, a five-member band with one of the most consistent public profiles amongst the Belarusan-language bands. Ulis members had been part of the rock scene since the earliest inception of the movement in the early 1980s and could comment on Belarusan rock with considerable hindsight. The members of this band provided detailed commentaries on the notion of image, the place of Belarusan culture in their music, their philosophy of rock music, and the advantages and limitations of the influence of their environment on their music and the rock scene in general.

DEFINING ULIS AND BELARUSAN ROCK

In a basement classroom of the Miensk Belarusan Lycée the five members of Ulis would meet every afternoon at four (Viačasłaŭ Korjan, guitar, Siarhiej Kraučanka, bass, Aleh Tumašaŭ, vocals, Siarhiej Knyš, percussion, Felix Aksienciev, lyrics). They would automatically step over amplifier and speaker cables, plug in their guitars and the microphone, play a few riffs, and then begin a run-through of their latest album, Tancy na dachu [Dances on the Roof].

Their studio demeanor was an indication of their level of professionalism. Between sets of their tunes they would stop for a chat or a beer, but the rehearsal package, the maintenance and honing of their present repertoire was obviously key. On the performance stage their postures were slightly more animated, especially Tumašaŭ's, who as front for the band was the

112   *Of Mermaids and Rock Singers*

most mobile. Overall, however, the band was tight, the posturing minimal, and the effect one of confident detachment. They were musicians who had experienced the Soviet rock scene, had doggedly paid their dues, were staunchly determined and realistic, and could enjoy the ease that comes with knowing certain success. They had established several indispensable criteria for that success: a signature sound, a reputation as veteran professionals, a discography, a certain fan base, and equally important, a well-connected and consistent sponsor.

Ulis boasted one of the most substantial portfolios of all the Miensk Belarusan-language bands. Unlike Pałac's Vydronak, who in promoting a new band spent as much time selling the band as he did composing, Ulis' members had recorded three albums by 1993, were regulars on television, and were about to leave for a concert tour in England.[7] As much as they were nurturing a domestic audience, it was clear that this group had the potential and the backing to establish an audience in western Europe.

Their views of rock life came from long-term involvement in the genre since the earliest days of a Belarusan rock movement. Three Ulis members (Kraučanka, Knyš, and Korjan) had been co-founders of the first Belarusan-language rock group that emerged in 1983, first under the name of Studio Seven and then as Bonda.[8] While Bonda's line-up ultimately changed due to creative differences, several members of the band eventually split to create two other groups Ulis and Krama, who together with Mroja, are still considered to be the backbone of the Belarusan rock movement. With a certain romanticism of rock still a driving force in their musician identities, Ulis' attitudes were balanced by a sense of realism about their opportunities, their context, and their responsibilities outside the stage and studio.

The group had become identified with the Belarusan cultural movement and was consciously part of a domestic popular culture. Their publicity materials described them as "the leading Belorussian [sic] rock-group of a new generation" and emphasized that the group "performs its own compositions in the Belorussian language."[9] For Ulis, identity and image merged with their definitions of rock music, the rocker lifestyle, and their context for making music. Belarusan-specific markers for that identity were acknowledged primarily in terms of language and its impact on melody.

Language choice, which was central to the overall definition of a Belarusan rock movement, was not referred to by these rockers as a reflection of a political ideal or of a national goal. All their comments reflected the creative potential in exploring the language within the rock genre. As bassist Kraučanka explained: "It [Belarusan] has not yet been fully explored in rock and roll. In English and in Russian there are already many words that have been overused, and from the point of view of understanding, of impact, Belarusan provides a wonderful language. You don't have to listen to it, it just comes to you" (1993).

Ulis: "America Is Where I Am"   113

Language choice also served to make another point for Ulis guitarist Korjan. For him, the basis of the character of traditional melody was language: "traditional music is tied to the language of that people . . . if the language is such it will define the music . . . it is a question of intuition."[10]

Lyricist Felix Aksienciev[11] emphasized that, as a poet, he could only write texts in Russian, but that as a writer of rock texts he could only write in Belarusan:

> For me the use of Belarusan is very straightforward. Music, the melody, simply calls for Belarusan texts. It is more natural. Sometimes in rehearsal we joke around and try to sing texts in Russian or English. It simply doesn't work and we get a good laugh. I think that the language is tied to the character of the music. It is tied to the past. Secondly we also wanted to create authentic Belarusan rock, rock that was natural for our country. Thirdly we have to remember that three members of Ulis began as members of Bonda [the first Belarusan-language rock band] and perhaps it is an extension of that tradition. It is difficult now to be original when you use Russian or English texts. It became very interesting contributing to a rock standard in another language.[12]

Rather than acting as an overt characteristic of their public image, a Belarusan identity was described by Ulis members as an inherent source of inspiration. They were careful to emphasize that the band did not function according to a predetermined strategy that they considered limiting to their creative development. They did not want their music marginalized according to one culture-specific analysis. Their rock and roll was part of a rock and roll community without national borders, either in intent or in context. For example, when I asked if they would sing in English, especially considering their upcoming introduction to British audiences, Kraučanka said that they were prepared to do so: "We are not going to shoot ourselves in the foot and say that we won't sing in English. But we will do it when it is necessary. For now we don't see the need" (1993).

Within their shared rock philosophy, Ulis members avoided all descriptions of their music and of their language choices solely on the basis of politics or nationalism. The choices that they were making were based on how the Belarusan language motivated them musically and satisfied their creative objectives. Language, a primary element of Ulis' style, was not a basis for defining their creative intent in terms of political or social messages. Aksienciev elaborated on the avoidance of one "concept" for the band. He did not like the term concept because it implied a lack of creative spontaneity. Most important for him were his religious, moral, and broad emotions that couldn't be expressed except through these words and through this music.

114 *Of Mermaids and Rock Singers*

> Groups that borrow a particular design subsequently ignore their own intuitions. But we didn't start out strategizing how to be different. We make the music that reflects what we want to say at the moment. Our first album [The Stranger 1991] was the most political because that was the nature of that time. Now we try to listen to what the millions of voices are saying around us. For me, art and artworks don't have political and social meaning but rather, spiritual and religious significance. I don't look elsewhere for an understanding of the world, it is a reflection of the inner person. But, it is difficult for me to interpret exactly what meaning these texts have at the moment of composition. I concentrate on the effect. It is only in hindsight that I can at times express the inspiration and meaning behind it (Aksienciev, September 1993).

The band's resistance to being interpreted according to one characteristic or one kind of motivation was explained in their definition of rock, which emphasized the creative and practical independence of the group.

Rock offered the true rocker a world view that included what bassist Kraućanka described as the autonomy of the group. The absence of industry mechanisms, and the early trials by fire that rock musicians experienced when, as he put it, "rock was half-legal," made ingenuity and persistence the indispensable elements for success:

> There were two reasons for the difficulties: Due to the attitudes in those days the music remained kind of half-legal and secondly, there wasn't any kind of support, no financial help. There was moral support, of course, from journalists . . . but this [laugh] was more bureaucratic . . . not really help. But I am not complaining, or saying that now we deserve something on the basis of our situation. As I see it, those of us who wanted to play did so, pursued the music, and we lived through very hard times. Because of these experiences I can say that I don't fear much now. I know that if I need something, I can do it with my own hands. Those musicians that emerge now are musicians, but they are not independent . . . someone is thinking and directing for them (Kraućanka, June 1993).

Despite the fact that Ulis was sponsored by one of the new independent businesses which had emerged in a post-Soviet environment, Kraućanka emphasized that the group was in complete control of their creative output and of their career choices. *Dainova Ltd.*, a computer firm, was highly visible as a sponsor of many Belarusan popular culture events throughout 1993. For Ulis, the firm provided "no-strings-attached" monies for touring and for cassette production, public relations, and performance. However, Ulis was not bound by a contract and had not cut a compact disk primarily because they had not been offered a contract that guaranteed their autonomy.

Ulis: "America Is Where I Am" 115

Perhaps due to the lifestyle that rock music required as a whole, Kraučanka's definition of rock emphasized a philosophy. Rock and roll was a religion, a question of calling. It is "an attempt to stand free and reach higher [. . .] to take care of my business where it is most important, in the soul" (June 1993) In this sense he could describe Belarusan rock in universal terms. As a world view, the definition of rock was not specific to style, to context, to conditions nor to professionalism.[13] This philosophy required a quasi-religious devotion. Guitarist Korjan was equally adamant about the all-encompassing nature of being a rock musician: "the group and the family is the same . . . I am totally committed. Rock and roll is a definition of life" (1993).

Kraučanka, Korjan, and lyricist Aksienciev emphasized the importance of being faithful to one's vision and creative needs. On this basis, which they most often articulated as sincerity, one could consider oneself a rocker. If a musician was motivated by anything else, i.e., commercialism, then the music would reveal it: "If a music is sincere, freely created—and this you can hear—then it is rock and roll. If it is done for money, then it is not rock and roll, and it is always clear" (1993).[14]

Sincerity and authenticity shaped an ideal definition of rock. It was nevertheless clear that style, context, conditions, and professionalism did impact on what Belarusan rock was accomplishing and, subsequently, what Ulis and fellow rockers were able to achieve on a broader world stage. Kraučanka revealed a frustration with the Belarusan rock context in relation to rock in other countries. He compared Belarusan rock to what was being produced abroad, explaining that domestic rock was "lower," not in the sense of quality, but according to opportunities for evolution and development, which might be defined by access to resources. As a result, the level of professionalism was necessarily below that of their Western counterparts. Without the consistent access to a studio, to a sound engineer who "can produce the sound that a musician really wants," the Belarusan rock group lacked options and polish: "We are young, but we have wasted much time by not having access to the same resources. If you listen to what is going on beyond our borders you can tell. At the same time, because we are isolated, perhaps we have retained more, we have hidden more within our soul. Certainly, if a person has all he desires, it is more difficult to think with the soul, you tend more towards the material. This is the plus we have from our situation" (Kraučanka, 1993).

This aspect of the rock scene presented a definite paradox. The lack of a music industry limited the resources available to these bands but also forced a certain independent development in the rock scene as a whole. Kraučanka's evaluation was, however, highly critical of Belarusan media sources. While he was careful to acknowledge that much had been done in radio and television because of the enthusiasm of certain individuals, he deplored the lack of standard, consistent, professional venues for rock music.

116   *Of Mermaids and Rock Singers*

In the same way that access to the resources of the music industry differentiated standards for Belarusan rock production from that of groups in Western countries, Kraučanka paralleled the lack of media know-how in Belarus to the slow evolution of a rock audience. The result was an audience more interested in watching Moscow-produced programming that boasted longevity, well-trained personnel, and certain commercial backing. The reaction of the Belarusan media was apparently apathetic: "In order for such interest and such programming to work you need to have a viable TV and radio industry in place. We don't, so we would need production, equipment, translators, program design, commercial interest. They [Belarusan media] say, here we don't have the money, and they [Moscow] have ten channels while we only have one. What are we supposed to do? These people want to have ten channels and money too. If you want something to happen [. . .] then you should expect to put in your own money, and then maybe, just maybe you can expect some financial return" (Kraučanka, 1993).

The underlying message in Kraučanka's analysis was the importance of personal commitment and personal risk. He repeatedly emphasized that what Ulis had achieved was the result of their own efforts. The criticism lay in a media attitude that bemoaned the lack of resources instead of pursuing a higher level of professional programming and of commercial monies for sponsorship. Ultimately the different media affected access to public exposure. In the end some, "mediocre groups get attention, and some excellent commandos (bands) will never be heard"(1993).

Korjan had similar views and, like Kraučanka, emphasized the autonomy of the group as well as the lack of systematized support: "The media doesn't do anything so that a musician can live normally . . . it all depends on the musician. TV shows groups that are pro or semi-pro but none of the people in TV are professionals. Rock and roll has more of an emotional support here, like in the 60s in the West" (1993).

Audience response, though acknowledged by band members, was differentiated from responses they had enjoyed in Western Europe. Commenting on what he saw as a general attitude in Belarus, Korjan remarked that the Belarusan public tended to display the same kind of apathy they had identified in the Belarusan media: "The public is the same . . . they look at Moscow and think it's great but they reject their own . . . a national public is not there."(1993). Korjan based his comments on the scope and level of audience response. Western rock audiences were definitely more numerous and therefore more supportive of their favorite groups. Rock concert behavior was also quite different: "We are a small republic and they [the Soviet system] really ruined it. They sit as though they were in the Philharmonia. Over 70 years they taught the public to be passive, they are afraid to laugh, cry, scream, they are afraid to show their reactions"(1993).

Ulis: "America Is Where I Am" 117

The quieter demeanor of Belarusan audiences was reflected in Ulis' stage style. Despite the energetic drive of their music and the heavy emphasis on guitar and drums, the group could not be described as extroverted or as having cock rock mannerisms.

The criticism of the Belarusan media and of domestic opportunities was based on firsthand experience in other performance contexts. Ulis had performed in Poland and in Germany, their fan club was based in Warsaw, and they were used to networking and self-promotion. They had a sense of what an industry should provide. This is most clear from their publicity materials, a six-page document with slick presentation, which emphasized the band's successes, available live-performance videos, some personal biographic information, and fan club address. It was clear that this information was not geared towards the fan, but towards members of a Western industry who might have an interest in promoting the band.

Ulis had defined itself despite a lack of an infrastructure, but also in response to it. The musicians were not only making the music, they were developing their own niche, their own private industry. They decided that "playing a concert for 100 rubles" was no longer in their best interest.[15] They were selective with regards to their performances while they acknowledged that Belarusans did not have the money to pay a fair price to hear them play.

The aspect of cosmetic image, the way in which the band chooses to present itself in the public sphere also recalls the band's cosmopolitan views of rock culture. Jeans, T-shirts, and black leather jackets are not only their everyday apparel but they are also used on the performance stage (Figure 6.1).

Kraučanka commented that following fads, or even creating them, placed a band in danger of going out of style and forcing the development of a new look. In avoiding a specific fashion statement they also avoided being associated with a specific trend. Of the two record covers, only the first, "The Stranger" offers a small photo of the band in a decidedly non-descript settings. The second *WhiteLongCloudLand* [sic], a literal description of a shared natural scene does not offer any photographs. The J-card of the cassette album *Dances on the Roof* was produced quickly for sale on their tour, again without an image of the musicians on the outer cover. The visual concepts behind their album styles, though carefully chosen, were also dependent on the band's resources.

The importance of commitment and autonomy were embodied in the group's collaborative approach to their musical style. Korjan, the rock veteran in the group and the main composer, emphasized that he consciously avoided following trends or being influenced by other rock bands. When asked about his influences, he mentioned an early interest in Nazareth, Toto,

Figure 6.1: Ulis in concert for the taping of the Belarusan TV program *Rock Island*, September 1993. L-R: Viačasłaŭ Korjan, guitar, Siarhiej Knyš, percussion, Aleh Tumašaŭ, vocals, Siarhiej Kraučanka, bass. Photographed by the author.

and Led Zeppelin. His current approach was not to listen to other bands because he did not want to produce music that copied the rock canon, and he did not want to be subconsciously influenced by other styles. When I asked him which other Belarusan rock he liked, he answered: "None. I only like what we do" (1993).

For Kraučanka, the style was qualified simply as having driving energy based on aggressive guitar. More detailed descriptions of musical style were based on the composition process which also supported the internal politics of the band. Korjan commented: "The melody is key, everything is based on the music. I take it so far. I know how it is on the guitar and I imply the rhythm and the harmonies that would work, and then we get together and marry the elements. Each member is the composer. We don't have a sense that this song is by this guy or that guy. If something doesn't work, then I make a suggestion and then we arrive at a moment [consensus]. If a group doesn't understand the song, they can't perform it" (1993).

Aksienciev emphasized that the words had to have a quality that is easily singable and that complement the melody with open sounds: Sometimes we simply sit and consider what sounds most suit natural speech, how many vowels there should be, so that it sounds spontaneous. It is certainly harder to start with a melody, but the words, as with all other parts of a song, have to be accepted by everyone. We all contribute to the sound" (1993).

The resulting texture of Ulis' music is rich but seldom overpowering. It is supported by a constant driving bass line and drums, and a complex and contrapuntal guitar part. There is little musical release within the body of

Ulis: "America Is Where I Am" 119

each song. The attempt is to project the listener forward, an effect that they maintain in their performances by playing their songs back to back. Tumašaŭ's vocal style is breathy and purposely strained, adding another layer of urgency to the musical effect.

The song "Ameryka" reflects many of the stylistic and philosophical characteristics that are typical of Ulis' style. As with many of their texts, this song is about a sense of place, the nature of identity, and about the interpretation of life's choices. In this song the words evaluate the placement of the singer and address the myth of *America* as a lifestyle, as an aspect of self-awareness, rather than a place that must be physically experienced. Aksienciev commented on the element of freedom, of empowerment, as being within the reach of the individual. As a result, one's immediate context could be mastered by a sense of consciousness and self-awareness.

"Ameryka," Ulis, *Dances on the Roof* (1993). Used by permission. Translated by the author.

> America is next to me
> Because I have not looked for it here
> My eyes are the sound
> I see the land beyond the fog
> Because America is not a country
> America is where I am
>
> Love me I am alive
> Take me where I am
> Bread and wine that is our fate
> The miracle of which you are dreaming
> Because America is not a dream
> America is where I am
>
> I listen to the voice of blood
> In a drop of water is the flow of a river
> I live here also now
> As if in a free state of America
>
> There is nothing to wait for anymore
> When I come to you
> You will perish with me
> Everlasting America

"Ameryka" offers listeners the opportunity to reevaluate their notion of an ideal *other* place. It is reflective of Ulis' experience outside the performance venues offered them in urban Belarus. Their other songs explore the effect on

120　　　　　　　　　　　　　　　　　Of Mermaids and Rock Singers

the self and on personal identity when one chooses to consciously reject his/her local environment in favor of an exotic "better" place.
Example 6.1: "Ameryka" Melody and Verse One. Transcribed by the author.

The melody of this song is sparse compared to the energy of the driven aggressive accompaniment. Tumašoŭ punctuates each line by aspirating slightly on the final note of each short phrase. Despite the seemingly interrupted distribution of the text, the melody is characterized by the triplet figures which are used in all but the final line of text. The result is the suggestion of a lyrical melody. In the transliteration of the first verse note that, with the exception of mm. 12 and 22, the end of each line of text is constructed on a vowel sound. While the Belarusan language contains five diphthongs in addition to six vowels, the language is characterized by many hard and soft consonant sounds and combinations that can appear at the end of a word. The text illustrates Korjan's and Aksienciev's focus on open, singable sounds.

The song *The Stranger*, from their first album of the same name (1991), suggests this loss of identity. The use of so many indicators of Western culture are contrasted with the sense of loss of self and isolation:

"The Stranger," Ulis, *The Stranger* (1989) Used by permission. Translated by the author.

> A stranger lives beside me
> He listens to U2

Ulis: "America Is Where I Am"

He searches for BBC at night
Just to listen

The stranger smokes Pall Mall
He watches *A Hard Day's Night*
He reads an old copy of the *Times*
There's an article about our land

I hear a nervous hum
I smoke too much
I always stroll alone
Myself, my own brother

A stranger lives beside me
I look in the mirror
There instead of my own face
I see only drops of rain

The meditative, self-searching character of their song texts contribute to Ulis' image. Always philosophical, at times enigmatic, the words suggest the image of the intellectual rocker who questions the implication of symbolic travel, and considers the loss of balance that can result when one ignores the importance of a local identity. Ulis' texts rarely address their mainly female audience and as a result, the band constructs a sense of distance between themselves and their fans. The fans, although certainly appreciated by the band members, were not catered to in their creative nor publicity strategies. Aksienciev was clear that, for them, the music was foremost and had to satisfy their own needs for expression. As Aksienciev said: "Maybe I risk insulting some of our fans, but I never think of the potential listener when I consider a text. If someone likes it, they relate to it, or if [the music] answers or generates questions, then I am pleased that it was useful, if not . . . then it is still ours" (1993).

Ownership and creative freedom are primary criteria in Ulis' definition of rock. This independence and the image of the rocker as artist are not only part of the rock image they construct for the public, but also the basis for the rock lifestyle they construct for themselves. Aware of the opportunities and venues that are missing from their urban context, privy to the resources that are available to bands in a Western environment, they navigate the domains of the authentic artist and of the commercial media. They try to follow their artistic mandate and, at least attempt to function according to the industry standards they have experienced abroad. Their polished, detached, and intellectual public image is also informed by their exploration of Belarusan as a basis for their rock. Ulis' cultural stance is based on what they consider to be the instinctive influence of language rather than on overt social and political positions. When I asked band members about the choice of name for the group, Kraučanka provide an answer that stresses the band's search for some

122

Of Mermaids and Rock Singers

basic common human experience: "The name came out of our interest in reading. We are all great readers and we were all inspired by James Joyce. Originally Ulis represented the romantic idea of being a traveler, something everyone has the desire to do. Now the original intent has been abstracted, our choice doesn't seem as precise" (Kraučanka, interview September 1993)

Ulis' evolution, their artistic goals, and their self-image continue to stress the idea of exploration guided by the internal needs of the band rather than by a willingness to sacrifice those needs in order to construct a bigger market and a larger audience. The reflections that they provided for this study serve to emphasize the central role of their philosophy that is the basis of their consistent and powerful image in the public sphere.

NOTES

[1] From 1993 cassette release *Dances on the Roof* (Dainova, n.n.).

[2] "Rock & Roll as a Cultural Practice," in *Present Tense: Rock & Roll and Culture,* ed. Anthony DeCurtis (Durham: Duke University Press, 1992), 122; hereafter cited in text.

[3] Interviews with members of Ulis, Miensk, September-October, 1993; hereafter cited in text.

[4] John Fiske, *Understanding Popular Culture* (London: Routledge, 1989), 1–4; hereafter cited in text.

[5] See Simon Frith, *Music for Pleasure: Essays in the Sociology of Pop* (New York: Routledge, 1988); hereafter cited in text; Roy Shuker, *Understanding Popular Music* (London: Routledge, 1994), 17–18; hereafter cited in text; Richard Middleton, *Studying Popular Music* (Philadelphia: Open University Press, 1990), 250–251.

[6] In 1993 interviews of Pałac were exclusively in Belarusan. When I was with them they were also careful to speak in Belarusan, although they spoke Russian amongst themselves. While they were publicly demonstrating a commitment to Belarusan culture, they were also trying to construct an image for my benefit.

[7] I was introduced to the group through an artist friend, Tania Markaviec who had arranged for me to sit in on one of their rehearsals. I vividly recall sitting beside lyricist Felix Aksienciev, and being acutely aware that this rocker environment was more closed and protected than that of the other groups I had worked with. The members of the band were used to journalists, they had been *interpreted* before.

My other encounters with the rock elite had been unabashedly casual. I had gone to rehearsals, sat backstage, socialized with them, eventually establishing some solid friendships that existed outside the studio and the stage. Ulis was altogether different. The members were into or past their mid-thirties, had families, and had separated their profession from their family lives. This was most clear towards the end of my stay when I invited them to dinner with their wives. Enlisting the help of my friend Tania, we prepared to receive ten guests in my small apartment. When they finally arrived I opened the door to find them on my threshold holding a crate of beer between them. Their wives were not with them,

Ulis: "America Is Where I Am"   123

and I found myself sitting in the living room with them holding a beer and trying to break the ice, while Tania grinned in the kitchen. I was clearly a feature of their professional life.

⁸ As Ulis bassist Kraučanka described, in the early eighties, those interested in rock were drawn to study communications technology, the closest degree program available that suited their musical interests. It was in this environment that would-be rockers came together, eventually forming the earliest bands (interview 1993). Member Korjan was an engineer in computer facilities, Kraučanka an electronic communications engineer, and Aksienciev a telecommunications engineer designer (Ulis, Publicity Brief, 1993).

⁹ Ulis, Publicity Brief, 1993. The biographical page offers some brief but telling information about each member. Both Korjan and Kraučanka specifically include their religious affiliation. As Catholics they contradict historical attempts to define all Belarusans according to Russian orthodoxy. Drummer Knyš's description emphasizes his interest in Belarusan culture, suggesting that this is a worthwhile and "cool" pursuit. The band's description of their own musical and performance style places an emphasis on "frankness" [sincerity], "soul," "emotion," and includes the mention of the effect from "Byelorussian melodics." The section entitled "The Press" offers a listing of the attention Ulis generated from the domestic and foreign press, primarily in the form of concert critiques. Their German reviews reproduced on this page describe the band as Russian, a typical conception of the uniformity of culture in pre- and post-Soviet countries. Ulis' portfolio also emphasizes their recordings, music festival performances, media interest, and projects abroad.

¹⁰ Interview with Viačaslaŭ Korjan, Miensk, June 1993; hereafter cited in text. In his interview, conducted in Russian, he clearly stated that the value of their music did not depend on the cultural implications of language choice. This was perhaps because I was a member of the Diaspora, whose rhetoric, strongly associated with a nation-conscious attitude, would undoubtedly frame my consideration of their music. I think that it was a reaction to Belarusan rock criticism in general. Rock journalism in Belarus had developed on a parallel path to the rock movement and had, in the years prior to and following Belarusan independence, contextualized rock music according to the Renaissance movement.

¹¹ Aksienciev, a published contemporary poet, started as a Russian-language poet who in the mid-1980s began writing in Belarusan. At the time he wrote several texts that were then used by Bonda. He began to be seriously committed to rock at the end of 1988 when Korjan proposed that he become involved with Ulis.

¹² Interview with Felix Aksienciev, Miensk, September 1993; hereafter cited in text.

¹³ In his article "Rock and Roll as Cultural Practice" (117–134) David Shumway explains that rock and roll is an elusive cultural practice without a specific definition by musical genre or specific text. Instead, rock is a cultural formation that "cannot be identified with any one of its many codes and practices" (118). In writing about rock and roll in an American and British context, Shumway proposes that rock should be considered a historically specific practice, reflecting specific

124 *Of Mermaids and Rock Singers*

modes of behavior from the performer and the listener (120–122). Shumway's lack of definition suits the Belarusan rock scene which, aside from a few common characteristics, exhibits so much variety that one model could not adequately describe the movement.

[14] The emphasis on sincerity is linked to the idea of authenticity. Roy Shuker writes: "Authenticity is underpinned by a series of oppositions: mainstream versus independent; pop versus rock; and commercialism versus creativity. [. . .] The uneasy alliance between art and commerce is frequently placed at the heart of rock history, but it must be seen as a false dichotomy. Rare is the performer who has not been concerned to ensure the fullest possible return on his talents, and a concern with marketability is not necessarily at odds with notions of authenticity or credibility" (1992, 36–37).

[15] In making this statement guitarist Korjan summarized the lack of financial support in the Belarusan media. Typically, radio programming would play a group's repertoire if it had been produced as a *phonogram*, a demo tape recorded in a professional studio on a sixteen-track reel to reel tape. Each group funded the production of these demos out-of-pocket, often paying 100 US for an all-night recording session in the Belarus Radio facilities. This was a monumental amount considering that a monthly salary averaged 30 US. Once produced, these tapes became a calling card and a means of publicizing the music on the air-waves. However, as with traditional performers, these groups had to be satisfied with the privilege of being played and did not receive royalties from air- time.

7.

From Bard to Rock Star:
Kasia Kamockaja

Rock and roll here, especially Belarusan-language rock and roll, was and remains the music of social protest

(Kasia Kamockaja, 1993)

ONE OF THE PERFORMANCE VENUES ESTABLISHED FOR BELARUSAN ROCK IS the annual festival Basovišča held in Biełastoččyna, eastern Poland, since 1990.[1] Organized by the Belarusan Student Organization BAS, the series of concerts take place on an outdoor stage in a forest glen. The theme and logo for the festival have been designed each year by long-time BAS member, artist Lavon Tarasevič. The logo he produced for the 1993 festival generated much criticism from the local community and from the cultural media, particularly the area's Belarusan-language newspaper "Niva." At first glance the image suggests a bird-like figure floating on a backdrop of blue sky (Figure 7.1). Upon closer inspection it is clear that the image depicts a smiling cartoon-style penis in flight. The image infuriated members of the local population, inciting acts of vandalism on additional props which Tarasevič had created for the festival. Although the logo is the result of one individual's vision of the rock experience, it illustrates a well-accepted aspect of rock as a predominantly male enterprise.

This chapter explores gender in Belarusan rock through the public evolution of Kasia Kamockaja, a successful bard who had crossed over into the rock genre as the lead singer of New Sky [Novaje Nieba]. Her position as the only established female rock musician allows for the exploration of her experiences, her opportunities, her treatment, and her choices in a creative environment defined by male performers and by a male-centered conception of rock music.

125

126 *Of Mermaids and Rock Singers*

Figure 7.1: Advertisement for the rock festival Basovišča 1993. The poster reads: "Belarusan Youth Music Festival [at] Haradok." Designed by Lavon Tarasevič. Courtesy of the artist. Used by permission.

GENDER AND BELARUSAN ROCK

Four of the five principal bands that were active in Miensk in 1993 were male, reflecting what John Shepherd (1986) labeled as the male hegemony inherent in Western rock music performance, audience development, and industry mechanisms since the inception of the genre.[2] Emerging bands mirrored the

From Bard to Rock Star 127

predominantly male make-up of the Western bands heard in eastern Europe and in the Soviet Union.

In the Soviet context listening to rock was not a passive activity amongst the more serious fans. A central aspect of fan behavior was the detailed interpretation of text and musical nuances heard on their pirated, underground recordings. In "Notes from a Rock Museum"(1990) Kolya Vasin, a St. Petersburg critic and rock enthusiast, describes the development of a youth rock subculture as a process of discovery.[3] The music of Western bands was disseminated through an increasingly varied and sophisticated cassette underground. The bands that had a significant impact somewhat reflect the historical canon of popular music in the West and indicate the availability of Western music as well as the tastes of its youth. Vasin writes:

> [1958]
>
> Haley's hit [Rock Around the Clock] became the anthem of Rock and one of its first slogans which was taken up by more than one generation of youth on both sides of the Atlantic;
>
> [1963–1970]
>
> There was an unbroken chain of discoveries [. . .] the Beatles—the Stones—the Animals—Dylan—the Cream—Hendrix—Led Zeppelin—the Doors—Jethro Tull—the Credence—the Deep Purple (33).

Vasin explains the excitement with which rock music enthusiasts listened to the music. He describes how every aspect of performance, creativity, instrumentation, and composition were part of the listener's experience. Part of their listening for pleasure was to define the nature of rock and roll. None of the bands listed by Vasin as influential Western imports during this initial period included female performers or soloists.[4]

In the late 1970s and in the 1980s, women performers were included in the roster of Western imports. Bands such as ABBA, and performers such as Debra Harry of Blondie broadened the gender definition of the rock musician, expanding the appearance of female performers in some eastern European countries. However, the rock scene in the Soviet Union remained predominantly male.[5]

Belarusan bands, as did most emerging rock bands in the then-Soviet republics, continue to reflect the same gender-specific make-up. Responses to questions about women in rock and the maleness of rock music were varied. Siarhiej Kraućanka, bassist with Ulis did not express a specifically male definition of rock. His interpretation of the issue was based on a comparison with the relative number of female performers amongst Western groups: "If you consider the number of Western groups that are male and the number of female artists, and then if you consider the number of Belarusan groups, then the fact that we have one [female group] reflects the same relationship"

128 *Of Mermaids and Rock Singers*

(1993). For *Ulis* guitarist Korjan, rock is quintessentially a male genre: "We [men] emerge out of another world. Women can't play guitar, drums, bass like a man, they don't have the same life experiences . . . they're not suited to rock, but pop music, yes" (1993). Lyricist Aksienciev echoed the sentiment saying that the life expectations of women are different, that "they have other concerns"(1993).

For Pałac's lead singer Aleh Chamienka, women were "too delicate" to perform in the rock genre and would not easily adapt to the lifestyle of the rocker. Chamienka made the connection between the absence of women in rock and a traditional Belarusan ideal of the female role and of femininity, as genteel and non-assertive. Women could not, and should not, vocally or musically challenge the male-defined aesthetic of rock music, rocker behavior, and rocker lifestyles.[6] He further suggested that the fraternity inherent between members of a rock group was always put at risk when women were included socially into the fold, let alone permitted to join in the music-making (June 1993).

The distancing of women from music-making process, as well as from the social aspects of the rock scene, is also an aspect of Western rock cultures. Roy Shuker emphasizes Sarah Cohen's research amongst rock groups in the Liverpool rock scene where: "women were not simply absent, but were actively excluded. All male bands tended to preserve the music as their domain, keeping the involvement of wives and girlfriends at a distance"(Shuker on Cohen 1994, 102).[7] Cohen writes, "On several occasions I was informed that two things split up a band: women and money. Many complained that women were a distraction at rehearsals because they created tension within the band and pressurized the band's members to talk to them or to take them home" (102).

Amongst Belarusan rockers, the demands of belonging to a rock group and of practicing for success interfered directly with the needs of relationships and family. Most of the rock musicians I had met were divorced. Some of the musicians who had children lived, practiced, and performed in Miensk while their wives lived in the village.[8] While certain musicians were protective of their families and had managed to combine the demands of their professions with consistent family lives, others saw the potential instability of personal relationships as a defining aspect of rock life and did not expect, nor want, permanent relationships. Those rock musicians who had successfully balanced rock relationships and personal relationships still did not actively include their wives in their professional activities.

Rock represented a late-night lifestyle, bus tours, daily rehearsals and planning sessions, argument, bickering and internal jealousies, months without pay and for some without proper food, and the ultimate reward: shared elation at the successful performance and subsequent critical recognition. The rock group is at once fragmented and united, a microcosm of familial loyalty

From Bard to Rock Star   129

and fragility overwhelmingly characterized by male relationships and brotherhoods. Women were an important part of the fan base, they could be a part of private life, but they were not easily allowed into the professional fold.

Ironically Pałac did experiment with including women in their live performances; as dancers in combination hip hop-cheer leading outfits. This addition to the performance was consistent with Pałac's experiment with the production of theatrical, visually-compelling performances. They were also clearly influenced by Western video such as M.C. Hammer's "Can't Touch This" (1992) which they played on the television in their rehearsal studio with some regularity. In general, if women were on stage they were part of the spectacle but were not central to the music itself, nor to the identity the band constructed for its public image.[9] Overall Chamienka's comments embraced a traditional view of rock, of the hardships of rock life as a *vie de Bohème*, and the incompatibility with a traditional Belarusan definition of femininity.

Women active in popular urban performance made music in staged variety genres [estradnaja muzyka], institutional ensembles, traditional folk ensembles [for example the Lićviny], and as bards; genres that were ideologically and stylistically more acceptable for women, and certainly more acceptable than rock performance in general. Kasia Kamockaja challenged this attitude when she left her bardic roots in order to publicly search for and define her brand of rock.

NOVAJE NIEBA'S KASIA KAMOCKAJA: FROM BARD TO ROCK STAR

A former candidate in ethnographic studies, once married to the well-known Belarusan bard Aleś Kamocky, Kasia Kamockaja began her transition from bard to rock star in 1991. Throughout that year her transition was evident in her stage image, in the evolution of Novaje Nieba's musical style, and in the determined and staunch political and social convictions that Kamockaja revealed in both her music and in her public interviews.

Kamockaja stood out amongst her male peers, confident and opinionated, as she constructed her rocker image and avant-garde style. When asked if her gender affected her experiences in the rock community she said, "For me it is only hard because I am a mother. From the emotional side, or in terms of discrimination, I don't feel this. It is the opposite, it is very pleasant for me" [Laugh] (1993).

Nevertheless she faced several critical hurdles as she reinvented herself as a rock musician. These hurdles were partly gender-based in that they reflected general attitudes about rock culture from within and from outside the movement.

Walking up Skaryna Boulevard one cold September evening, Kasia and I bumped into an acquaintance of hers from the literary intelligentsia. He questioned Kamockaja for abandoning her bard activities for the less favorable rock genre, commenting that what she had produced as a bard was more "serious" and that she should refocus her energies on that style of expression (September 1993). A bard clearly had more credence as a legitimate artist because of the literary, poetic, and often political aspects of bardic music. Moreover, bardic performances took place in the House of Literature [Dom Literataraŭ], their output was considered intellectual and, perhaps most significantly in Kamockaja's case, bards escaped the kind of suspicions about morality, lifestyle, and commercialism associated with rock musicians.[10]

Kamockaja's second challenge did not emanate from the bard/intelligentsia set but rather from within the ranks of Belarusan rock music itself. Her decision to shift musical categories seemingly defied the process of gaining legitimacy recognized by bands, fans, and journalists in rock music circles. Her public saw her transition to rock as problematic. Journalists were slow to recategorize her and her musical style, in part because it was musically different from the other rock groups on the scene. When I first interviewed journalist Nadzia Kudrejka (Youth Radio, Miensk) about the active rock groups in Miensk, she included Kamockaja as an afterthought, "even though she is in the group Novaje Nieba, she is still a bard" (interview May 1993). Kudrejka was responding to the first manifestation of Novaje Nieba. Initially a four-member band, the group was still solidly entrenched in bardic style with an added rock and roll beat. Early descriptions of Kamockaja's style emphasize experimentation with orchestral strings and a broad range of instruments. She described the group as a musical laboratory where experimentation and style evolution allowed for a continuous exploration of musical style.[11]

In 1993, Kamockaja's band, Novaje Nieba, began to perform regularly and joined bands that were clear veterans of the rock scene (Mroja, Krama, Ulis and Miascovy Čas). In her description of her evolution from bard to rocker, Kamockaja emphasized her learning experiences in rock. When I first spoke to her and Lavon Volski early in 1993, Novaje Nieba had changed musicians, had redefined their musical style, and were in the process of recording a new tape [phonogram]: "Earlier we had bard songs with a band as back-up. This was not working. I didn't have any experience in singing rock. After I started to experiment with my voice, it was clear that even our guitarist didn't have any rock experience. [. . .] We changed musicians and deserted the traditional concept of bard-like traditional Belarusan song. Eventually we found a style we were comfortable with" (1993).

When Kamockaja reinvented Novaje Nieba in 1992, she did so with one solid link to legitimacy in the rock hierarchy. Included in the group were members of Mroja (Dream) who were clear veterans in the Belarusan rock scene, had a solid fan base, and had long been respected by the rock community. Lavon Volski was, with Kamockaja, a defining force for the new

From Bard to Rock Star   131

group. Nevertheless, it was often clear that the members of Novaje Nieba were not treated like the other Belarusan rock groups. Prior to a televised concert entitled "Rock Against the Revolution" in October 1993, the other participating groups were given time for sound checks and equipment set-up. Kamockaja was offered five minutes after all of the other groups had cleared. Her reaction was that she refused to perform without a sound check. The technicians gave her more time. This was a risky move considering the national exposure such a concert would provide. Kamockaja's own talents and abilities aside, it seemed that her admission into the rock community would have been even more difficult without the support from Mroja's reputation and the participation of Volski and his band members.

From the perspective of audience development Novaje Nieba and Mroja did not compete for the same public attention. Mroja enjoyed a fan-base that had developed over the group's ten-year existence. The consistency of their hard rock style had also secured their popularity amongst what Volski described as a "varied audience mainly of young people." Kamockaja explained: "For Novaje Nieba we have an audience mainly of students. The music is different. People who have interest in Belarus, but who don't find they fit into the traditional renaissance musical choices. We have, I don't know, an underground audience. The kind that feels connected to artists, more general. But for Mroja, their audience is more nationally aware" (1993).

Mroja's fans associated the group's music with a national and a political consciousness. Novaje Nieba could not be guaranteed that same fan base. Volski explained that at first Novaje Nieba's music did not appeal to popular Belarusan audiences. He admitted: "I have to say that Novaje Nieba doesn't play popular music. With the change of style it is very hard to lift ourselves into popularity" (1993). Kamockaja described the style as "non-traditional avant-garde music," a style that was not familiar to Belarusan audiences. Volski added: [we have] "a spontaneous approach to composition, we don't have a strategy per se"(1993). The experimental aspect of the style of Novaje Nieba and their willingness to model the group as an artistic and creative collective was unique amongst the key Belarusan groups. They invited other musicians to participate in their music-making experiments, performance, and recording projects.

By 1993 Kamockaja and Novaje Nieba did carve a niche in the Belarusan rock scene. That year performance venues for rock music increased and as a result rock groups received more public exposure. Kamockaja's performance image became more consistent and her musical style became more familiar to listeners. Equally important, Novaje Nieba was developing a reputation associated with contemporary commentary that would define Kamockaja 's image as a socially conscious performer and allow her to combine the political essence of her bardic roots with her emerging style of rock music.

132 *Of Mermaids and Rock Singers*

IMAGE, BELONGING, AND ASSOCIATION

The look of a band, their choice of elaborate costume or their emphasis on street clothes can contribute to the image of a group, to associations about the musical meaning, and to the listeners interpretation of the performance. Belarusan bands could be casual (Krama's choice of jeans and shirts), could suggest a rocker fashion (Ulis' leather jackets), could design clothing specific to the bands intended public image, such as Pałac's appropriations of traditional dress, or could adopt the established look associated with their musical style (long waist-length hair amongst Mroja-members which reflected their hard-rock style). While clothing does not "make" the band, rock fashion has had an enormous impact on the public attention given some artists. As a woman performing on a male stage, Kamockaja experimented with her stage look throughout the summer of 1993.

My first view of Novaje Nieba in performance was in Małademcna 93, a well-established annual Festival of Belarusan Song and Poetry. Novaje Nieba and other rock bands were to play in a two-day program of music that centered upon a song competition in the estradnaja musical genre. The rock community considered this performance venue as desirable because of the public exposure and, as Kamockaja mentioned, the availability of "good equipment"(April 1993). Performing a midnight concert, Novaje Nieba were dwarfed on an enormous outdoor stage. Kamockaja stood slightly in front of her fellow musicians, acoustic guitar in hand. She stayed behind her mike for most of the set, a static and conservative figure, reflecting the performance style of the bard, the poet/storyteller (See Figure 7.2). Her visual image changed remarkably over the course of that summer. By September she had sheared her blond hair, favored black jeans and leather jackets, and most often held the mike as she used the stage and her body language to project the music. Her fashion now announced her clear membership in the rock genre: incorporating some of the accepted uniform worn by other rockers (black leather jackets), and de-emphasizing those attributes that announced a stereotypical femininity, especially her long wavy blond hair (Figure 7.3). She has kept the style as a consistent part of her image even in 1999.

The early casual stage image, which works well for other bands seemed to undermine Kamockaja's authority on stage. She was trying to convince the public on many levels: that her *avant-garde* music was worthy of their attention and that her position as a female front for an all-male band was a viable combination in rock. The short hair, black uniform, and her dark glasses proclaimed her own positioning as a member of the rock community and visually stressed an association with rock performance.

As Kamockaja's physical look evolved, Novaje Nieba's music began to reflect a cohesiveness of style, without sacrificing the experimentation that defined their early musical mandate. They drew from a variety of styles

From Bard to Rock Star 133

Figure 7.2: Kasia Kamockaja in concert, May 1993, Maładečna, Belarus. Photographed by the author.

Figure 7.3: Kasia Kamockaja in concert, September 1993, Miensk, Belarus. Photographed by the author.

134 *Of Mermaids and Rock Singers*

including 1950s-rock 'n' roll, reggae, and music tinged with 1970s psychedelic rock overtones. Kamockaja and her fellow musicians drew from an impressive repertoire of musical expertise (as do many bands in Belarus who learned their craft from listening to imported records). The structure of the songs is one of the musical aspects that distinguish Kamockaja and Novaje Nieba from other Belarusan bands and, while the text is central to the song, the instrumental treatments are equally important.

While most Belarusan rock draws on a strophic architecture, a verse refrain arrangement with musical interlude, Novaje Nieba will often begin a song with a drawn-out instrumental section and then ease into an economical vocal section and a return to instrumentals. Kamockaja's strong resonant alto, unusual when compared to preferred traditional female vocal range, punctuates the texture as a part of the overall musical soundscape which includes electronic keyboard, guitar, bass, percussion (often two musicians), acoustic guitar, and male vocals. The texts, when not penned by the band, are taken from the works of contemporary young Belarusan poets. Always choosing socially conscious texts, the group reflects the moods of their cultural and national environment. The song "Terrible Beauty" [Žachlivaja Pryhažość from *Son i tramvaj* [Sleep in the Trolley], Kovcheg 1994] was recorded in early 1993 and is a dark statement of loss and helplessness as a result of apathy, the difficulties of urban life, and the continuing impact of the Chernobyl disaster:

"Terrible Beauty" [Žachlivaja Pryhažość], Novaje Nieba, *Son i tramvaj*. Translated by the author. Used by permission.

> Our dances are nothing more than
> a sharp casual movement.
> A barely visible gesture
> Of skinny nervous hands.
> The day ends and at six o'clock
> You will notice yourself
> How the crowd will swallow you
> Like a bottle of wine.
>
> The fog of the square quarters
> Poisoned by wind [reference to Chernobyl]
> Is floating on the evil city
> Terrible beauty
>
> Our dances are nothing more than
> the language of mute people
> In this city noisy with cars
> It is easier to speak this way
> The day will end and at six o'clock
> The city will fill the crowd
> With saws, axes, nails, hammers, screws...

From Bard to Rock Star

> The fog of the square quarters [apartment blocks]
> Poisoned by wind
> Is floating on the evil city
> Terrible beauty
>
> I have seen them
> Walking through the gray dusk

This song, though not aggressively political, hinted at the kind of themes that would eventually define the music of Novaje Nieba. The words emphasize the powerless individual lost in an overpowering yet compelling urban landscape. References to dances and language reflect the actions and the voices that might serve to bring change or to assert individual will. In this text dance is reduced to futile gestures: "no more than a sharp casual movement" or "the language of mute people." The symbolic city offers anonymity, a general noise that drowns out individual longing, and finally transforms its inhabitants into an apathetic mechanical population. References to Chernobyl [poisoned by wind is floating on the evil city] and the preference for linguistic conformity [it is easier to speak this way] provide a sobering representation of an urban cultural and social climate.

This text is framed by contrasting musical segments. Instrumental sections are dominated by a punctuated pattern played on electronic keyboard that suggests the rhythm of regular mechanical motion, an accelerated interpretation of a march. Kamockaja sings the main verses with clipped diction enhancing the mechanized character of the music as a whole. The aggressive stress of each syllable and the constricted range of the verse melody establish a musical contrast with the refrain. The refrain, based on some descending motion and dramatic leaps is not performed in a clipped style. Instead, the instrumental and vocal treatment suggest a lyrical point of relief against the percussive verse sections. Kamockaja, doubled by Volski, repeats the word "beauty" [pryhažosc] which is set to a descending line followed by an ascending sustained fifth. The ambiguity of a tonal center, the leaps, and the displaced stresses oppose the initial effect of the refrain as a respite from the suggested urban energy of the verses. The effect is that of an angry lament (Example 7.1).

Example 7.1: Refrain excerpt from Novaje Nieba's Žachlivaja Pryhažość from *Son i tramvaj*. Transcribed by the author.

136   *Of Mermaids and Rock Singers*

By 1995, an established experimental musical style and a more confident stage image began to fulfill the public's expectations of Kamockaja and her group. Her reputation also began to be defined as aggressively political. Novaje Nieba's most celebrated underground hit illustrates this aspect of the group's style which was publicly critical of the emerging politics of the time.

1994 was a pivotal political year in Belarus. The energy of the cultural Renaissance had established the official use of the Belarusan language in education and in the media. Belarusans who had been exposed to a Belarusan-aware education were exploring and supporting a Belarusan identity on both personal and national levels. The climate for such exploration changed substantially with the election of a new president. Alaksandar Lukašenka, a Soviet-style politician, began to reintroduce much of the cultural policy that had defined the Soviet era. He banned Belarusan in the school systems, reorganized the media as a Russian-language reflection of his policy, and started to campaign for the reunification with Russia. As Alexandra Goujon has theorized, he appealed mainly to voters who perceived the Soviet system as more stable and more economically viable (1999).

Released in 1995, the song "President GO Home," (*Go Home*, Kovcheg 1995), delivers a wave of angry musical energy, an aggressiveness that denies Kamockaja's earlier preference for ballad-style songs. The music, a demand for populist President Lukašenka to go home, back to Russia, contains a recurring guitar gesture, a wa wa guitar that sounds like empty repetitive political rhetoric. Even the sequential quality of the musical line suggests the lack of musical direction, a potential comment about contemporary politics in Belarus. The words are equally a powerful criticism of Lukašenka's political intent, of the population's inability to detect his strategies, and of their lack of conviction in generating political change:

"President GO Home," Novaje Nieba (*Go Home*, Novaje Nieba 1995). Translated by the author. Used by permission.

> They look at the red sky and hope for rain
> They look at the dry earth and hope for a harvest
> But you and me, we believe in freedom
> Even if we can't drink it like a beer
> This is why we repeat these three words
> President GO home . . .

Needless to say, this was most definitely an underground hit. It was summarily banned from radio play. With this song Kamockaja and her band aggressively defined the social and political responsibility which informed their style. "President GO Home" caught the attention of Belarusan youth and of the Western European Press. Both were reacting to Lukašenka through civil protest and through media analysis. Lukašenka outlawed the public dis-

From Bard to Rock Star   137

play of the historical Belarusan flag, replacing it with a Soviet version. The militia was under orders to confiscate pins, flags, and banners, as well as any representation of the white-red-white flag. In response, Belarusan youth found ways to defy the new policy. At soccer games, where before Lukašenka, the crowd would wave Belarusan flags in support of their teams, Belarusan youth now used face paint to paint the flag on their cheeks, daring the militia to take the flags away (interview Tryhubovic 1995). Such acts of defiance became increasingly dangerous as Lukašenka began a campaign of human rights violations by imprisoning anyone who defied his edicts.

It is clear that Kamockaja and Novaje Nieba took a risk with this song and with all of their persistent Belarusan-language music. While she is now clearly a member of the rock community, Kamockaja remains a rocker on the fringe defining success according to the consistency of her message. Unlike many of the bands that now revert to Russian-language interviews because of political censorship and media pressure, Kamockaja continues to publicly support a Belarusan-conscious attitude. In her cultural rebellion she alone seems to uphold the traditional romantic ideal of the rocker as an idealistic rebel.

Kamockaja's musical evolution and the political facet to her public persona remain unique in the Belarusan rock movement. In 1999, the bard-come-rocker is the spokesperson of a cultural movement that began in the 1980s and reached a peak in pre-Lukašenka Belarus. Kamockaja has not only established herself as a member of the Belarusan rock community, she has established herself in another traditionally male-defined context as well. Her political voice, though often subjugated to the underground, remains prominent in the public sphere. She projects the image of conviction, strength, and principle dismissing any notions that her gender limits her artistic intent and her public impact.

Her position established, she continues to function in an increasingly hostile political environment. Her third release, *My Country* [Maja Kraina, Kobcheg 1997], remains faithful to her established public image. In a 1999 interview published in the newspaper Svaboda, Kamockaja defined Belarusan rock:

> It is worth looking at Belarusan rock if only because it is different from rock in other countries. Presently in Belarus the government is enforcing a concrete anti-national campaign [. . .]. That is why rock and roll here, and especially Belarusan-language rock and roll satisfies those functions that rock and roll used to have in the beginning of the movement. This music is a social protest and only in Belarus does it retain this national goal. In other post-Soviet countries the political situation is not as limiting, in the West rock has focused on anti-drug and Aids research. But this is normal, the better a person lives the less he wants to protest.[12]

138   *Of Mermaids and Rock Singers*

Kamockaja, a unique figure in a male-dominated genre, has defined an image, a musical style, and a social mandate that has been accepted by the rock community and by a growing number of underground fans. Fellow musicians contribute to Belarusan rock according to traditional resources (Pałac) or according to conceptions of music and language articulated as a rocker aesthetic rather than a medium for social commentary (Ulis). Kamockaja has gained credibility from her consistent public stance and her unwillingness to change the musical experimentation that has come to define Novaje Nieba.

NOTES

[1] The region of Biełastoččyna in Eastern Poland is connected historically, ethnographically, and linguistically to Belarus. The communities found at the eastern border of modern Poland comprise a substantial Belarusan population with its own newspaper [Niva], organizations, and schools [Belarusan Lycée in Hajnaŭka]. The Belarusan Student Organization [BAS] was organized by students of the Belarusan lycée who have been active in exploring Belarusan culture, music, and language issues since the Solidarity movement in Poland in the early 1980s. BAS was particularly interested in opening connections with their counterparts in Miensk and expanding their membership in their own communities. In 1990 they organized the first Belarusan Rock Festival Basovišča and have since funded the publication of rock anthologies, organized fan clubs for Belarusan rock groups, and incorporated Belarusan music into local radio programming.

[2] Shepherd, John "A Theoretical Analysis for the Sociomusicological Analysis of Popular Music." *Popular Music* 2: 145–178. In his chapter "The Absent Woman," Roy Shuker writes "the masculine emphasis within rock culture, and the relative absence of female performers, has been a traditional aspect of rock" (1994, 101). Shuker further offers key analyses by other popular culture theorists that describe the maleness of rock as : (1) a way of limiting the opportunities for women in the music industry (Chapple and Garofalo 1977, as cited in Shuker), (2) reflecting a male model that is consciously sexist in its use of women in lyrics and in visual representations (Shuker, 1994), and (3) defining the social experience of rock from performer to audience as a primarily male activity (Cohen 1991). In the 1990s women have emerged as powerful figures in the Western music industry in almost every genre from hip hop, rap, to the more traditional R&B ballad styles, and Pop. Madonna's constant self re-invention, and artists such as Alanis Morrisette and Jewel who are known for their vocal styles and their ironic, aggressive lyrics, reflect a more than delicate female perspective. Sarah MacLaughlin's initiation of the *Lilith Fair* concerts have also surprised the music industry with their continued success. The industry had predicted that an all-female line-up would not attract a significant audience, assuming that the strength of popular music sales depended on the activities of male performers.

[3] Kolya Vasin, "Notes from a Rock Museum," In *Soviet Rock* (Moscow: Progress Publishers, 1991), 30–46.

From Bard to Rock Star 139

[4] For example the Polish band Manaam included a female lead vocalist, Olga Jackowska, in 1978 (Rybak 1990, 184–186). Rybak does mention a canceled Leningrad concert which was to headline Santana and Joan Baez (164) and the success of Tina Turner in Bulgaria in 1980 (194). Sabrina Ramet highlights the appearance of two all-female rock groups, Loretta and Lochness in Slovakia (1991, 70). Analyzing rock in 1980s Hungary, Lázló Kürti writes that: "the most intriguing aspect of new bands was their near total composition of male performers and singers" ('"How Can I Be a Human Being?" Culture Youth and Musical Opposition in Hungary" In *Rocking the State*, Ed. Sabrina P. Ramet (Boulder: Westview Press, 1991), 88.

[5] A listing of the "best known groups and solo artists" in Russia (principally Leningrad and Moscow) includes one female fronted group called Bravo, who were active in the 1980s. See *Soviet Rock: 25 years in the underground + 5 years of freedom* (1991, 197–206).

[6] These comments are ironic considering Chamienka's appropriation of traditional female vocal style as his own signature vocal delivery (see Chapter Five).

[7] Sarah Cohen, *Rock Culture in Liverpool: Popular Music in the Making* (Oxford: Clarendon, 1991), 218.

[8] Some musicians explained such arrangements as the result of residency limits for the city of Miensk. Although many of the rock musicians were not Miensk natives, they had received residency papers when they became university and conservatory students in the city.

[9] The eventual inclusion of a female vocalist [Veronika Kruhłova], would prove to generate palpable friction amongst Pałac's members.

[10] Despite their public successes, and the strength of their messages in the public sphere, rock musicians were fringe performers and, despite the post-Soviet climate, were still considered to be outside social norms. In 1993, Opposition leader Zianon Paźniak (representing the Belarusan Popular Front Party), lost the ear of many young voters when he publicly questioned not only the morality of rock music and musicians, but mentioned the "lack of artistic value" in the genre.

[11] Pop Muzyka 1(42): 55.

[12] Svaboda, Naviny, 1999: 29(560).

8

National Republic Of Mroja [Dream]: Quotation and the Kangaroo

I N 1995 THE VETERAN BELARUSAN-LANGUAGE ROCK BAND MROJA [DREAM] modified their name. The change emphasizes the group's long-standing commitment to contemporary political and cultural commentary. Mroja's new name, Narodnaja Respublika Mroja [National Republic of Mroja or NRM] was a direct response to the state of the nation after the then newly elected President Lukašenka began to revert to Soviet-era cultural and political policies. The band's emphasis on a *national republic* was a symbolic challenge, a criticism of Lukašenka's attempts to channel post-sovereignty Belarus back into a territorial, political, and cultural affiliation with Russia. The name change also chastised Belarusans who, incredulous of Lukašenka's influence, were to see the assertion of their renaissance movement sustained through the convictions of a rock band. NRM's focus on the national movement and on Belarusan language rights has been evident since their debut performances in the early 1980s, when a group of art students from a Miensk art college came together to form the band.[1] Lead singer Lavon Volski acknowledges that the band's long standing fan base associates NRM with national and language-rights issues. Volski commented on the popularity and the style of NRM: ". . . when Mroja started we had a small audience. But our music was seen as more original, partly because of language choice.[2] Our audience has been steadily growing" [and] "Well, Mroja has existed for the past ten years and our style hasn't really changed. Even in American terms our style is really hard rock, traditional. But we try to use the melodic Belarusan style in our songs" (May 1993).

NRM's music is unique to Belarusan-language rock. Their musical style and stage manner reflect the influence of Western heavy metal tradition. Their stage presence is aggressive and animated, reflecting the movements

141

142   *Of Mermaids and Rock Singers*

and the look associated with the hard rock genre. Lead singer Lavon Volski shapes his vocal style through exaggerated diction and a raw assertive vocal quality. Volski's on-stage attitude, as well as that of fellow band members, reflect the energized pulsating movements of cock rock performance. Lavon Volski's stage image contradicts the quiet introspective style that he projects when off stage. He is a gifted chameleon changing his performance persona to suit the intended effect of the song and/or the image of a band. This is most evident in his transformation from cock-rocker to avant-garde performance artist as a member of Kasia Kamockaja's Novaje Nieba.

The performance style and the musical connections to the hard rock genre are evident in much of NRM's repertoire. The Belarusan-language texts reflect the high literary standards associated with eastern European rock in general.[3] In addition to these characteristics NRM manipulates music and text to create complex, highly referential songs that reflect a pathos for contemporary Belarusan experience through the use of multiple musical texts. Although their repertoire is vast, the song "Aŭstralijskaja Polka"[4] (*28th Star* 1990) will serve to illustrate the musical and texted references that characterize the most powerful examples of NRM's music. Aŭstralijskaja Polka is a musical commentary on the impact of the Chernobyl nuclear accident in Belarus. The text, the chosen genre [polka], and the incorporation of musical quotations and references result in an eclectic and powerful example of NRM's musical fusions.[5]

As the title suggests Aŭstralijskaja Polka is a polka, a genre associated with the traditional repertoires of Eastern and Central Europe. Mroja's selection of this genre continues the formal and stylistic link between contemporary music and traditional genres. The use of traditional songs as a framework for stylistic experimentation reflects the kind of appropriations heard in the Pieśniary. In NRM, texture and various idioms (classical/jazz/folk) are varied throughout the composition as a strategy of musical form and development. More importantly in the case of this song, the choice of rhythmic and formal qualities of the polka is ironic and serves to stress tragedy rather than the traditional light-hearted themes usually associated with the genre.

The polka is a celebratory genre. It invites listeners to dance and, in the Belarusan tradition, most commonly includes carefree texts of romance and courtship. In contrast, the text of Mroja's polka is charged with irony; it is not about romance but about choices. Sung in the first person, it tells of a young man's struggle to decide between staying in Belarus and relocating to Australia. The need for the choice, the Chernobyl fallout, is only made explicit in the fourth verse of the song.

After the 1986 Chernobyl nuclear fall-out, one of the proposed solutions offered by many nations was the partial relocation of the population. Some of the offers were funded by the Belarusan Diaspora, including that communi-

National Republic of Mroja [Dream]

ty in Australia. This rock polka evaluates the reasons for choosing Australia over Belarus by comparing the quality of life in each context:

> Excerpt "Aŭstralijskaja Polka" Mroja (28th *Star*). Used by permission. Translation by the author.
>
> Verse 4:
> There you have kangaroos and duck-billed platypuses
> You've never seen anything like them in your life
> Here radiation devastates the nation
> Red wine isn't enough to make us happy here [to fix this situation...]
>
> Verse 8:
> I am a patriot I told them at the station
> I told them as well that I will soon die
> I prefer **our own** radiation [my emphasis]
> It is worth more than foreign kangaroos.

Thus the formal construction of the chosen polka genre provides a layer of meaning. Here it is informed by the traditional 'celebratory' function of the polka and its application to a tragic event. It can also be argued that polka as 'meaning' relates to the courageous spirit and national conviction of the singer. Whether it is a commentary on post-Chernobyl choice or on the strength of human conviction, the choice of the polka as a framework for the Chernobyl theme adds to the irony of the song.

The musical elements of the polka are formally accurate and especially effective performed by electric guitar, bass, drums, and Volski's hard-edged vocals. The song begins with a brief use of guitar feedback that unexpectedly leads into an eight measure introduction in a strict 2/4 with a background drone (Example 8.1). The emphasis on beat two is typical of polka patterns and is supported by traditional choreography where the footwork accentuates beat two of the measure according to a two eighthnotes - one quarter pattern. This pattern also dictates the text layout for verse and for the chorus (Examples 8.2 and 8.3).

Example 8.1: Introduction and interlude segment for NRM's "Aŭstralijskaja Polka". Transcribed by the author.

Example 8.2: "Aŭstralijskaja Polka" (Verse 1). As the bass drum emphasizes the offbeats, the guitar line provides a forward-moving counterpoint to the polka-like vocal line. Transcribed by the author.

National Republic of Mroja [Dream]

Example 8.3: "Aŭstralijskaja Polka" (chorus). The chorus provides a contrast to the thicker texture of the verses. The vocals drop down an octave and together with instrumental doubling provide an accented homorhythmic segment that interrupts the intense forward motion created by the guitar part that underlies each verse. The choral text is sung once and is immediately repeated without text. Transcribed by the author.

Beyond the form, Mroja's Polka contains other types of borrowing. These appear as episodes in the overall musical texture and as such, also function as dramatic devices to inform the text. As the text transcription shows (Schema 8.1), the song includes six verses which appear in pairs. These are separated by the refrain and the repetition of the introduction. Between each verse pair, Mroja has included other techniques of 'style' incorporation. The first of these is melodic quotation. The melody chosen for this section comes from the traditional polka repertoire. It is a significant choice because this traditional piece, known as "Lavonicha," holds iconic meaning for Belarusans. It is the national dance of Belarus and has come to produce an anthem-like response from performers and audiences alike. In the Mroja example, the symbolic significance of the song enhances the message of the text. The six-measure quotation appears after the singer says: "There our ziemlaki (fellow Belarusans) await us." The "Lavonicha," quote is a musical signpost for a shared identity and for the perceived nationalism of Belarusan immigrant communities.

Example 8.4: "Lavonicha": Six-measure phrase as heard in "Aŭstralijskaja Polka". Transcribed by the author.

Between verses three and four the listener hears another type of quotation. In this section the singer is comparing the downfalls of Belarus to the 'wonderful' things offered by Australia. The light-hearted verse ends with the exclamation that Australia gave us the group AC/DC. Suddenly Mroja moves away from the musical texture established up to this point and breaks into a sixteen measure *stylistic* quote of AC/DC. This is achieved without interruption of the overall metrical and rhythmic feel of the song. Verses 5 and 6 are also divided by a similar device.

Perhaps the most dramatic use of quotation comes at the end of the text for the Aŭstralijskaja Polka. It is at the end of the song that the speaker voices his desire to die "with our own radiation/Its worth more than foreign kangaroos." The somber nature of this decision is emphasized by a complete change in both style, gesture, and idiom. As the last statement, Mroja offers a section in an eight bar blues form. Within the last four measures the group performs the last quote heard in the song. This final quote is taken from the Beatles' "Hey Jude" (Example 8.5). Rather than quoting from the beginning of a musical segment, Mroja chooses to quote from the last four measures of the melody. The dramatic effect of this final choice certainly lies in the complete change of musical character. However, Mroja are also revealing their association between a tragic context, heroic choices, and the meaning that they interpret in this appropriated Beatles song. This last quote, as the others heard in this piece, reveal the importance of quotation as a communication technique which draws on the referential power of musical gesture.

Example 8.5: "Aŭstralijskaja Polka" final phrase based on the quotation from the Beatle's "Hey Jude." The musical choice may have been dictated by the words of the last four measures of each verse [Remember to let her into your heart then you can start to make it better (Lennon/McCartney 1968)].

Schema 8.1: Mroja: "Aŭstralijskaja Polka" (*28th Star*). Used by permission. Translation by M. P. Survilla.

Intro: eight bars [Example 8.1]
Verse One [Example 8.2]
My friends stopped me in the club and said
What are you doing sitting here in these conditions
Better to come with us to Australia
There they await us our *ziemlaki* (fellow Belarusans)

Lavonicha quote (complete six measures from first phrase of song) {Example 8.4}

There the coral glows
There you have golden [sands] and ocean waves
And here, what do you have? only warm beer–

National Republic of Mroja [Dream] 147

And the woman who, for the moment, stays with you.
Refrain: 8 measures [Example 8.3]

> Our heart councils us
> Towards luminous Australia

Interlude: from intro 8 measures

There Belarusans are very wealthy
There – AC/DC were born (the popular Australian hard-rock group that emerged in the 1970s)

AC/DC stylistic quote 16 measures

There you have kangaroos and duck-billed platypuses
You've never seen anything like them in your life
Here radiation devastates the nation
Red wine isn't enough to make us happy here [to fix this situation...]

Refrain: 8 measures

Our heart councils us
> Towards luminous Australia

Interlude: from intro 8 measures

I spent a whole week in France changing my mind
My hands and my legs trembling
You already transferred yourself to a foreign land
But with conviction I told myself - no!

8 measures **heroic** quote

I am a patriot I told them at the station
I told them as well that I will soon die
I prefer **our own** radiation [my emphasis]
It is worth more than foreign kangaroos. *

–extension of last bar to 4 beat/measure –blues eight bars in slow 4 - last four bars of piece are a quotation from the Beatles' 'Hey Jude' [example 8.5]

In popular music, style is not so much an element of taxonomic definition as it is a marker of both individual expressions, social climates, and cultural interactions. Beyond the importance given to language choice and to traditional repertoires, Belarusan rockers combine musical and stylistic resources in a variety of ways. NRM uses traditional forms, the quotation of traditional melodies within new compositions (Lavonicha), the quotation of trademark styles not as imitations but as a means of emphasizing and informing the text (AC/DC style quote), and the quotation of materials from

148 *Of Mermaids and Rock Singers*

Western repertoires ("Hey Jude") as a way to underscore meaning by referential means.

This close reading of Mroja's "Aŭstralijskaja Polka" parallels Dettmar and Richey's *intertextual* reading of popular music where "the musical and lyrical texts [are] associative, allusive, or even quotational" (1999, 3). The source pool for such constructions and for the subsequent associations that inform the listener/fan are tied to the assumption that both performer and audience are aware of past constructions and past meanings, of the established iconographies that are part of popular music past and present. The reference to, borrowing of, and recontextualizing of musicians, styles, and songs adds to the "multiple dimensions [of a] verbal and aural polyphony"(ibid., 5) that challenge the reading of popular music. NRM is therefore challenging and enticing their listeners. The multiple borrowings reach beyond simple quotation and demand that both performers and audience be conscious of various musical and extra-musical meanings in order to "read" the texts in this polka-lament.

NOTES

[1] By 1984 they had recorded a cassette album entitled "The Old Temple." Three members were engaged in military service between 1984 and 1986. The group reunited and released three more albums before 1991: "Sight" (1989), "Studio BM" (1988), and "28th Star" (1990, Melodiya C60 30401 001). Since 1991 they have consistently performed and produced cassette albums (see discography).

[2] Mroja's album "28th Star" illustrates the group's emphasis on Belarusan-language rights. The album cover is bilingual with all information in Belarusan and in English. Underneath the list of songs the band has included the statement "All songs in the Belarusan language."

[3] See Chapter Four pages X–X.

[4] This example appears in part in Survilla, "Rock in Belarus," In *Rocking the State,* Ed. Sabrina Ramet (Boulder: Westview, 1994), 236–238.

[5] This example was used as a basis for a presentation entitled "Quotations for a Kangaroo: Multi-textuality and Style in Belarusian Rock," at the Society For Ethnomusicology Conference for the session "Cross Cultural Perspectives in the Analysis of Popular Music," Seattle, Washington, October 25th, 1992.

9

Rock and Revolution: Performance and the Mediation of Rock

You have a comfortable position in relation to us all. Even if we all stop playing, you will still be there doing your job.

(Siarhiej Kraučanka, Ulis, 1993)

SINCE THE MID-1980s, MUSIC IN URBAN BELARUS HAS REFLECTED AND OFTEN intensified the movement towards cultural and national assertion known as the Belarusan Renaissance [Adradžeńnie]. This climate of renewal has prompted performers, journalists, scholars, and audiences to search for the parameters of Belarusan expression. Cultural exploration has been characterized by several factors. Scholars and journalists evaluate the impact of Soviet ideology on traditional folk repertoires and offer commentaries in the public sphere. They engage in the popularization of the Belarusan language by choosing to use it and/or by addressing language trends in public forums. Performers also make a statement according to their language choice. Mediators active in this cultural renaissance are also keenly aware of the effect of Western trends on Belarusan culture. Commentaries on Western influences reflect polarized viewpoints that contrast an enthusiasm for the exploration of non-Belarusan expression with questions about the loss of cultural authenticity. Responses to the Soviet legacy, language reform, and the influences of Western trends are all bound to changing political mandates and cultural policies that can define the mediation of culture in the public sphere. For example, rocker Kasia Kamockaja was banned from performing at the MałAdečna 98 song Festival because her public support of Belarusan sovereignty and culture were in direct contrast to the cultural policies of president Lukašenka. The decision to exclude Kamockaja was made by the Festival organizers because, by their own admission, they were afraid of Lukašenka's response.[1] Audiences are informed by this medi-

149

150   Of Mermaids and Rock Singers

ation and further the process of evaluating and defining the role of contemporary Belarusan culture in their private and their professional lives.

The cultural processes and the strategists that attempt to sway public sentiment are neither hidden nor subtle on the post-sovereignty urban stage. In the same way that Soviet cultural policy mandated aggressive cultural assimilation, those active in the Belarusan public sphere in 1993 were actively soliciting a specific cultural reaction. The goal was to entice the public towards political and cultural self-determination. The potential of a new political climate offered the opportunity to reevaluate personal and cultural identities. Most of what was offered in the public sphere, from political speeches to children's programming, to televised song festivals were contextualized according to a "new" Belarus.

ROCK AND REVOLUTION: PERFORMANCE AND THE MEDIATION OF ROCK

> How much do you make in a concert?
> *Laughter* . . . Well, once we're finished with any expenses, we usually have enough for a pack of cigarettes.
> (Kasia Kamockaja, Novaje Nieba, 1993)

The performance venues open to Belarusan rock increased slightly in 1993. Where rockers could count on perhaps one major performance every three months in the early nineties, by the Spring of that year rock music was heard live or on television at least twice every month (Volski, interview 1993). Some of the performance venues were conceptualized as annual rock festivals and had already become key events in the rock calendar.[2] Other performances were one-time events. None of the concerts headlined one group in solo performance. Concerts gathered the rock community, promoted solidarity amongst the groups, and helped to support the idea of an intimate and strong rock fellowship.[3]

It was clear that these concerts provided rock bands with the opportunity to play, to elaborate on their public image, to encourage a public, and to satisfy existing fans. As the quote above suggests, none of these musicians expected to gain financially from their efforts.[4] Rock concert audiences could expect to see the same core rock groups no matter what the venue. The appearance of these core bands was the singular consistency that rock fans could expect in going to a concert. The events were defined by a lack of a uniform liturgy and by the absence of standardized format.

Rock performers reached their public through a sporadic system of concert venues. Some venues, such as the national Belarusan Song Festivals in Maładečna, were organized to highlight other styles of performance. The Maładečna '93 Festival served as a competition for staged variety balladeers. Though rock groups were asked to perform, their position in the perform-

Rock and Revolution

ance hierarchy was evidently quite low. I recall first seeing members of Ulis and Mroja in a Maładečna park close to the central outdoor stage. They apparently had been assigned a large gazebo-like structure for their performances but the organizers had overlooked choosing a stage with an electrical source. Eventually they were offered the main stage but only once the main festival program had been completed. The groups waited backstage until personnel finished dismantling equipment and television cameras and finally began to play their concert at midnight. Rather than discouraging the audience, the anticipation seemed to energize the crowd and they responded with satisfying enthusiasm.

Other concert opportunities were defined by the level of sponsorship, the character of an already established music festival, or by the particular calendrical date that might inspire a specific theme. The 1993 concert schedule listed below is organized according to the different character of these events (Table 9.1). At those concerts where the rock community piggy-backed onto a performance defined by another genre, the rock presentations were not overtly contextualized by any specific type of theme or political commentary.

In Maładečna, rock was considered outside the boundaries of the officially-accepted estradnaja style.[5] In this venue, rock was an after-hours concert experience. The audience that waited in the dark for the concert to begin could draw on their anticipation and impatience for some ritual energy. What was unique about Maładečna is that the public was also privy to the construction of the clandestine-like environment, one reminiscent of the adolescent longing for the time when adults finally go to bed. They saw the dismantling of the orchestral stage, and the unplugging of television cameras, and they saw their rock stars setting up the stage. This window on what is typically a backstage aspect of rock performance shaped the concert as an intimate experience.

Maładečna's midnight concert was similar to a Western concert environment. The crowd was loud in its appreciation as they sat in the chill of a May night. Members of the militia wandered in front of and behind the stage anticipating crowd control that was not necessary. An enthusiastic fan managed to reach the stage and was asking performers to autograph his shirt as they tried to perform. In a gesture taken from rock concert ritual, Pałac's Chamienka suggested that the crowd keep warm by holding up their lighters. Overall, the performers played to a surprisingly well-behaved crowd. Unlike in a Western-style crowd however, the sea of faces in Maładečna was punctuated with waving Belarusan flags. The scene hinted at the strong association between rock and the celebration of nation.

* * *

There is a distinction to be made here between the assertion and the celebration of national sentiment. The positive cultural environment enjoyed by

Table 9.1: Summary of Rock Concert Activity in Belarus (1993)

Concert	Sponsor	Mediation	Venue	Theme/Implied Image of Rock	Rock Specific/Other
Maładečna '93 May	Combination of state and private sponsorship	Celebration of Belarusan Song and Competition	Outdoor stage constructed for the event	Marginalized by organizers non-official status	No
Slavianski Bazar (Viciebsk) July	State and private	Slavic Song Festival and Competition	Various auditoriums and outdoor stages	None*	No
Rock Island (Miensk) May)	Belarus Television	Rock as a club style performance	Studio setting Belarus TV	Social experience	Yes
Rok Na Vychadnych (Miensk) September	Private	Rock concert as an end-of-summer youth celebration	Belarus Dome—circular tent-like sports complex in Miensk outskirts	Stress-release	Yes
Rok Supraĉ Revalucyjaŭ (Miensk) October	Belarusan Youth radio and Kovcheg	Political/National Consciousness	Auditorium of Miensk foreign language Institute	Political activism (overt)	Yes
Veteran-Day concert October	Unknown	Political rally	Steps of the Miensk Opera	Political activism (implied)	Yes–after a series of political speeches

*Veronika Kruhłova sang a selection by Pałac- member Juraś Vydronak as part of the song competition but rock was not central to the event.

Rock and Revolution 153

Belarusans in 1993 generated a different kind of energy than the national consciousness associated with rock in the pre-sovereignty and post-sovereignty years. The mood in 1993 was celebratory, the association between rock and an assertion of identity was well-established and came to the forefront of the movement in 1994.

The development and the encouragement of such associations has already been considered from the perspective of the rock ideologies that drive each group. Novaje Nieba, Narodnaja Respublika Mroja, Ulis, and Krama either explicitly identify their music as a link to social and political consciousness, or imply the importance of a Belarusan identity through the use of language. The rebellious, underground origins of rock and the general climate of cultural exploration also facilitated such cultural and national associations. Some concert organizers chose to contribute to these associations and structure concerts around national themes. Others tried to encourage the growth of a rock following by designing concerts around an ambiance, a strategized ritual space that the public could then associate with rock and the concert experience.

While Belarus Radio provided Belarusan rockers the most public exposure for their music, the television medium offered the public a different kind of mediated performance. The television show "Rock Island" was produced by Belarus Television and highlighted not only Belarusan-language bands, but English-language Jazz-based groups such as Zindjian, as well as some Russian-language groups. The show was filmed in different kinds of concert spaces which were manipulated in order to suggest the sophisticated level of rock, of rock venues, as well as the high level of program production.[6]

In 1993, Ulis, Krama, and Pałac were showcased in two "Rock Island" programs. The two programs were differentiated by the implied setting for the performance, the amount of control the producers had in constructing the concert ambiance, and the subsequent image of rock and rockers that was constructed for the public. The first of these programs tried to imply a casual concert space by suggesting the intimate setting of a bar/night club. The bands were encouraged to invite their friends and family to fill the tables that had been arranged in one of the studios of Belarus TV. The station also provided beer for both the performers and for the audience, hoping to encourage a festive mood. Cameras rolling and music playing, the audience contributed to the club scene by expressing their enthusiasm and dancing in front of the groups. Musicians and audience shared the implied intimacy of the space that was darkly lit, crowded with tables, and was devoid of a separation between the performers and their audience. The beer, the music, the company, and the unusual context all contributed to the club environment. From the point of view of the producers, this concert construction and this ritual space was a relative success. The groups were presented as accessible, the concert experience was intimate and desirable, and at no time were the per-

154   Of Mermaids and Rock Singers

formers or the audience overly assertive or out-of-control. Of course, no one
at home noticed that one of the drummers was so drunk that he fell off his
chair and dropped his sticks. The television cameras carefully mediated the
event.

The second taping of the program was not intimate in nature and therefore seemed harder to control. The set had been constructed on the stage of
the Miensk Military "Dom" [House/Center], and the production staff was
hoping for a big crowd. The bands had their dressing rooms backstage and
arrived for sound checks throughout the afternoon. The main stage prop was
as dramatic as the club set had been subtle. Enormous massive white letters
spelling "rock" filled the back of the space. Lighting technicians were check-
ing floods and spotlights, and the sound engineer was busy accommodating
the needs of each band. The resulting stage show was smooth and professional. While the bands performed with their usual technical and expressive
abilities, this taping venue backfired. Although the taping had been advertised throughout the city, the producers had chosen a late afternoon start for
the concert. The velvet-backed seats of the formal auditorium were hardly
filled by show time. The producers eventually invited a few military cadet
classes to sit in on the concert to suggest the presence of a numerous and
enthusiastic public. On camera the effect was somewhat successful.
However, it seemed that these bands were missing a public with which to
connect. As a result, the performances lacked the energy generated from the
interaction between the performer and the crowd.

"Rock Island" producers were trying to promote the acceptance of rock
and to encourage the growth of rock-centered programming. They were ultimately striving to normalize the rock genre for general Belarusan audiences,
to bring rock from its place in the cultural underground and place it in the
media mainstream. Other concert organizers were intent on the same goal.
However, their strategies emphasized the rebellious, the national, and the
sometimes outrageous aspects associated with rock and rockers.

Villi Simaška, a head producer with Belarusan Youth Programming
[Biełaruskaje Maładziožnaje Radyjo] had been committed to the promotion of
Belarusan-language rock well before sovereignty and Belarusan-language
legislation. He continued to manage rock interviews for the radio in 1993. His
attempt to give rock credibility while still preserving its social edge was
apparent on many occasions. Simaška was however exceptionally respected
amongst the rock community. He was not only a supportive and scrupulous
professional, but he was also a fan, and therefore his enthusiasm gave him
credibility amongst performers and amongst rock audiences.

The most explicitly political performance by these rockers was at a concert that was aggressively anti-Soviet and nationalistic. Simaška together
with Victor Čyzin, public relations director of the publicity and production
wing of Youth Radio, Kovcheg, as well as most of the Belarusan-language

Figure 9.1: Rock Against the Revolution [Rok Suprać Revalucyjaŭ] Concert Logo. Design by Lavon Volsky. Used by permission of the artist. (as used for the J-Card from the cassette-album *Rock Against the Revolution: Concert*, Kovcheg 1994).

bands cooperated in this construction of rock as a political and social expression.[7]

The concert was held in the auditorium of the Foreign Language Institute in central Miensk. The auditorium lacked the official trappings of a classical concert hall. The seats were wooden, the walls painted an institutional green, and the stage, though adequate, was neither large nor well-equipped. Against the backdrop of the black velvet curtain on the stage the organizers had hung an enormous red poster that announced the theme of the concert: a cartoon parody of Lenin playing an electric guitar with the words "Rock Against the Revolution" (Figure 9.1). However humorous, the image served to proclaim that this concert was conceived as a political state-

156 Of Mermaids and Rock Singers

ment, and that the performers and the audience would be participants and witnesses to both political protest and celebration. The obviously comical likeness was a blatant critique of the Soviet-era infatuation with the likeness of Lenin. The Revolution, touted and celebrated by Soviet propaganda as the true beginning of that country's history, was the focus of the protest. The ability and freedom to protest was the basis for celebration.

The concert, though conceptualized as a public deconstruction of Lenin's Bolshevik Revolution, did not demand a serious or militant response from the performers nor from the audience. Villi Simaška was the MC for the evening and set the tone for the event. He introduced all of the groups and then brought them out on stage for a quick interview after each performance. Kasia Kamockaja and I (I had been invited to perform with Novaje Nieba for the evening), were reintroduced and asked to make a public toast over several shots of vodka. The appropriation of the toasting ritual onto the rock stage shaped the event in two ways. It added a familiar personal character to the event, offering the audience the opportunity to witness an intimate gesture from their rock idols. At the same time, the toast represented a formal recognition of the significance of the concert's theme. At times kitchy, at times poignant, the concert suggested the playfulness of the rock genre, and the intellectual and national overtones of the movement as a whole.

Ulis, Krama, Novaje Nieba, and Mroja all performed that evening. As a final gesture of group solidarity, members of these bands came together for the last tune and sang the song Sluckaja Brama [The Gates of Slutsk, Bonda, Siarhiej Knysh] which was made popular by the first Belarusan-language band Bonda. The text draws on certain historical associations that are significant to the theme of the concert. The historical significance of the city of Slutsk[8] is also tied to the defense of Belarus against the Bolsheviks. In 1920, the leadership of the Belarusan Democratic Republic organized the Slutsk Brigade, an army of 10,000 ill-equipped volunteers who tried to hold back the advancing Bolshevik army. After five weeks of battle and tremendous losses the Brigade was defeated. The battle and its historical site are part of anti-Bolshevik symbolism and provided a powerful climax to the anti-Revolution concert.

The refrain for the song is sung to a low-register chant-like melody. The last line of the refrain, "I am your guard," places the rock singer at the site of battle as he adopts the role of protector. The historical significance of the song, its origins in the early part of the Belarusan-language rock movement, and the implied connection between the rocker and the guardian were emphasized further in the television broadcast of the concert. The rehearsal for the final song had been taped in the rehearsal studio shared by Mroja and Novaje Nieba. Crowded into the room in the back of the Miensk Philharmonia, band members coordinated instrumentals and vocals while

Rock and Revolution

Belarus TV looked on. The entire concert was also broadcast on national television.

The capacity crowd responded to the concert with loud enthusiasm. In the smoky auditorium a few Belarusan flags waived between numbers. The reach of the concert, its political message, and its politically conscious construction of the rock movement reached a national audience. There was nothing ambiguous about the kind of associations that were being suggested about rock.

The mediation of rock through rock concert venues is the main resource for contextualizing the rock movement and its musicians for both local and national audiences. Advertising campaigns for recordings and performances, associated with music industry mediation, are not part of the Belarusan rock context. The intent of the rocker in defining his/her performance space is therefore often secondary to the strategies of the media that frame their televised performances, or of song festival organizers who present rock in relation to other popular genres. In concert, rock is constructed according to: (1) the nature of the performance venue, (2) the implied value given to rock within the presentation, (3) live broadcast versus mediated taping of programming, and (4) the use of an overt theme to establish a clear association between rock and a cultural, social, or political idea.

Despite the variety of venues, and the occasional loss of control over the representation of their music, rockers continued to perform, sometimes blurring the impact of their self-defined image. Ulis, whose rock philosophy is articulated as non-political, performed at the "Revolution" concert. Pałac, whose membership in the rock community was still questioned by established bands, skirted the border between the acceptable and the non-acceptable by playing in the Maładečna Festival as well as in the midnight rock concert. Kamockaja was not invited to play in the *Rock Island* tapings.

It is therefore difficult to consistently reconcile the messages being mediated by concert organizers and by the rockers themselves. It is clear that some of the most unified messages have a strong basis in the cultural Renaissance movement. This, together with the association between rock and the urban cultural underground, continue to encourage a nationalistic understanding of the rock concert as a public demonstration, as a public celebration of nation, and as a potential opportunity for the public expression of new identities.

* * *

As a movement, Belarusan rock announced a conceptual connection with Belarusan culture and self-determination from its inception. The pro-West, youth rebellion associations encouraged the official Soviet response to the genre which Kolya Vasin labels as *rockophobia* (1991, 32–33). Belarusan rockers began by choosing a subjugated language, and by recognizing and communicating the value of a Belarusan aesthetic. For those invested in

158   Of Mermaids and Rock Singers

Belarusan popular culture, first impressions of the rock movement were specifically articulated in relation to cultural assertion (Martynienka and Mialhuj, 1991).

The potency of political and cultural processes in post-Soviet Belarus provides a unique and often problematic backdrop for musicians making rock music. Rebellion was only partly about challenging cultural policy. The most significant rebellion was against public opinion that had been shaped by a colonialist legacy and continued to dominate attitudes towards Belarusan culture and language. In order to respond to the music, audiences had to overcome the negative associations with the prototypical rock musician and had to conquer negative sentiments about the value of indigenous language and culture. At the height of independence activism (1989–1990), evaluations of rock as cultural expression became tied to social and cultural awareness of the musician. The result was a brand of social criticism that differentiated bands and their music according to connections with national consciousness. Bands were approved if they were considered sincere or nationally-aware. By extension, rock journalists often used a nationalist framework to interpret the music and the expressive intent of the musician.[9] The prominence of cultural reinvention in the public sphere threatened to pigeonhole the rock genre into the anti-establishment category so popular in social criticism.

While the late eighties were characterized by the push for independence, the beginning of the next decade would be characterized by the deconstruction of past attitudes and the initial construction of a new confident psyche for the nation. Some of the first Belarusan rock bands that emerged in the 1980s were aware of the momentum of that time. They had been inspired by it and had served to generate much of the public energy. These bands, and new additions to the rock community eventually placed themselves and their music against the backdrop of the construction of nation. For example, Mroja [NRM] began as a clandestine rock band singing in a marginalized language. Their music and their language choice shaped their fan-base and determined their reputation as supporters of the national renaissance movement. Their choice of language was in itself a powerful symbol of their convictions. Eventually, their repertoire would also reflect an anti-establishment (read anti-Soviet) position. Their song "Aŭstralijskaja Polka" was a rare public treatment of the dangers of Chernobyl at a time when Soviet officials were denying the continuing impact of the catastrophe. Ulis connects the pro-Belarusan character of their music of the late 1980s with the national climate of those times. While their music became more introspective in later releases, they maintain their connection with the state of the nation by exploring the modern Belarusan identity in their texts and in their choice of language. By 1993 it was evident that contemporary cultural issues informed audiences

Rock and Revolution 159

and musicians at some point in the dialogue between music-maker and music consumer.

The bands which defined the Belarusan rock movement in the early nineties adapted Belarusan resources and implied cultural assertion in a variety of ways. It became clear that the associations with Belarusan language and culture that these bands constructed and implied did not necessarily signal a singular nationalistic message. Pałac's public image and their overt borrowing from traditional repertoires would seem to suggest that this group of musicians was particularly invested in disseminating a cultural and political message. Their use of Belarusan in interviews, their enthusiastic public descriptions of their expedition efforts, and their performance image dominated by traditional dress implied that they were fully invested in the cultural renaissance movement. However, this band which most overtly advertised a Belarusan identity was least articulate about the politics of the time and seemed to avoid performances at events that were framed by a political message, for example the *Rock Against the Revolution* concert. Composer and manager Juraś Vydronak commented that they did not want to become embroiled in political debate (September 1993). Nevertheless they did not object when their music gained notoriety and public attention as a result of interpretations based on the renaissance movement.

The band Ulis, which had emerged at the cusp of political change, were clearly articulate about the effects of their music on political and cultural attitudes. They acknowledged that their first album, *The Stranger*, reflected the cultural momentum of the late eighties. However, subsequent releases, as well as the band's philosophy, were indicative of a lifestyle definition and of an artistic and aesthetic development that they considered separate from the socialist interpretations typical of post-sovereignty Belarusan criticism (interview Korjan 1993). Ulis' position reflected their appreciation of a Belarusan language aesthetic that they saw as informing and defining their musical style. Their goal was to create Belarusan rock and their Belarusan-specific choices were a natural extension of their cultural identifies and musical experience. Other than language choice, Ulis' performance did not advertise an ethnic/cultural image.

Kasia Kamockaja and Novaje Nieba evolved out of the bardic genre, a song tradition that was literary in style and very often political in theme. Kamockaja's self-fashioning into a member of the rock community emphasized her interest in musical experimentation, an avant-garde style, but equally emphasized a public position that was overtly political. She is the most assertive about current cultural and political issues and considers Belarusan rock music to be a fundamentally political genre, a venue for social and cultural commentary: "This music is a social protest and only in Belarus does it retain this nationalist goal" [as compared to the rock produced in other post-Soviet states] ("Naviny," 560).

160   Of Mermaids and Rock Singers

Mroja, the oldest veteran rock band can be seen to reflect various intents. Their self-described hard rock style can include some stylistic surprises. Their 1989 song "Aŭstralijskaja Polka" (28th Star) combines the instrumental style of the hard rock genre with the rhythmic familiarity of the traditional polka. Their connection to the political climate in Belarus is emphasized through their topical themes and the commentaries that emerge in their music as well as their name [National Republic of Dream].

These bands demonstrate that Belarusan-language rock bands do not interchangeably represent a single political stance or cultural aesthetic. The application of an all-encompassing politically-based definition of the Belarusan rock movement is therefore problematic. Individual inspirations and expressive intent reflect a general membership in a rock movement, but their self-fashioning, the images these bands offer in the public sphere are varied. As Pałac demonstrates, overt use of cultural symbols and costumes do not necessarily reflect a political position. Musical approaches also reflect preferences for different musical styles and a menagerie of appropriations from both Western and local musical practice. These bands are in a constant state of stylistic evolution. They are linked by lifestyle, by language choice, and by logistic challenges. In addition, a band may agree to construct a particular public image, but the group is still a collection of individuals. These members might invest in the philosophy of the band in differing degrees.

For the Pieśniary, the Belarusan language, the costuming, and the use of traditional repertoire served to construct an image of a band at once invested in a specific traditional culture and in Soviet anti-rock rhetoric. It was member Lavon Bartkievič who most consistently articulated a commitment to the Belarusan language and supported an aesthetic ideal based on a valuing of traditional musical repertoire. Despite Pałac's avoidance of any overt political intentions, members Veronika Kruhłova and Dzima Vajciuškievič were politically active outside the activities of the band. They participated in pro-Democracy election campaigns and were aware of the potential impact of current policies and planned referendums. In 1996 both Kruhłova and Vajciuškievič would create a new band called Kriwi (a reference to the Krivichans, a tribe who inhabited the Belarusan territory in the ninth century). The music of this new group would also recontextualize traditional elements within a contemporary musical framework. The political position of this band, and their overt support of Belarusan self-determination would become a clear aspect of their image.

The interpretation of these Belarusan bands requires that the reading of the music and of an implied intent be reflective of musical experimentation, the impact of a changing urban context, and the opportunities available to record and to perform. With the 1994 election of Alaksandar Lukašenka, the momentum which had developed as a result of the Belarusan cultural renaissance was summarily stopped. Symbols of cultural identity were out-

Rock and Revolution 161

lawed and education and language reforms were nullified. The Belarusan language was barely heard in the media. Pro-democracy political groups were harassed, demonstrators were incarcerated, and supporters of the cultural renaissance found themselves in the still familiar environment of the urban underground. Belarusan rock bands were again being heard against the backdrop of political instability. For many groups, the challenges of functioning under the cultural restrictions of the new regime were an extension of their already established political awareness. Kamockaja recorded *President Go Home* (1995) and Mroja became the National Republic of Mroja. Rock critics were once again contextualizing rock according to the issues of the current political moment, acknowledging that the key act of rebellion by these bands was to continue singing in the Belarusan language.

NOTES

[1] *Svaboda,* "Naviny" 1999: 29(560).

[2] For example Basoviśča, in eastern Poland.

[3] The Rock Festival is a central aspect of Western rock performance. Roy Shuker points out that throughout the sixties these festival venues played "a central role in the myth making of rock, especially through creating the ideology of a rock community" (1992: 209).

[4] Some band members sought other work in order to subsidize their music, some working for Belarus radio, or in the case of one Palac musician playing for funerals and other religious services. None of the musicians emphasized this aspect of their lifestyles. For them, being a rocker also forcibly required some economic hardship.

[5] Despite the less-than central role given to rock in the festival, rockers had agreed to perform because of the prestige associated with the event and, as Kamockaja emphasized, it gave them a chance to "play on good equipment" (interview 1993).

[6] See V. Korjan and S. Kraŭchanka's comments about the Belarusan media, and television programming, and their impact on rock groups (also see Chapter Six,).

[7] Palac was not present at this concert. At the time, they seemed to avoid any explicit association between their music and political events.

[8] The city of Slutsk, found in South-central Belarus, dates back to the 6th century and is considered a significant city-center in the economic and cultural development of those principalities that eventually defined Belarus. In 1441 the city obtained municipal self-rule (Zaprudnik 1994, 70).

[9] The influence of the cultural renaissance on rock criticism is most obvious in *Through the Prism of Rock* (1991) by Miensk journalists Vitaŭt Martynienka and Anatol Mialhuj. In this source melody, text, performance, and musicians are considered through the "prism" of cultural consciousness that serves as a marker for authenticity and musical value.

Bibliography

Adamovič, A. "The Kupała-Kołas Century 1882–1982." *Journal of Byelorussian Studies* 5, no. 2 (1982): 5–26.

Adorno, Theodor. "On Popular Music." In *On the Record*, 301–314. New York: Pantheon, 1990.

Aivazian, A.A. *Rok 1955/1991*. St. Petersburg: Trial, 1992.

Alexander, Jeffery C. "Bringing Democracy Back In: Universalistic Solidarity and the Civic Sphere." In *Intellectuals and Politics: Social Theory in a Changing World*. Vol. 5, *Key Issues in Sociological Theory*, ed. Charles C. Lemert, 157–176. Newberry Park: Sage, 1991.

Allen, Robert, ed. *Channels of Discourse*. Chapel Hill: University of North Carolina Press, 1987.

American Folklife Center. *Ethnic Recordings in America: A Neglected Heritage*. Washington: Library of Congress, 1982.

Anderson, Benedict. *Imagined Communities: Reflections on the Origin and Spread of Nationalism*. London: Verso, 1983.

Arsiennieva, Natalla. Miž bierahami: *Selected Poetry of Natalla Arsiennieva 1920–1970*. New York: Byelorussian Institute of Arts and Sciences Inc., 1979.

Ashcroft, Bill, et al. *The Post-Colonial Studies Reader*. London: Routledge, 1995.

Ashis, Nandy. *The Intimate Enemy: Loss and Recovery of Self Under Colonialism*. Oxford: Oxford University Press, 1983.

Bahdanovič, Maksim. "Apocryf." In *Vianok* (Garland of Poetic Heritage), 234–236. Munich & New York: Baćkauśćyna, Byelorussian Institute of Arts and Sciences, 1960.

Bandarchyk, Vasilii, et al. *Balady u dzviukh knihakh*. Minsk: Navuka i Tekhnika, 1978.

164 Bibliography

Barszczewski, A. "Romantic Elements in Kołas' 'Symon Muzyka.'" *Journal of Byelorussian Studies* 5, no. 2 (1982): 27–43.

Bartashevich, Halina, and L. Salavei.*Vesnavyia pesni*. Minsk: Navuka i tekhnika, 1979.

Becker, A.L. "An Essay on Translating the Art of Music." In *Karawitan: Source Readings in Javanese Gamelan and Vocal Music*, ed. Judith Becker. Vol. 2. Ann Arbor: University of Michigan Press, 1984.

Belbéoch, Bella, and Roger Belbéoch. "La Catastrophe de Tchernobyl: Eléments pour un bilan." *Stratégies énergétiques, Biosphère & Société* (1990): 53–58.

Bykaŭ, Vasil. "Demakracyja pakul niazdolnaja procistajać kamunafašyzmu." *Svaboda* 22 (1995).

Bird, Thomas E., ed. *Zapisy 17: Proceedings of the Twenty-fifth Anniversary Symposium of the Byelorussian Institute of Arts and Sciences, February 1977*. New York: St. Sophia Press, 1983.

Blum, Stephen. "Ethnomusicologists and Modern Music History." In *Ethnomusicology and Modern Music History*, 1–20. Urbana: University of Chicago Press, 1991.

Bohlman, Philip. *The Study of Folk Music in the Modern World*. Bloomington: Indiana University Press, 1988.

——— "Pilgrimage, Politics, and the Musical Remapping of the New Europe." *Ethnomusicology* 40, no. 3 (1996): 375–412.

Brackett, David. *Interpreting Popular Music*. Cambridge: Cambridge University Press, 1995.

Bright, Brenda-Jo. *Looking High and Low: Art and Cultural Identity*. Tucson: University of Arizona Press, 1995.

Broughton, Simon, et al. *World Music: The Rough Guide*. London: Penguin, 1994.

Broŭka, P.U., et al. *Bielaruskaja Savieckaja Encyklapedyja*. Miensk: Akademija Navuk BSSR, 1973.

Brown, J.F. *Surge to Freedom: the End of Communist Rule in Eastern Europe*. Durham: Duke University Press, 1991.

Brunt, Rosalind. "Engaging with the Popular: Audiences for Mass Culture and What to Say about Them." In *Cultural Studies*, ed. Lawrence Grossberg, Carrie Nelson, and Paula Treichler, 69–76. London: Routledge, 1992.

"Byelorussians." In *The Canadian Family Tree: Canada's Peoples*. Prepared by the Multiculturalism Directorate, Department of the Secretary of State, Don Mills, 38–42. Ontario: Corpus, 1979.

Calder, Jeff. "Living by Night in the Land of Opportunity." In *Present Tense Rock & Roll and Culture*, ed. Anthony DeCurtis, 271–301. Durham: Duke University Press, 1992.

Bibliography

165

Carew, Jan. "The African and the Indian Presence: Some Aspects of Historical Distortion." *Race and Class* 27, no. 1 (1985): 29–44.

Chambers, Ian. *Border Dialogues: Journeys in Postmodernity*. London: Routledge, 1990.

Clem, Ralph S. "Belorussians." In *The Nationalities Question in the Soviet Union*, ed. Graham Smith, 109–122. London: Longman, 1990.

Chatterjee, Partha. "Nationalism as a Problem." In *Nationalist Thought and the Colonial World: A Derivative Discource*. Japan and London: Zeb Books for United Nations University, 1986.

Clifford, James. *The Predicament of Culture: Twentieth Century Ethnography, Literature and Art*. Cambridge: Harvard University Press, 1988.

Clifford, James, and George E. Marcus, eds. *Writing Culture: The Poetics and Politics of Ethnography*. Berkeley: University of California Press, 1987.

Colton, Timothy, and Robert Legvold, eds. *After the Soviet Union: From Empire to Nations*. New York: Norton, 1992.

Cushman, Thomas. *Notes from Underground: Rock Music Counterculture in Russia*. New York: State University of New York Press, 1998.

Cutler, Chris. "What is Popular Music." In *Popular Music Perspectives 2: Papers from the Second International Conference on Popular Music Studies, Reggio Emilia, September 19–24, 1983*. Göteborg: IASPM, 1985.

Davis, Martha Ellen. "Careers, 'Alternative Careers,' and the Unity Between Theory and Practice in Ethnomusicology." *Ethnomusicology* 36, no. 3 (1992): 361–387.

DeCurtis, Anthony, ed. *Present Tense: Rock & Roll and Culture*. Durham: Duke University Press, 1992.

Denisoff, Serge R. "Massification and Popular Music: A Review." *Journal of Popular Culture* 9, no. 4 (1976): 886–894.

Dettmar, Kevin D.H., and William Richey, eds. *Reading Rock and Roll*. New York: Columbia University Press, 1993.

Dingley, James, and Arnold McMillin, eds. *Occasional Papers in Belarusan Studies*. No. 1. London: School of Slavonic and Eastern European Studies, University of London, 1995.

Dovnar-Zapolsky, M. "The Basis of White-Russia's State Individuality." In *Byelorussian Statehood: Reader and Bibliography*, ed. Vitaut Kipel and Zora Kipel. 1911. Reprint, New York: Byelorussian Institute of Arts and Sciences, 1988.

Drinker, Sophie. *Music and Women: The Story of Women in Their Relation to Music*. 1948. Reprint, New York: University of New York Press, 1995.

Dugin, Alexander. "The Phenomenon of Rock in the USSR." In *Soviet Rock: 25 years in the underground +five years of freedom*. Moscow: Progress Publishers, 1990.

Elatov, V. *Ladovyie Osnovy Belorusskoi Narodnoi Muziki*. Miensk: Navuka i Tekhnika, 1964.

166 Bibliography

Ewen, Stuart. *All Consuming Images: The Politics of Style in Contemporary Culture*. New York: Basic Books, 1988.

Fanon, Franz. *A Dying Colonialism*. New York: Grove Weidensfeld, 1965.

Feshbach, Murray, and Alfred Friendly. *Ecocide in the USSR: Health and Nature Under Siege*. New York: Basic Books, 1992.

Fiadosik, A.C., ed. *Paezija Bielaruskaha Ziemliarodnaha Kaliendara*. Vol. 10, Biełaruskaja Narodnaja Tvorćaść. Miensk: Navuka i Technika, 1992.

Fischer, Michael, M. J. "Ethnicity and the Post-Modern Arts of Memory." In *Writing Culture: The Poetics and Politics of Ethnography*, ed. James Clifford and George Marcus. Berkeley: University of California Press, 1987.

Fiske, John. *Understanding Popular Culture*. London: Routledge, 1989.

———"Cultural Studies and the Culture of Everyday Life." In *Cultural Studies*, ed. Lawrence Grossberg, Carrie Nelson, and Paula Treichler, 174–181. London: Routledge, 1992.

——— *Reading the Popular*. London: Routledge, 1995.

Flacks, Dick. "Making History and Making Theory: Notes on How Intellectuals Seek Relevance." In *Intellectuals and Politics*, 3–18. Vol. 5, *Key Issues in Sociological Theory*, ed. Charles C. Lemert. London: Sage Publications, 1992.

Foucault, Michel. "What Is an Author?" In *The Foucault Reader*, 101–120. New York: Random House, 1984.

Frith, Simon. *Sound Effects: Youth Leisure, and the Politics of Rock 'n' Roll*. New York: Pantheon Books, 1981.

——— "Towards an Aesthetic of Popular Music." In *Music and Society: The Politics of Composition, Performance, and Reception*, ed. Richard Leppert and Susan McClary, 133–149. London: Cambridge University Press, 1987.

——— *Music for Pleasure: Essays in the Sociology of Pop*. New York: Routledge, 1988.

——— "The Cultural Study of Popular Music." In *Cultural Studies*, ed. Lawrence Grossberg, Carrie Nelson, and Paula Treichler, 174–182. London: Routledge, 1992.

——— *Performing Rites: In the Value of Popular Music*. Cambridge: Harvard University Press, 1996.

Frith, Simon, and Andrew Goodwin, eds. *On Record: Rock Pop and the Written Word*. New York: Pantheon, 1990.

Garofalo, Reebee, ed. *Rockin' the Boat: Mass Music and Mass Movements*. Boston: South End Press, 1992.

Garth, Terry. *A subject and name index to articles on the Slavonic and East European langauges and literatures, music and theatre, libraries and the press, contained in English-language journals, 1920–1975*. Nottingham: University Library, University of Nottingham, 1976.

Geertz, Clifford. *Local Knowledge*. New York: Basic Books, 1983.

Bibliography 167

Giroux, Henry A. *Border Crossings: Cultural Workers and the Politics of Education.* New York: Routledge, 1992.

Glazer, Nathan, and Daniel P. Moynihan, eds. *Ethnicity: Theory and Experience.* Cambridge: Harvard University Press, 1975.

Golde, Peggy. *Women in the Field: Anthropological Experiences.* 2nd ed. Berkeley: University of California Press, 1970.

Grenier, L., and J. Guilbault. "Authority Revisited: Methodological Issues in Anthropology and Popular Music Studies." Paper presented at the Thirty-fourth Annual Meeting of the Society for Ethnomusicology, Boston, Mass., November 8–12, 1989.

Gross, Jan Tomasz. *Revolution from Abroad: The Soviet Conquest of Poland, West Ukraine and West Belorussia.* New Jersey: Princeton University, 1988.

Guilbault, Jocelyne. *Zouk: World Music in the West Indies.* With Gage Averill, Édouard Benoit, and Gregory Rabess. Chicago: University of Chicago Press, 1993.

Hall, Stuart. "Cultural Studies and its Theoretical Legacies." In *Cultural Studies,* ed. Lawrence Grossberg, Carrie Nelson, and Paula Treichler, 277–287. London: Routledge, 1992.

Harris, Marvin. *Cows, Pigs, Wars, and Witches.* New York: Vintage, 1974.

Hebdige, Dick. "Style as Homology and Signifying Practice." In *On the Record.* 56–65. New York: Pantheon, 1990.

Heider, Karl G. *Ethnographic Film.* Austin: University of Texas Press, 1999.

Henry, Paget, and Carl Stone, eds. *The Newer Caribbean: Decolonization, Democracy, and Development.* Philadelphia: Institute for the Study of Human Issues, 1983.

Hollis, Susan Tower, Linda Pershing, and M. Jane Young, eds. *Feminist Theory and the Study of Folklore.* Illinois: University of Illinois Press, 1993.

Horoško, Leŭ. "Kastuś Kalinoŭski." *Journal of Byelorussian Studies* 1, no. 1 (1965): 30–35.

Horowitz, Donald L. *Ethnic Groups in Conflict.* Berkeley: University of California Press, 1985.

Hosking, Geoffrey. *The First Socialist Society: A History of the Soviet Union from Within.* Cambridge: Harvard University Press, 1985.

Hutchison, John, and Anthony Smith, eds. *Nationalism.* Oxford: Oxford University Press, 1994.

Ignatieff, Michael. *Blood and Belonging.* New York: Farrar, Straus, and Giroux, 1993.

Isaacs, Harold R. "Basic Group Identity: The Idols of the Tribe." In *Ethnicity: Theory and Experience,* ed. Nathan Glazer and Daniel P. Moynihan, 29–52. Cambridge: Harvard University Press, 1975.

Janovič, Sakrat. *Miniatures.* Ed. and Trans. Shirin Akiner. London: The Anglo-Byelorussian Society, 1984.

168 Bibliography

Jedlicki, Jerzy. "Heritage and Collective Responsibility." In *The Political Responsibility of Intellectuals*, ed. Ian MacLean, Alan Montefiore, and Peter Winch, 53–76. Cambridge: Cambridge University Press, 1990.

Jemal, Geydar. "The Roots." In *Soviet Rock*, 11–28. Moscow: Progress Publishers, 1990.

Kartomi, Margaret. "The Processes and Results of Musical Culture Contact: A Discussion of Terminology and Concepts." *Ethnomusicology* 25, no. 2 (1981): 227–249.

Keil, Charles. "Participatory Discrepancies and the Power of Music." *Cultural Anthropology* 2, no. 3 (1987): 275–283.

Kennedy, Michael D. *Professionals, Power, and Solidarity in Poland: A Critical Sociology of Soviet-type Society*. London: Cambridge University Press, 1991.

Kipel, Vitaut. "Byelorussians." In *The New Jersey Ethnic Experience*, ed. Barbara Cunningham, 88–107. Union City, New Jersey: Wm. H. Wise and Co., 1977.

——— *Byelorussian Americans and Their Communities in Cleveland*. Cleveland: Cleveland Ethnic Heritage Studies, Cleveland State University, 1982.

——— "The Early Byelorussian Presence in America." In *Zapisy 17: Proceedings of the Twenty-fifth Anniversary Symposium of the Byelorussian Institute of Arts and Sciences, February 1977*, 113–131. New York: St. Sophia Press, 1983.

Kołas, Jakub. *Symon Muzyka* (Simon the Musician). Minsk: Belarus, 1972.

Konoplya, E.F. "Global Ecological Consequences of the Chernobyl Nuclear Explosion." Radiobiology Institute of the Belarusian Academy of Sciences, 1992.

Koskoff, Ellen, ed. *Women and Music in Cross-Cultural Perspective*. Urbana: University of Illinois Press, 1987.

Krader, Barbara. "Slavic Folk Music; Forms of Singing and Self-Identity." *Society for Ethnomusicology* 31, no. 1 (1987): 9–17.

Kreūski, J. "Kastuś Kalinoūski: Anti-Russian Uprising of 1863." *Belarusian Review* (spring 1993): 13–14.

Kulikovič, V. *The Whiteruthenian Music*. New York: Byelorussian Institute of Arts and Sciences, 1953.

——— *Byelorussian Songs and Dances*. Cleveland: Byelorussian Youth Association, 1960.

——— *Kaladouščyki*. Cleveland: Byelorussian Youth Association, 1961.

——— *Rodnyja Matyvy*. New York: Byelorussian Institute of Arts and Sciences, 1967.

Lane, David. *Soviet Society Under Perestroika*. London: Unwin Hyman, 1990.

Lemert, Charles C. "Intellectuals and Politics: Social Theory in a Changing World." In *Key Issues in Sociological Theory*. Vol 5. London: Sage Publications, 1991.

Bibliography 169

"Letters to Gorbachev: New Documents from Soviet Byelorussia." London: Association of Byelorussians in Great Britain, 1987.

Lewis, George, H. "Popular Music: Symbolic Resource and Transformer in Society." *International Review of the Aesthetics and Sociology of Music* 13, no. 2 (1982): 183–189.

Lićvinka, Vasil. *Sviaty i Abrady*. Minsk: Belarus, 1998.

Lozka, Aleś. *Bielaruski narodny kaliandar*. Minsk: Polymia, 1993.

———— *Bielaruskaja Batlejka: Kaliandarnyja i abradnyja hulni*. Minsk: Technalohija, 1997.

Lubachko, Ivan S. *Belorussia Under Soviet Rule, 1917–1957*. Lexington: University Press of Kentucky, 1972.

Łuckievič, Anton. "A Summary Glance into the History and the Situation of White Russia." In *Byelorussian Statehood: Reader and Bibliography*, ed. Vitaut Kipel and Zora Kipel. 1919. Reprint, New York: Byelorussian Institute of Arts and Sciences, 1988.

Lysloff, René T.A. "Mozart in Mirrorshades: Ethnomusicology, Technology, and the Politics of Representation." *Society for Ethnomusicology* 41, no. 2 (1997): 206–219.

MacLean, Ian, et al. *The Political Responsibility of Intellectuals*. Cambridge: Cambridge University Press, 1990.

Manuel, Peter. "Marxism, Nationalism, and Popular Music in Revolutionary Cuba." *Popular Music* 6, no. 2 (1987): 161–178.

Marples, David R. *Belarus: From Soviet Rule to Nuclear Catastrophe*. Edmonton: University of Alberta Press, 1997.

Martynienka, Vitaŭt, and Anatol Mialhuj. Praz rok-pryzmu: zbornik artykułau i intervju [Through the Prism of Rock]. English introduction by Maria Paula Survilla. New York: Byelorussian Institute of Arts and Sciences, 1989.

Mažejka, Z.J. *Pesni beloruskoho Paazer'ia*. Minsk: Nauka i tekhnika, 1981.

———— *Pesni Bieloruskogo Polesia 1 & 2*. Moscow: Sovietski Kompozitor, 1984.

———— *Kaliendarno-pesennaia kul'tura Belorussii: opyt sistemno-tipologicheskogo issledovanniia*. Miensk: Nauka i tekhnika, 1985.

———— *Bielaruskaja Etnamuzykalohija*. Minsk: Technalohija, 1997.

———— "Belarus." In *The Garland Encyclopedia of World Music*, ed.Tim Rice, James Porter, Chris Goertzen. Vol. 8. New York: Garland, 2000.

McClary, Susan. *Feminine Endings: Music, Gender, and Sexuality*. Minneapolis: University of Minnesota Press, 1991.

———— "Same as it Ever Was: Youth Culture and Music." In *Microphone Fiends: Youth Music Youth Culture*, ed. Andrew Ross and Tricia Rose, 29–40. New York: Routledge, 1994.

McMillin, Arnold B. *Die Literatur der Weissrussen: A History of Byelorussian Literature from its Origins to the Present Day*. Giessen: Wilhem Schmitz, 1977.

Bibliography

Medvedev, Grigori. *No Breathing Room: The Aftermath of Chernobyl*. New York: Basic Books, 1993.

Merriam, Alan P. *The Anthropology of Music*. Evanston, Ill.: North Western University Press, 1964.

Middleton, Richard. *Studying Popular Music*. Philadelphia: Open University Press, 1990.

Minh-ha, Trinh. *The Moon Waxes Red: Representation, Gender and Cultural Politics*. New York: Routledge, 1991.

Montefiore, Alan. "The Political Responsibility of Intellectuals." In *The Political Responsibility of Intellectuals*, ed. Ian MacLean, Alan Montefiore, and Peter Winch, 201–228. Cambridge: Cambridge University Press, 1990.

Mucharynskaja, L.C. Biełaruskaja Narodnaja Pieśnia. Minsk: Navuka i tekhnika, 1977.

Nazina, Inna. *Belorusskie narodnye muzykal'nye instrumenty*. Minsk: Navuka i tekhnika, 1979.

——— *Belorusskie narodnye muzykal'nye instrumenty: strunnye*. Minsk: Navuka i tekhnika, 1982.

——— Žanićba Ciareški. Minsk: Navuka i tekhnika, 1993.

Ong, Walter. *Orality and Literacy: The Technologizing of the Word*. London: Methuen, 1982.

Paget, Henry. *The Newer Caribbean: Decolonization, Democracy, and Development*. Ed. Paget Henry and Carl Stone. Philadelphia: Institute for the Study of Human Issues, 1983.

Parsons, Talcott. "Some Theoretical Considerations on the Nature and Trends of Change of Ethnicity." In *Ethnicity: Theory and Experience*, ed. Nathan Glazer and Daniel P. Moynihan, 53–83. Cambridge: Harvard, 1975.

Pashkievich, Valentyna. *Fundamental Byelorussian*. Toronto: Harmony, 1974.

Patry-Tamushanski, R. "Byelorussian Renaissance Verse." *Journal of Byelorussian Studies* 1, no. 1 (1965): 23–29.

Paźniak, Zianon. *Kurapaty*. Miensk: Niezaležnaja vydavieckaja kampanija "Technalohija", 1994.

Picarda, Guy. "The Origins of Renaissance Polyphony." *Journal of Byelorussian Studies* 1, no. 2 (1965): 92–102.

——— *Minsk : a historical guide and short administrative, professional and commercial directory*. Minsk: Technalohija, 1994.

Pond, Irina. "Soviet Rock Lyrics: Their Content and Poetics." *Popular Music and Society* 11, no. 4 (1987): 75–92.

Pratt, Mary Louise. *Imperial Eyes: Travel Writing and Transculturation*. New York: Routledge, 1992.

Price, Joe, ed. *Byelorussian Review: Quarterly Information Bulletin*. California: Byelorussian-American Association, Inc., 1989.

Bibliography

Ramet, Sabrina. *Social Currents in Eastern Europe: The Sources and Meaning of the Great Transformation.* Durham: Duke University Press, 1991.

Ramet, Sabrina, ed. *Rocking the State.* Oxford: Westview Press, 1994.

Ramet, Sabrina, Sergei Zamascikov, and Robert Bird. "The Soviet Rock Scene." In *Rocking the State.* Oxford: Westview Press, 1994.

Rapawy, Stephen. "Nationality Composition of the Soviet Population." *Nationalities Papers* 8, no. 1 (1985): 70–83.

Rice, Timothy. "Eastern Europe." *Ethnomusicology* 29, no. 1 (1985): 151–153.

Rich, Vera, trans. *The Images Swarm Free: A Bilingual Selection of Poetry by Maksim Bahdanovič, Aleś Harun, and Žmitrok Biadula.* Ed. Arnold McMillan. London: The Anglo-Byelorussian Society, 1982.

Rich, Vera. "Maksim Bahdanovič in Byelorussian Literature." *Journal of Byelorussian Studies* I, no.1 (1965): 36–50.

——— *Like Fire Like Water: An Anthology of Byelorussian Poetry from 1828 to the Present Day.* London: George Allen & Unwin Ltd, 1971.

Royce-Peterson, Anya. *Ethnic Identity: Strategies of Diversity.* Bloomington: Indiana University Press, 1999.

Rushdie, Salman. "India At Five-O: The Anniversary of the End of British Rule is Being Greeted with Shoulder-Shrugging Sourness. And it's No Wonder."*Time* (August 11, 1997): 40–42.

——— *Imaginary Homelands: Essays and Criticism 1981–1991.* Granta: Viking-Penguin, 1997.

Ryback, Timothy. *Rock Around the Bloc.* New York and Oxford: Oxford University Press, 1990.

Sazyc, Joe. "Record Review." *Byelorussian Youth* 5, no. 43–44 (1974): 24.

Sadouski, John. *A History of Byelorussians in Canada.* Belleville, Ontario: Mika Publishing, 1981.

Said, Edward W. *Orientalism.* New York: Vintage, 1979.

Salaraŭ, Siarhej. "Navinka." *Naša Niva* (90) August 25. 1997.

Savicki, Stanisłaŭ. "A Historical Conspectus of the Sources of Byelorussian Law." *Journal of Byelorussian Studies* 1, no. 2 (1966): 110–112.

Schramm, Adelaide Reyes. "Ethnic Music, the Urban Area, and Ethnomusicology." *Sociologus* 29 (1979): 1–17.

Schwarz, Boris. *Music and Musical Life in Soviet Russia (1917–1981).* Bloomington: Indiana University Press, 1980.

Shepherd, John. "A Theoretical Analysis for the Sociomusicological Analysis of Popular Music." *Popular Music* 2 (1982): 145–178.

Shils, Edward. *Tradition.* Chicago: University of Chicago Press, 1981.

Shuker, Roy. *Understanding Popular Music.* London: Routledge, 1994.

——— *Key Concepts in Popular Music.* London: Routledge, 1998.

Shumway, David R. "Rock & Roll as a Cultural Practice." In *Present Tense: Rock & Roll and Culture*, ed. Anthony DeCurtis, 117–134. Durham: Duke University Press, 1992.

172 Bibliography

Siŭčyk, Viktar. *The Unknown War Against Belarus: A Secret Page of Modern History*. Minsk: Navukova-Papuliarnaje Vydannie, 1993.

Slobin, Mark. "Micromusics of the West: A Comparative Approach." *Ethnomusicology* 1 (1998): 1–87.

Soljenitsyne, Alexander. "L'hypocrisie du XXe siècle finissant." *L'express*, 2407 (1997): 50–52.

Stocking, George W., ed. *Objects and Others: Essays on Museums and Material Culture*. Madison: University of Wisconsin Press, 1985.

Survilla, Maria Paula. *Music and Identity: Balarusans Making Music in North America*. Master's thesis, University of Michigan, 1990.

———. "Introduction." In . Praz rok-pryzmu: zbornik artykułau i intervju [Through the Prism of Rock], by Vitaŭt Martynienka and Anatol Mialhuj. New York: Byelorussian Institute of Arts and Sciences, 1991.

———. "From Affirmation to Aesthetics: Belarus as Subject in Poetic and Musical Texts." In *Zapisy 20*, 43–49. New York: Belarusan Institute of Arts and Sciences, 1992.

———. "Rock Music in Belarus." In *Rocking the State*, ed. Sabrina Ramet, 219–242. Oxford: Westview Press, 1993.

———. "Belarus." In *The Garland Encyclopedia of World Music*, ed.Tim Rice, James Porter, Chris Goertzen. Vol. 8. New York: Garland, 2000.

Svaboda. "Jak zaŭždy, tolki horš." 4 (1996).

Swiss, Thomas, John Sloop, and Andrew Herman, eds. *Mapping the Beat: Popular Music and Contemporary Theory*. Oxford: Blackwell Publishers, 2000.

Szemere, Anna "The Politics of Marginality: A Rock Musical Subculture in Socialist Hungary in the Early 1980s." In *Rockin' the Boat*, ed. Reebee Garofalo, 92–114. Boston: South End Press, 1992.

Thornton, Sarah. "Moral Panic, The Media and British Rave Culture." In *Microphone Fiends: Youth Music Youth Culture*, ed. Andrew Ross and Tricia Rose, 176–192.New York: Routledge, 1994.

Titon, Jeff Todd. "Music, the Public Interest, and the Practice of Ethnomusicology." *Ethnomusicology* 36, no. 3 (1992): 315–321.

Trimillos, Ricardo D. "Music and Ethnic Identity: Strategies Among Overseas Filipino Youth." *Yearbook for Traditional Music* 18 (1986): 9–20.

Troitsky, Artemy. *Back in the U.S.S.R.: The True Story of Rock in Russia*. London: Omnibus Press, 1987.

———. "The Tree." In *Soviet Rock*. 29–62. Moscow: Progress Publishers, 1990.

Urban, Michael. "The Folklore of State Socialism: Semiotics and the Study of the Soviet State." *Soviet Studies* 25 (1983): 471–86.

Vakar, Nicolas P. *Belorussia: The Making of a Nation, A Case Study*. Harvard University Press, 1956.

Vasin, Kolya. "Notes from a Rock Museum." In *Soviet Rock*. 30–46. Moscow: Progress Publishers, 1990.

Bibliography

Volski, Lavon, and Jura Čyzin, eds. Biełaruski Rok-n-rol Teksty: Bonda, Krama, Mroja, Novaje Nieba, Ulis. Miensk: Kovcheg, 1994.

Wagner, Roy. *The Invention of Culture*. Chicago: University of Chicago Press, 1981.

Walser, Robert. *Running with the Devil: Power Gender and Madness in Heavy Metal Music*. Hanover and London: Wesleyan University Press, 1993.

Weber, Max. "The Nation." In *Nationalism*, ed. John Hutchison and Anthony Smith, 21–25. Oxford: Oxford University Press, 1994.

Wicke, Peter. "Rock Music: a Musical-Aesthetic Study." *Popular Music Journal* 2 (1982): 219–243.

——— "The Times They Are A-Changing: Rock Music and Political Change in East Germany." In *Rockin' the Boat*, ed. Reebee Garofalo, 81–92. Boston: South End Press, 1992.

Wolfe, Janet. *Aesthetics and the Sociology of Art*. London: George Allen & Unwin, 1983.

Jaškievič, Siarhiej. "Prablemy nacyianalnaj adukacyi." Hołas Radzimy 41, 2339 (1993).

Zajaravaŭ, V.A. ed. *Paleskaje Viasielle* . Minsk: Universiteckaje, 1984.

Zaprudnik, Jan. "Developments in Belorussia Since 1964." In *Nationalism in the U.S.S.R. in the Era of Brezhnev & Kosygin*, ed. George W. Simmonds, 105–115. Detroit: University of Detroit Press, 1977.

——— "Soviet Documentation of Byelorussia's History." In *Zapisy 17: Proceedings of the Twenty-fifth Anniversary Symposium of the Byelorussian Institute of Arts and Sciences February 1977*. New York: St. Sophia Press, 1983.

——— "Belorussian Reawakening." *Problems of Communism* 38 (Jul/Aug 1989): 36–52.

——— *Belarus at a Crossroads in History*. Boulder: Westview Press, 1993.

——— *Historical Dictionary of Belarus*. No. 28, *Historical Dictionaries*. Metuchin, New Jersey: Scarecrow Press, 1999.

Zaslavskaya, Tatyana. *The Second Socialist Revolution: An Alternative Soviet Strategy*. Bloomington: Indiana University Press, 1990.

Zemtovsky, Izaly. "An Attempt at a Synthetic Paradigm." *Ethnomusicology* 41, no. 2 (1997): 185–205.

Discography

Krama

Kamendant. Miensk, Kovcheg 1995 n.n.
Hej tam nalivaj. Miensk, Kovcheg 1994 n.n.
Chvory na rok-n-rol. Miensk, Kovcheg 1993 n.n.

Novaje Nieba

Maja Kraina. Miensk: Kovcheg, 03096, 1996.
Go Home. Miensk: Novaje Nieba, 1995, n.n.
Son i tramvaj. Miensk: Kovcheg. n.n.

Marchenko, Uri

Kaliendarnie Pesni Belorusskogo Polesia. Melodya C20 19893 001.
———, and L. Petrova
Traditsionnie Pesni Polesia. Melodya C20 28043 005.

Mroja (NRM)

Odzirdzidzina. Miensk: Kovcheg, 03396, 1996.
Łałałała *1995*. Miensk: Kovcheg, 00295, 1995.
Vybranyja pieśni *1989-1993*. Miensk, 1993.
28th Star. Melodija, C60 30401 001, 1990.

Mozheiko, Zinaida, et al.

Biełaruski Muzykalny Falklor. Melodija M30 49231 009.

Pałac

Palace Folk-Modern Palac. Vigma 0360.

Pieśniary

Pesniary: Byelorussian Traditional Song. Melodija 33 C60-11287-88, 1988.

Ulis.

Błukańnie. Minsk: Kovcheg, 02096, 1995.
Dances on the Roof '93. Minsk: Dainova, 1993, n.n.
Čužanica. Moscow: Melodija, 1991.
Kraina Doūhaj Biełaj Chmary. Warsaw: Polskie Nagrania, 1990, n.n.

Index

ABBA, 127
AC/DC, 145–146
activism, 44
Adradžeńnie [Renaissance], 77, 149, 158–159
Aksienciev, Felix, 111, 113, 114, 115, 118, 121
album covers
    Pałac, *102*
    Pieśniary, *70–71*
    Ulis, 117
American Bandstand, 62
"Ameryka," 119–120,
Anderson, Benedict, 6–7
anthem response, xxiv, 145
"Aŭstralijskaja Polka," xiii, 80, 142–148, 158
audience response, 116, 121, 131, 150–151
authenticity, 11–12, 50, 85n.32, 87–89, 105n. 17, 115, 124n. 14, 149
authorship, 102–103

Bahdanovič, Alena and Vacłaŭ, xvii, 3
bard, 63–64, 79–80, 130
Bartkievič, Lavon, 69

BAS [Belarusan Student Organization], 125, 138n.1
Basovišćca, 125–126, 138n. 1
    poster, 126
bayan, 63
Becker, Judith and A.L., 57n. 1
Belarus
    post-sovereignty critiques, 5, 12n. 3
    terminology, xxviiin. 4, 21–22,
    historiography, "Golden Era", 22–27
Belarus TV, 153
Belarusan Academy of Sciences, 32, 103
Belarusan language
    attitudes and use, xxv, 29, 32, 44, 48–49, 136, 149
    education, 28, 32
    in Grand Duchy of Litva, 25–26
    identity, 49–50
    "Law About Languages," 19
    media, 11
    publications, 50, 59n. 21
    religious affiliation, 28
    rock, 65, 77–80, 93, 112, 113, 122,

Index

137, 141
Soviet policy, 36n. 9
Stalin, 7
Belarusan Institute of Culture, 47, 50, 63, 88
Belarusan Popular Front, 36n. 7, 47
Belarusan rock, 77, 80, 114, 115
 commercialism, 130
 concert circuit, 125–126, 150–153
 criticism, 80–82
 group dynamics, 110–111
 journalism, 85n. 30, 85n. 35, 158–159, 161, 161n. 6,
 lifestyle, 79–80, 128–130
 recording industry, 81, 114, 115–117, 124n. 15
 social activism, 137, 153
 texts, 79–80
Belarusaness, xxi, xxvi, 11
Biełakou, Juraś, 100
Biełaruskaje Maładziožnaje Radyjo [Belarusan Youth Radio], xix, 64, 78, 93, 153
Biełastoĉcyna, 125–126, 138n. 1
Blondie, 127
Bolsheviks, 31–32
 Revolution, 19
Bonda, 156
Bujło, Kanstancyja, xxiii
Bukĉa, 54
Byelorussian Soviet Socialist Republic, 31, 35n. 1
Bykau, Vasil, 9

calendrical ritual, 11–12, 62, 92–94, 105n. 15
Chamienka, Aleh, 88–90, 93–94, 100
Chatterjee, Partha, 7
Chernobyl, 33–34, *34*, 39n. 42, 53–55,

60n. 26, 89–90, 134–135, 142, 158
Ciareŝĉanka, Valžyna, 64
Clifford, James, 5, 47–48, 57n. 1, 58n. 2
cohesion, 57n. 1
colonialism, 17, 158
colonization, 20, 27–29, 31
consumer products, 51–53
cultural re-invention, 47
currency exchange, 59, see ruble
cymbalom, 63
Ĉyzin, Victor, 154–155

Dainova Ltd., 114
Damy Kultury, 70, 90
democracy, 45–46, *46*
Diaspora, Belarusan xxiv-xxvi, 15n. 21
discos, 66
Dugin, Alexander, 67

economic change, 11–12
emigration, 38n. 33
estradnaja muzyka, 61–62, 64, 132
ethnicity, 14n. 7
ethnocide, 32
ethnography, critiques, 63
ethnographic expeditions, 84n. 19, 88–89, 104
ethnomusicology, xxvi- xxvii
 public ethnomusicologist, xxviiin. 5

Fanon, Franz, 4
fans, 94, 121
 listening, 127
flag, Belarusan, xxiv, 20, 137, 157, 151, 160
Frith, Simon, xxiv, 85n. 32, 85n. 33, 106n. 23
folk-modern, 43, 89, 101, 106n. 23

Index   179

Geertz, Clifford, 57n. 1
gender
    in Pałac's "Rusałki," 92–95
    Belarusan rock scene, 125–129
    electric guitar, 106n. 23
    family functions, 105n. 16
    rock membership 128, 137, 138n. 2
    women in performance, 129, 132
Go Home, 136–137
Gorbachev, Mikhail, 18, 35n. 6
Grand Duchy of Litva, 19, 23–27

Hamzovič, Rehina, 63
Hrannaja Niadziela, 92
"Hey Jude," 146
Horowitz, Donald, 7

identity, xxiv, 6–7, 43–44, 47, 145, 153, 159–160
    and mediation, 5–12
    and language, 49–50
    colonial, 27–29
    construction, 11–12, 19
    ethnography, 104n. 5
    post-colonial, 20
    Russian, 10
intelligentsia, xxv, 30, 32, 36, 77
image, 109, 116–117, 121, 129, 132, 141–142, 15160
Institute of Belarusan Culture [1922], 32
independence, 20, 31, 35n. 5
intellectuals, 19
internat, 110
intertextual readings, 148
Intourist Hotels, 61

Janava, 90–92

Jemal, Geydar, 67–68

kalektyvy, 61
Kalinoŭski, Kastuś, 29
Kamockaja, Kasia, xvii, 78–81, 125–139, *133*, 142, 149–150, 156–157, 159, 161
Kamotski Aleś, 64, 129
Karabach, Dzima, 88
KGB, 67
Kipel, Vitaut, 21, 28, 30, 38n. 33
    and Zora, 23
Knyš Siarhiej, 111, 118, 156
Komsomol, 66
Korjan, Viačasłaŭ, 64, 111,113, 114, 115, 116, 118, 128
Kovcheg, 154
Krama 41, 80, 130, 156
Kraučanka, Siarhiej, 67, 109, 111, 112, 113, 114, 115, 116, 118, 127
Kreŭski, J., 29
Kriwi, 160
Krudastoŭ, Alaksandar, 48
Kruhłova, Veronika, xvii, 90, 160
Kudrejka, Nadzia, 64, 79, 130
Kultrabotniki, 90
Kumejša, Rita, xix
Kupala, Janka, 30
Kupalle, xxi
Kurapaty, 33

"Lavonicha," 145
"Law About Culture," 59n. 17
"Law About Education," 59n. 17
Lenin, 47
"Letter of the Twenty-Eight," 36
Lićviny, 129
Lićvinka, Vasil xviii, 63, 103n. 3
Lithuania, 23–24, 26

180

Litva, 26
lounge bands, 61–62
Lozka, Aleś, xvii, 92
"Lublu naš kraj," xxiii
Lukašenka, Alaksandar, 8–12, 15n. 24,
    31, 34, 37n. 14, 136–137, 149,
    160–161
lyrics
    and melody, 113
lyricists, 80, 113

Maja kraina [My country], 137
Maładečna, 93, 64, 132, 149–150, 157
Maładečna, 98, 150
Markaviec, Tania, xviii, 122n. 7
market, 46, 51–53, 58n. 8
Marples, David, 12n. 3, 31, 39n. 42,
Martynienka and Mialhuj, 67, 85n. 30,
    161n. 6,
Mažejka, Zinajda, xvii, 50, 63, 103n. 2,
    105n.17
media coverage
    Belarus, 8–11
mediation, 101
Melodiya, 69, 81
mermaid, see rusałka
Miascovy Čas, 130
Miensk 1, 42–44
Miensk Belarusan Lycée, 111
migration,
    Soviet policy, 18
    Tribal, 22
    Post-Chernobyl relocation, 33
Minh-ha, Trih. T, xxvii
movement at differentiation, 7, 50, 59n.
    19
Mroja, See NRM
Muljavin Uładzimir 68
Mužyckaja Praŭda [Peasant's Truth], 29
Naša Niva [Our Soil], 30, 31

"Na Hrannoj Niadzieli," xi, 92
nationalism, 6–8; 13,n.4, 15n. 22
nationhood, 4, 5, 10
national consciousness, 32, 34–35
    in literature, 30, 79–80
    policy, 59n. 17
Novaje Nieba, xii, 110–111, 125, 130,
    156, 159
NRM, 110–111, 130–131, 141, 156,
    160–161

Official nationalism, 7
Orthodoxy, Christian, 22, 25, 28, 58n.
    10

Pahonia xxiv, 20, 36n. 10,
Pałac xii, 43, 80, 87–107, 110, 112, 159
Palešsie, 89
Panfiluk, Yolanta and Mirasłava, xvii
participant observation, 90
Paźniak Zianon, 33, 39n. 39, 139n. 10
"Pierapiołačka", 72–76
Pieśniarok 76
Pieśniary, xi, 68–76, 70, 71, 160
Pieśniekievič, H. 103n.4
poetry, 30, 79
polka, 142
Polonization, 25–28
popular music, 64, 131
post-colonialism, 31
post-sovereignty, see Belarus
"Prezydent idzi damoŭ," [President go
    home], xii, 136–137, 161
publicity, 123n. 9

Rada, First All-Belarusan Congress 31,
    39n. 38,
Radio Club Folklore, 105n.17
Ramet, Sabrina Petra, 66, 80
rap ["Rusałki"], 89, 94–95

Index

181

religious categorization, 25, 28, 38n. 33
Rich Vera, 30
Rock Island, 118, 153–154, 157
rockophobia, 157
Rok Suprać Revalucyjaŭ [Rock Against the Revolution], 131, 154–157, 159
  Poster, 155
ruble, 59n. 12, 60n. 24
Ruś, 21–22
Rusałka [mermaid], 87, 92–99, 105n. 15
"Rusałk,i" 87, 92–101,
  lyrics, 96
Rushdie, Salman, xxvi, xxviii
Russian rock, 67–68
Russification, 7, 20, 32
Ryback, Timothy, 65–66, 69–70

Sadouski, John, 25, 28
Shepherd, John, 126
Shuker, Roy, 124n. 14
Shumway, David, 109, 123n. 13
Sielviasiuk, Valenty, xvii
Simaška, Villi, xvii, 78, 84n.28, 154, 156
Sitnica, Ryhor, 43
Siŭčyk, Vitaŭt, 25–27
Skaryna, Fransičak, xxviii n. 3, 25
Słavianski Bazar, 64
"Sluckaja Brama," [Gates of Slutsk], 156–157
social histories, 51
Sokalau-Vojuš, Siaržuk, 64
Soljenitsyne, Alexander, 10
Son i tramvaj [Sleep in the Trolley], 134–135
Soviet jazz, 66
Soviet rock, 65–67, 83n. 10
Soviet Union fall, 18
Sovietization, xxixn. 7, 12,

staged folklore, 61, 63, 84
Stalin, Great Terror, 32–33
"Stand in the Doorway," 41, 56
State University of Belarus, 50
Stołbuny, 90
Svaboda, 137
Sviata, 63, 67

Tancy na dachu [Dances on the Roof], 111, 117
Tarasevič, Lavon, 125–126
terminology, see Belarus
"The Stranger," 120–121
The Stranger, 159
"To the Enemies of Things Byelorussian," 30
Treaty of Riga, 31
Troitsky, Artemy, 66
Tryhubovič, Valancina, xvii, 47, 59n. 14, 137
Tumašaŭ, Aleh 111, 118

Ulis, xii, 64, 80, *118*, 127, 130, 156, 159
Uniate, 25, 28
Union of Brest, 25–26
Union of Lublin, 25, XXn. 26
urban
  communities, 42
  lifestyles, 44–45, 58n. 4
  mediators, 63

Vajciuškievič, Dzima, xvii, 90, 160
Vasin, Kolya, 127, 157
VIA 66, 68–70
Viačorki 63, 103n. 3
viasielle [wedding celebration], 88–89
Vodka on Ice, 41
Volski, Lavon, xvii, 78–81, 130–131
Vydronak, Juraś, xvii, 88–90, 159

Walser, Robert, 106n. 23
wealth, 43, 47, 58n. 4
West, perceptions, 46, 53, 60n. 25

"Žachlivaja Pryhažoćś" [Terrible
Beauty], 134–135
Zaprudnik, Jan, 5, 12n. 3, 22–25, 28,
36n. 9, 37n. 17, 51